T0305055

Sustainable Entrepreneurship and
Entrepreneurial Ecosystems

Sustainable Entrepreneurship

and Entrepreneurial Ecosystems

Frontiers in European Entrepreneurship Research

Edited by

Eddy Laveren

Professor, University of Antwerp and Antwerp Management School, Belgium

Robert Blackburn

Professor, University of Liverpool Management School, UK

Cyrine Ben-Hafaïedh

Professor, IESEG School of Management, France

Cristina Díaz-García

Professor, University of Castilla-La Mancha, Spain

Ángela González-Moreno

Professor, University of Castilla-La Mancha, Spain

IN ASSOCIATION WITH THE ECSB

 Edward Elgar
PUBLISHING

Cheltenham, UK • Northampton, MA, USA

Published by
Edward Elgar Publishing Limited
The Lypiatts
15 Lansdown Road
Cheltenham
Glos GL50 2JA
UK

Edward Elgar Publishing, Inc.
William Pratt House
9 Dewey Court
Northampton
Massachusetts 01060
USA

A catalogue record for this book
is available from the British Library

Library of Congress Control Number: 2020942938

This book is available electronically in the **Elgar**online
Business subject collection
http://dx.doi.org/10.4337/9781839109690

ISBN 978 1 83910 968 3 (cased)
ISBN 978 1 83910 969 0 (eBook)

Printed and bound by CPI Group (UK) Ltd, Croydon, CR0 4YY

Contents

Contributors

Olga Belousova, University of Groningen Centre of Entrepreneurship (The Netherlands).

Cyrine Ben-Hafaïedh, IESEG School of Management (France).

Jennie Cederholm Björklund, Halmstad University, Centre for Innovation, Entrepreneurship and Learning Research / The Rural Economy and Agricultural Society (Sweden).

Robert Blackburn, University of Liverpool Management School (UK).

Clara Cardone-Riportella, Pablo de Olavide University, Seville (Spain).

María C. Cuerva, Faculty of Economics and Business Administration, University of Castilla-La Mancha (Spain).

Cristina Díaz-García, Faculty of Economics and Business Administration, University of Castilla-La Mancha (Spain).

Isabel Feito-Ruiz, Faculty of Economics and Business, University of León (Spain).

Ángela González-Moreno, Faculty of Economics and Business Administration, University of Castilla-La Mancha (Spain).

Aard J. Groen, University of Groningen Centre of Entrepreneurship (The Netherlands).

Henri Hakala, School of Business and Management, Lappeenranta University of Technology (Finland).

Dagmar Ylva Hattenberg, University of Groningen Centre of Entrepreneurship (The Netherlands).

Jeaneth Johansson, Halmstad University, Centre for Innovation, Entrepreneurship and Learning Research/ Luleå University of Technology, Entrepreneuship & Innovation (Sweden).

Annu Kotiranta, Research Institute of the Finnish Economy (Finland).

Katja Lahikainen, School of Engineering Science, Industrial Engineering and Management, Lappeenranta University of Technology (Finland).

Eddy Laveren, Department of Accounting and Finance, University of Antwerp and Antwerp Management School (Belgium).

Kaisu Puumalainen, School of Business and Management, Lappeenranta University of Technology (Finland).

Francisco José Sáez-Martínez, Faculty of Economics and Business Administration, University of Castilla-La Mancha (Spain).

Kirsi Snellman, School of Business and Management, Lappeenranta University of Technology (Finland).

Ángela Triguero, Faculty of Economics and Business Administration, University of Castilla-La Mancha (Spain).

Saila Tykkyläinen, Impact Business (Finland).

David Urbano, School of Economics and Business, Universitat Autonoma de Barcelona (Spain).

Anna Vuorio, School of Business and Management, Lappeenranta University of Technology (Finland).

Acknowledgements

We would like to thank Edward Elgar Publishing for their encouragement and support in the development of this book. We are also grateful for the reviewers listed below who helped in the selection and development of the chapters:

Cyrine Ben-Hafaïedh, IESEG School of Management, France
Robert Blackburn, University of Liverpool Management School, UK
Silvia Costa, University College Groningen, The Netherlands
Cristina Díaz-García, University of Castilla-La Mancha, Spain
Fréderic Dufays, KU Leuven, Belgium
Hermann Frank, WU Vienna University of Economics and Business, Austria
Ángela González-Moreno, University of Castilla-La Mancha, Spain
Jarna Heinonen, University of Turku, Finland
Julie Hermans, Université de Louvain – Mons, Belgium
Breda Kenny, Cork Institute of Technology, Ireland
Effie Kesidou, University of Leeds, UK
Norris Krueger, Ohio State University, USA
Eddy Laveren, University of Antwerp and Antwerp Management School, Belgium
Colin Mason, University of Glasgow, UK
Yannis Pierrakis, Universitat Internacional de Catalunya, Spain
Matilde Ruiz-Arroyo, University of Granada, Spain
Michael Schaper, Institute of South East Asian Studies – Yusof Ishak Institute, Singapore
Laura Spence, Royal Holloway University of London, UK
Edwin Weesie, HU Business School Utrecht, The Netherlands

1. An introduction to *Sustainable Entrepreneurship and Entrepreneurial Ecosystems*

Eddy Laveren, Robert Blackburn, Cyrine Ben-Hafaïedh, Cristina Díaz-García and Ángela González-Moreno

INTRODUCING THE CHAPTERS

This volume presents nine chapters that demonstrate examples of excellent research in the field of sustainable entrepreneurship and entrepreneurial ecosystems. Sustainable entrepreneurship is widely acknowledged as the answer to the environmental and social challenges that society has faced in recent years (Filser et al., 2019, p. 3). Strategic sustainability decisions are characterized by their importance and the high stakes they entail for several stakeholders. Thus, businesses have a responsibility to participate in setting the agenda for a more sustainable future and it is important to learn more about the factors that drive sustainable entrepreneurship and strategic sustainable decision-making. The entrepreneurial ecosystem (EE) has a significant impact on shaping the entrepreneur's evaluation of prospects that can potentially be realized, since entrepreneurial decisions are inevitably dependent on how individuals judge their entrepreneurial ecosystem.

An entrepreneurial ecosystem can be defined as 'a dynamic community of inter-dependent actors (entrepreneurs, suppliers, buyer, government, etc.) and system-level institutional, informational and socioeconomic contexts' (Audretsch and Belitski, 2016, p. 4). The distinctive features of entrepreneurial ecosystems are that they both enable entrepreneurs to identify market opportunities, and offer local resources, including support and finance, to new, high-growth ventures (Spigel and Harrison, 2018). The success of entrepreneurial ecosystems is based on the interaction of material, social and cultural attributes that provide benefits and resources to entrepreneurs. In regional entrepreneurial ecosystems, universities can be considered as one of the key material attributes. The main social attributes include networks, holders of investment capital, mentors, deal-makers and talented workers. The cultural attributes consist of attitudes and histories of entrepreneurship. In a similar vein, Brush (2014) states that the key dimensions of ecosystems are stakeholders, resources, infrastructure and culture. The stakeholders include internal and external stakeholders that have different needs, connections and motivations. Resources include, for example, intellectual knowledge and research capabilities, physical facilities, and monetary and human resources. The infrastructure includes elements related to connectivity, for example technological platforms as well as formal and informal networks. Culture includes norms, values and traditions. The interdependent and multilevel nature of entrepreneurial ecosystems implies the notion of potentially crucial synergistic effects of systems' components, including cross-level interactions (Isenberg, 2011; Prahalad, 2005; Spigel, 2017). Of course, entrepreneurs and their firms are essential ingredients and an outcome of successful entrepreneurship ecosystems (Isenberg, 2011). Volkman et al. (2019, p. 1) highlight that: 'while the concept of entrepreneurial ecosystems is now a prominent topic and an important stream in entrepreneurship research, the question of how ecosystems can specifically promote sustainable entrepreneurship and contribute to the Sustainable Development Goals (SDGs) set by the United Nations is a neglected issue'.

This book contributes to filling this gap and aims to serve at the nexus of contextualization of entrepreneurship and sustainability. The chapters in this book are organized in three parts. In Part I, four chapters are presented regarding sustainability or sustainable entrepreneurship. In Part II, two chapters present the entrepreneurial ecosystem orientation as an explanatory factor of entrepreneurial behaviour. In Part III, three chapters give attention to entrepreneurial conditions and behaviour.

PART I: SUSTAINABLE ENTREPRENEURSHIP

Four chapters (2–5) make up Part I of this book, all focused on sustainable entrepreneurship. Chapter 2 focuses on the concept of the 'circular economy' (CE) as the production model that leads to sustainable results, highlighting both its increasing relevance in entrepreneurship and strategic management journals, and the barriers that European small and medium-sized enterprises (SMEs) encounter within this circular production model. Chapter 3 examines how different combinations of perceived opportunities (including sustainable value) require entrepreneurs to use different decision-logics (effectuation and causation), and how the entrepreneurial mindsets relate to predictive performance regarding competitors (making the opportunity more or less interesting to pursue). Chapter 4 focuses on the drivers of eco-innovations in food and beverage firms. These firms are characterized by their high environmental impact, and therefore many firms feel pressured to engage in eco-process innovations. Chapter 5 focuses on understanding how emotion affects strategic sustainability decision-making.

In Chapter 2, Cristina Díaz-García, Ángela González-Moreno and Francisco José Sáez-Martínez analyse the challenges and enablers of businesses to adopt circular economic activities. The authors' starting point is that the linear economy is unsustainable, surpassing the physical limits of the planet, and a shift towards a CE is inevitable. Apart from a more efficient use of resources (materials and waste, energy, water) and products that generate economic gains, the implementation of circular economy business models leads to the creation of entrepreneurial opportunities, the stimulus of innovation and the improvement of environmental protection. The model has been already treated in ecological economics, but it has some important additional contributions to make. These include the importance of materials in the product value chain retaining the highest value possible (for reuse, refurbishment/repair and remanufacturing; and only later for raw material utilization, the main focus in traditional recycling), and that products should be in economic circulation for as long as possible, emphasizing the benefits of the sharing economy.

Despite an increase in academic research on CE in recent years (especially since 2015), and considering that the bulk of knowledge on this issue previously has been developed by policy-makers and practitioners, authors have argued that the literature is unorganized, superficial (remaining largely unexplored) and lacking an economic-business perspective. However, more recently the literature and debates on sustainability have broadened from the domain of environmental management journals to entrepreneurship and strategic management journals. This broadening has also led to a new focus on issues such as sustainability, innovation (for competitiveness) and especially innovation in business models. Within the topic of CE, different sub-topics may be identified. One of these is the challenges and enablers of adopting circular economic activities. In Chapter 2, the authors draw upon the Flash Eurobarometer 441 on European SMEs and the CE. Their literature review and data analysis lead to some implications for policy-makers and academics regarding the importance of SMEs' engagement in the circular economy in this moment of climate emergency.

According to Anna Maija Vuorio and Kaisu Puumalainen in Chapter 3, sustainable entrepreneurship is a particular form of entrepreneurship through which three types of value are created: social, environmental and economic. These types of value creation could also characterize potential entrepreneurial opportunities. However, there is only limited evidence about the attributes of potential entrepreneurial opportunities that include sustainable value creation. Furthermore, although decision-making logics (effectuation versus causation) have gained considerable attention in the entrepreneurship literature, there seems to be a lack of studies that focus on decision-making in sustainable entrepreneurship. Additionally, there is limited evidence about entrepreneurial opportunity recognition in sustainable entrepreneurship and the dimensions of a potential entrepreneurial opportunity.

Furthermore, Vuorio and Puumalainen aim to shed light on how decision-making logics and perceptions of entrepreneurial opportunities (novelty, uncertainty, economic value and sustainable value) shape venture performance. Findings in the literature on the impacts of effectuation and causation have been mixed and there is only limited evidence on how these two logics may be utilized in the context of sustainability incentives. Furthermore, Muñoz and Cohen (2018) have put forward a call for alternative methodological approaches to study sustainable entrepreneurship, and thus a machine learning approach is applied in this chapter. Data from 301 Finnish owner-managers in SMEs is analysed using an artificial neural network. First, three alternative mindsets are shown combining the two decision-making logics and dimensions of potential entrepreneurial opportunities. Only one of the mindsets (flexible planner) perceives opportunities, that enable sustainable value creation and are at the same time innovative and uncertain, conditions which are associated with decision-logics of planning and consideration of how much a person can lose combined with flexibility. Second, how these mindsets are connected to different performance outcomes is analysed. The results show that a flexible planner mindset and a networking planner combining causation and elements of effectuation are connected to the perception of better performance compared to competitors' performance. Conversely, an experimenter mindset including only experimentation as an element of effectuation is linked to the perception of worse performance compared to competitors' performance. The empirical results contribute to the literature by using two different decision-making logics and provide evidence to show how these are used, under different conditions together with causation and effectuation, to shape perceptions about performance outcomes. It is a hopeful result that the mindset which detects opportunities enabling sustainable value is also connected with a prediction of better performance than competitors, since this might motivate more potential entrepreneurs to take the leap to sustainable entrepreneurship.

In Chapter 4, María C. Cuerva, Ángela Triguero and Francisco José Sáez-Martínez focus on the food and beverage sector, which is characterized by its high environmental impact and level of emissions because of resource inefficiencies and high rates of food waste, and thus require a transition towards more sustainable practices. Therefore, the sector is pressured to face an eco-innovation challenge including the recovery and treatment of waste, improved production processes, better distribution methods and new packaging solutions. The authors analyse the drivers of eco-process innovations in the food and beverage industry taking into account the internal capabilities of the firms and the use of external knowledge sources. The chapter is based on a survey of 279 Spanish food firms. By the specification of probit models, it is shown that the use and the frequency of collaborations with different external partners has a positive effect on the probability of adopting eco-process innovations by food firms. Furthermore, the study reveals that the use of external knowledge from universities, consultants and other external agents is more decisive than collaborations with customers or providers. Finally, a U-shaped relation between age and eco-process innovations is confirmed in this sector. This implies that the adoption of eco-process innovations by food firms is affected both by internal firm characteristics (size, age, financial and technological capabilities) and firms' openness (measured through a diverse collaboration puzzle of external knowledge sources).

The objective of Chapter 5, by Kirsi Snellman and Henri Hakala, is to understand how emotion affects strategic sustainability decision-making. Considering that businesses have a responsibility to participate in setting the agenda for a more sustainable future, it is important to learn more about the factors that drive strategic sustainable decision-making, including the impact of emotions. While emotion may be the enemy of good decisions, other researchers suggest that emotion and reason are complementary in good decisions. Hence, this chapter investigates how emotions affect strategic sustainability decision-making. Drawing on interviews with 23 owner-managers of sustainability 'trailblazing' SMEs, the authors illuminate how emotions complement thinking and rational analysis in sustainability decision-making. This happens through three interrelated elements that link emotion with ethical considerations: sensitizing, sensing and selecting. Sensitizing is associated with an initial awareness of the ethical dilemma; sensing with establishing a global sense of a whole; and selecting with making the ultimate right/good choice. The authors propose a model in which emotion acts as an ethical compass for managers who are subject to multiple forces when making strategic sustainability decisions. The authors' findings indicate that strategic sustainability decisions reflect not only rational reasons and facts, but also associated emotions in addressing ethical dilemmas and an unknown future. The authors suggest that without emotions, there is no readiness to change, nor a willingness to move forward in the strategic decision-making process.

PART II: ENTREPRENEURIAL ECOSYSTEMS

The two chapters of Part II focus on two specific entrepreneurial ecosystems (EEs): university-based EE (Chapter 6) and Swedish agricultural support EE (Chapter 7). In both cases, institutional members have to be focused to guide highly pressured entrepreneurs towards establishing sustainable businesses while operating in highly competitive and complex markets.

Recently, universities have been identified as important contributors in entrepreneurial ecosystems. Universities can provide a large variety of resources to entrepreneurial ecosystems: new technologies that create entrepreneurial opportunities, human capital (teaching and other education activities), knowledge capital (technology and research) and entrepreneurship capital (creation of spin-offs, and entrepreneurial mindset). Additionally, universities may play an important role in creating and connecting entrepreneurs in their networks, thereby enabling entrepreneurs to acquire resources, knowledge and support from the actors of the entrepreneurial ecosystem. University-based entrepreneurship ecosystems can be researched as sub-systems of larger regional or local entrepreneurial ecosystems or as entrepreneurial ecosystems on their own.

In Chapter 6, Katja Lahikainen focuses on investigating a university-based entrepreneurial ecosystem on its own. A university-based entrepreneurial ecosystem (U-BEE) is defined as the strategic and collective actions of various organizational components in order to maximize both the entrepreneurial and the innovative contributions of universities (Hayter, 2016). The chapter aims to discover the underlying factors that influence the emergence of a U-BEE. Current research on U-BEEs focuses largely on organizational-level studies from the university point of view. This study contributes to the existing research by providing new insights to the immature theory development on U-BEEs by giving voice to individuals and comparing the different perspectives of the university and company actors towards the university as a producer of new knowledge, start-ups, entrepreneurs and a skilled workforce.

Lahikainen employs a qualitative case study approach and follows the inductive thematic analysis method. The study is based on 22 thematic in-depth interviews with company and university actors belonging to an emerging U-BEE around a Finnish university campus. The analysis shows that entrepreneurship promotion in the U-BEE is not only about new business creation; rather, the most important role of the university in the ecosystem is to educate entrepreneurs and the high-quality workforce. The emergence of the U-BEE is fostered by scientific excellence, focusing on creating strong dyadic relationships between the university and company actors. However, strong dyadic relationships can also act as a hindering factor, since they might lead to the one-sided development of a specific industrial field. The study suggests that the current theories on U-BEEs should place more weight on entrepreneurial culture and social relations, as well as acknowledge that students are important intermediaries and members in a U-BEE. From the practitioner point of view, the analysis implies that the centralization of entrepreneurship-related functions may lead to additional bureaucracy that might hinder the emergence of U-BEEs.

The agricultural entrepreneurial ecosystem operates much in the shadow of what reflects 'real' entrepreneurship and is often neglected in the traditional entrepreneurship literature. Agricultural entrepreneurs globally face the pressure to transform into entrepreneurial models to improve innovativeness and to seek new opportunities and new ways of doing things in the highly competitive landscape. In Chapter 7, Jennie Cederholm Björklund and Jeaneth Johansson acknowledge the situational boundaries embedded in the context of the Swedish agricultural entrepreneurial support ecosystem The key actors in this ecosystem consist of governmental agencies, agricultural advisory organizations, agricultural member organizations and rural societies, among others. At the macro level, the agricultural entrepreneurship support ecosystem may be divided into a governmental system and an advisory system. Parts of the agricultural support ecosystem are studied from different perspectives, but there is no overall picture and understanding of the roles and the challenges faced by advisors in the ecosystem. Agricultural advisors have been subject to much critique, both in practice and in the literature, for not answering agricultural entrepreneurs' needs for support in the ongoing industry transformation. Advisors expect to guide highly pressured agricultural entrepreneurs operating in complex settings towards sustainable businesses in highly competitive markets.

The chapter answers the call to further contextualize agricultural entrepreneurship research by highlighting the specific context of the entrepreneurial agricultural support system in general, and the advisory support system in particular. The researchers collected data by attending 16 meetings involving participation of 34 key actor organizations in the agricultural entrepreneurship support system. These observations were complemented with follow-up semi-structured interviews with key actors and further exploration of the advisors' roles and challenges in the agricultural ecosystem, through the lens of complexity leadership theory (CLT). According to CLT, leadership is considered a phenomenon involving social interactions that causes a shift from emphasizing the human capital of the advisor and the entrepreneurs in the system, to emphasizing social capital. The authors look into advisors' relational leadership and connectedness in the agriculture entrepreneurial support ecosystem and explore the advisors' leadership in coordinating formal and informal work when operating in dynamic agricultural entrepreneurship environments. The authors identify an emergent need for innovation in the leadership of advisory work, and conceptualize enabling mechanisms to accomplish such change. They conclude with the development of a conceptual model that outlines the mechanisms fostering and hindering the support ecosystem's adoption of the new practices and innovation required by the external society.

The results indicate the need to create an adaptive space for reflection and learning. This space is a relational environment and not necessarily a physical place, that can give innovation the opportunity to flourish through enabling leadership.

PART III: ENTREPRENEURIAL CONDITIONS

In Part III, three chapters are presented that examine conditions predicting entrepreneurial activity or behaviour amongst postgraduate students (Chapter 8) and employees within organizations (Chapter 9) and how, during the economic recession, social enterprises outperform other enterprises in creating inclusive growth, contributing to solve prevalent societal and environmental challenges (Chapter 10).

In Chapter 8, Clara Cardone-Riportella, Isabel Feito-Ruiz and David Urbano investigate whether the family business background of postgraduate students determines their entrepreneurial intention and behaviour. These students may start their own business, continue as a successor in the next generation of the family business, or work for others outside the family firm. Social cognitive career theory argues that a career choice is a function of the interaction between entrepreneurial self-efficacy, outcome expectations and personal goals. The interaction of these constructs leads to the formation of entrepreneurial intention. Based on social cognitive career theory, evidence from a study of 190 former students of a business administration international postgraduate programme, taught in Spain, indicates that students with a family business background have more entrepreneurial self-efficacy and more entrepreneurial intention than those without this background. However, in terms of entrepreneurial behaviour (starting a new business or being a successor), the direct effect of a family business background is not significant, but the indirect and total effect through entrepreneurial intention is positive and significant. Overall, therefore, these results show that intention precedes behaviour, and that past experience in a family business may influence future behavioural intentions and determine professional career choice.

In Chapter 9, Dagmar Ylva Hattenberg, Olga Belousova and Aard J. Groen explore to what extent organizational conditions stimulate the entrepreneurial mindset (EMS). Employees are at the heart of an organization. The ability and willingness of individuals to rapidly sense, act and mobilize in response to a judgemental decision under uncertainty about a possible opportunity for gain, has the potential to aid organizations in sustaining their competitive advantage in an increasingly competitive environment. The entrepreneurial mindset captures whether one perceives oneself to have the skillset and abilities to act entrepreneurially.

The scientific knowledge base regarding EMS in an organizational context continues to be fragmented, especially regarding what organizations can do in terms of their environmental conditions to stimulate employees' EMS. EMS is first theorized to be active amongst managers, increasing entrepreneurial initiative and the competitiveness of organizations by influencing their organizational members. The next step is to understand how the EMS of employees can be influenced by organizations. Using a survey method within a Dutch pharmaceutical family firm with offices spread over five countries and three continents, followed by semi-structured interviews with 12 employees, an investigation of EMS in an organizational context is carried out to further understand its interaction with organizational conditions. The results indicate that organizational conditions stimulate the EMS. This implies that organizations can undertake action to influence employees' EMS, for which propositions are formulated.

Chapter 10, by Annu Kotiranta, Saila Tykkyläinen and Kaisu Puumalainen, aims to investigate the growth trajectories of social enterprises in different economic cycles. Social enterprises are seen by politicians and academics as playing an important part in developing more resilient economies and creating inclusive growth. The global economic crisis of 2008 accelerated discussion among European politicians on the potential of social enterprises to contribute to solving prevalent societal and environmental challenges. It has been argued that social enterprises must continue to grow in order to match the scope of these challenges. However, previous research on the topic has not provided compelling evidence on the large-scale effects of social enterprise growth. The results in Chapter 10 are based on robust quantitative methods and matched samples of Finnish SMEs and social enterprises. The authors show that, during the economic recession, social enterprises outperformed other enterprises. Thus, the study provides new evidence on social enterprises' growth performance and contributes to the literature by applying theoretical insights from firm growth research.

OUTLOOK

Entrepreneurship research regarding sustainable entrepreneurship and eco-systems appears to be evolving and it is intended that this volume adds to this literature, as well as stimulates further research agendas and methodological approaches. Overall, the book demonstrates the vibrancy of research on entrepreneurship and its nexus with the literatures on sustainability and entrepreneurial ecosystems. The chapters present new scientific evidence in the field, together with research-informed policy and practical implications. They also demonstrate the variety of research methods in the field.

REFERENCES

Audretsch, D.B. and M. Belitski (2016), 'Entrepreneurial ecosystems in cities: establishing the framework conditions', *Journal of Technology Transfer*. https://doi.org/10.1007/s10961-016-9473-8.

Brush, Candida G. (2014), 'Exploring the concept of an entrepreneurship education ecosystem', in Sherry Hoskinson and Donald F. Kuratko (eds), *Innovative Pathways for University Entrepreneurship in the 21st Century*, Bingley, UK: Emerald Group Publishing, pp. 25–39.

Filser, M., S. Kraus, N. Roig-Tierno, N. Kailer and U. Fisher (2019), 'Entrepreneurship as catalyst for sustainable development: opening the black box', *Sustainability*, **11**, 4503. doi: 10.3390/su11164503.

Hayter, C. (2016), 'A trajectory of early-stage spinoff success: the role of knowledge intermediaries within an entrepreneurial university ecosystem', *Small Business Economics*, **47** (3), 633–656.

Isenberg, D.J. (2011), 'The entrepreneurship ecosystem strategy as a new paradigm for economic policy: principles for cultivating entrepreneurship', Babson Entrepreneurship Ecosystem Project, Babson College, MA.

Muñoz, P. and B. Cohen (2018), 'Sustainable entrepreneurship research: taking stock and looking ahead', *Business Strategy and the Environment*, **27** (3), 300–322.

Prahalad, C.K. (2005), *The Fortune at the Bottom of the Pyramid: Eradicating Poverty through Profits*, Saddle River, NJ: Wharton School Publishing.

Spigel, B. (2017), 'The relational organization of entrepreneurial ecosystems', *Entrepreneurship Theory and Practice*, **41** (1), 49–72.

Spigel, B. and R. Harrison (2018), 'Toward a process theory of entrepreneurial ecosystems', *Strategic Entrepreneurship Journal*, **12** (1), 151–168.

Volkmann, C., K. Fichter, M. Klofsten and D.B. Audretsch (2019), 'Sustainable entrepreneurial ecosystems: an emerging field of research', *Small Business Economics*. https://doi.org/10.1007/s11187-019-00253-7.

PART I

Sustainable entrepreneurship

2. Circular economy and SMEs: insights and EU situation

Cristina Díaz-García, Ángela González-Moreno and Francisco José Sáez-Martínez

INTRODUCTION

It has been proved that the current dominant production model 'extract–produce–use–dump' – that is, the linear flow of materials and energy from nature to the human economy – is unsustainable, and therefore an alternative cyclical model has gained relevance: the 'circular economy' (CE), which is in line with environmental sustainability (COM, 2014; COM, 2015; CIRAIG, 2015). This model is offered as a solution to the environmental crisis giving an efficient and competitive alternative to economic linear development (allowing more value to be achieved and for a longer period) generating, in addition, sustainable development. Korhonen et al. (2018) cite recent estimations by the European Commission that circular economy-type economic transitions could create €600 billion annual economic gains for the European Union (EU) manufacturing sector alone, and the global economy would benefit by US$1000 billion annually. Therefore, it is attracting the attention of governments and businesses around the world.

Sustainable development was originally defined as 'development that meets the needs of the present without compromising the ability of future generations to meet their own needs', having three dimensions: economic, ecological and social (WCED, 1987). Within this global frame of sustainability, the circular economy is defined as 'restorative and regenerative by design and aims to keep products, components and materials at their highest utility and value at all times, seeks to ultimately decouple global economic development from finite resource consumption' (Ellen MacArthur Foundation, 2015, p. 2). In a CE model, 'the value of products, materials and resources is maintained in the economy for as long as possible, and the generation of waste minimised . . . to develop a sustainable, low carbon, resource efficient and competitive economy' (European Commission, 2015). The aim is closing the circle: design, production, consumption and waste management, especially transforming waste in resources. It is feasible to improve the processes of production so that resources are used more efficiently and generate less waste, and at the same time entrepreneurial opportunities are created, innovation stimulated and environmental protection improved.

Since 2014, the number of studies which focused on this topic has increased exponentially (see Figure 2.1). However, the majority of developments on CE to date have been led by practitioners, the business community and policy-makers and the scientific literature on the circular economy is still 'superficial and unorganized', therefore 'it remains largely unexplored' (Korhonen et al., 2018, p. 37). Furthermore, some authors propose that research has focused on reducing waste, resource efficiency and environmental impact, neglecting an economic and business perspective, and for this reason, since advantages for industries are not explicit, implementation at industrial level has been hindered (Lieder and Rashid, 2016). Urbinati et al. (2017, p. 488) suggest that developing a comprehensive understanding of the role that the circular economy can play from a business model perspective is crucial, and especially 'nowadays when there are empirical evidences highlighting the lack of public awareness on the potential of Circular Economy and few incentives for companies to translate in practical actions the concept of Circular Economy'.

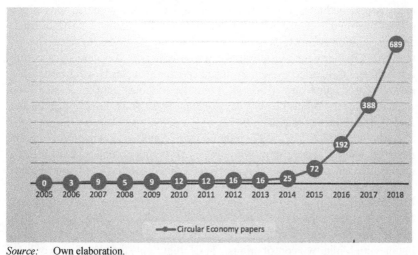

Source: Own elaboration.

Figure 2.1   *Number of papers published in Web of Science*

The chapter is structured as follows. First, a brief literature review; then a more detailed review of the challenges that firms confront when engaging in circular economy activities is introduced. This is followed by a short discussion of the findings from Flash Eurobarometer 441 on European small and medium-sized enterprises (SMEs) and the CE, and some final remarks.

THEORETICAL FRAMEWORK

Urgency of Adopting a CE model

Korhonen et al. (2018) refer to a parent natural system from which resources and energy are extracted to be used in the human economic subsystem that operates within it. In the latter, physical flows of materials and energy follow a linear fashion, since once produced and consumed the goods, wastes and emissions are dumped back into the environment in harmful concentrations. Brown (2006) shows that the global natural ecosystem (life-supporting parent) is shrinking on an accelerated path in size and volume, in both quantitative terms (deserts are expanding; sea level is rising, reducing the land area; and 75 per cent of the energy consumed is based on non-renewable sources) and qualitative terms (potential of the earth's ecosystems to provide life-sustaining functions, the environment cannot assimilate the level of emissions). At the same time, the human economic subsystem is growing both in population (also of livestock, including cattle) and in per capita consumption. So, this linear production model is encountering a head-on collision, it is unsustainable; and the solution seems to be a model in which the flows are reversed, that is, the CE. 'Circular economy limits the throughput flow to a level that nature tolerates and utilises ecosystem cycles in economic cycles by respecting their natural reproduction rates. Successful circular economy contributes to all the three dimensions of sustainable development (economic, environmental and social)' (Korhonen et al., 2018, p. 39).

Korhonen et al. (2018, p. 37) propose that, 'Ecological economics may be the most fruitful source from which the new practical, policy and business orientated concept of CE could find scientific and theoretical support and guidance', due to its long tradition in recycling and other concepts related to CE, on both the macroeconomic and the microeconomic levels (that is, eco-efficiency or 'inter-system ecology'). In this sense, the authors state that there is little that is truly new in the CE concept in terms of sustainability science research, but they highlight two contributions: '1) CE highlights the importance of high value and high quality material cycles in a new manner and 2) shows the possibilities of the sharing economy alongside sustainable production for a more sustainable production-consumption culture' (Korhonen et al., 2018, p. 45). 'The "sharing economy" may bring significant efficiency improvements involving as much as it is possible of the existing material capacity in economic systems into efficient use' (Korhonen et al., 2018, p. 41). The authors propose three limits to the CE concept: thermodynamic limits (entropy), spatial and temporary system boundary limitations, and potential rebound effects. With regard to the first limit, they argue that despite the limits posed by entropy (Second Law of Thermodynamics: 'recycling will always require energy and will always be incomplete generating wastes and side-products of its own') and the theory that everything can be recycled (with renewable – infinite – energy from the sun), it is clear that the CE can generate radical improvements to the linear production–consumption model simply by arranging the physical flows. With regard to the second limit, and despite being conscious of the difficulties of the assessment, they recommend that each CE project should be considered for its contribution to global net sustainability (compared to the situation before the project and globally, as the physical flows of materials and energy cross organizational, administrative and geographical boundaries) and considering the long-term environmental impacts. The rebound effects relate to the fact that CE business models (BMs) should have as a result an increase of production efficiency, leading to a decrease in production costs and probably a decrease in the prices of end-products which, in turn, would boost consumption. Therefore, if economic growth must be allowed, the growth of the physical scale of the economy (measured in physical material and energy flow footprints) should be limited to the sustainability limit of the supporting system (nature).

The central idea of the CE is that materials in the product value chain and life cycle should retain the highest value as possible and that products should be in economic circulation for as long as possible. Materials have to be used in as high-value applications as possible: they should first be recovered for reuse, refurbishment and repair; then for remanufacturing (demanding less resources and energy, these processes are more economic); and only later for raw material utilization (the main focus in traditional recycling); with energy combustion and landfill disposal being the very last options. In this sense, waste generation within the production phase can be prevented, for example, through improvement of material efficiency, the use of processes that generate less waste or innovation in products and services (that is, designs that ease recycling); in the phase of distribution, through good supply planning and stocks, use of marketing strategies that do not promote waste (for example, offers must be avoided of the 'buy one and get two' type that tend to generate waste by encouraging unnecessary food purchases), or using less wasteful packaging; and in the consumption phase, using products that are less waste-intensive during their life cycles. Promoting sharing and renting models of use, or using reverse logistics, are concepts that enhance sharing the function of the product between many users, and thereby reduce consumption levels (EEA, 2016).

It is clear that this change in the business landscape modifies the ways of working and generating value, and therefore it is placing new demands on the skills and abilities of a company's resource base that support the strategies aiming to obtain a competitive advantage from the exploitation of sustainable opportunities (Lahti et al., 2018). Thus, 'the forum for the debate on sustainability has moved from environmental management journals to entrepreneurship and strategic management journals, where the issues of sustainability, innovation, and competitiveness are central' (Parida and Wincent, 2019, p. 2).

Results from a Recent Literature Review

Recently, Rosa et al. (2019) have done a systematic literature review on circular business models (CBMs), reviewing 283 articles identifying seven areas of research: best practices (5 archetypes), classification methods (9), adoption-oriented challenges (5), decision-support tools (4 types, depending on the intent), and three other additional research areas: life-cycle assessments, performance comparison and rapid experimentation.

The CBM 'best practice archetypes' are: paradigm-based (3 articles), service-based (1), product-based (3), sector-based (13), and pattern-based (8). As can be seen by the number of articles, the most frequently recurrent themes are: sector-based best practices – guiding companies belonging to specific industries (mainly electric and electronic equipment); and pattern-based best practices – indicating general and innovative patterns aiming to help companies in addressing the CE, that is, reinventing BMs; identifying different types of product–people interactions; describing 3R-based (reuse, remanufacturing and recycling) guidelines for adopting CE; presenting CE-related competitive advantages; implementing innovation practices for closing materials loops; methods for adopting reuse principles.

With regards to classification methods and innovation frameworks (identifying ways to be circular), the authors identified three groups of papers depending on the frameworks they refer to: (1) the ReSOLVE framework, proposed by the Ellen MacArthur Foundation (2015) (five articles); (2) the Business Model Canvas (BMC) methodology, proposed by Osterwalder and Pigneur (2010) (eight articles); and (3) papers proposing hybrid models, exploiting both the previous ideas (ten papers classified in seven different approaches). Following their revision, they conclude that the Business Model Canvas is the most diffused classification framework.

Another CBM research area focuses on decision-support tools, which they classify according to the final intent of the tool: (1) sustainability check – tools for checking the sustainability level of companies and making the transition towards the CE easier (7 articles); (2) problem-solving – tools able to solve a delicated issue related with CE (3 articles); (3) scenario analysis – tools for helping to understand inconsistencies and/or lack of clarity existing in descriptions of reuse options (2 articles); (4) linear/circular comparisons – that is, comparing remanufacturing and production in terms of economic and environmental attractiveness (3 articles). They conclude that the most used circularity decision-making tool is the sustainability check, and argue that it might be because its use is simpler for companies in order to verify that circularity is applied in a correct way (the other tools might require a bigger effort to be adopted into practice).

With regard to the CE challenges, they find articles related to barriers, and others related to enablers, classifying these in five categories: (1) sustainability – general perspective without considering any sector or issue; (2) supply chain – macroscopic level; (3) company; (4) information and communication technology (ICT); and (5) lean-based ones. Rosa et al. (2019) conclude that most of the studies focus their attention on challenges while approaching circularity at micro level (company), either adopting the general lens of sustainability or focusing on the ICT dimension (as enabler). However, the supply chain and lean dimensions appear to be still neglected. We will look at this research area in greater depth below, focusing on SMEs.

Circular Economy: Challenges and Enablers for SMEs

As with many other business issues, the challenges faced by SMEs can be found both internally and externally (see Figure 2.2 for a summary, and Table 2.1 for a compilation of the studies researching the different challenges). Beginning with the internal challenges, these all have to do with resources and capabilities: organizational, technical or financial. The organizational challenges are multiple, but one of the most important ones is the need for strategic capabilities to define a new strategy and structure for the firm. It is necessary to completely rethink the way in which the firm does business or generates value, that is, the business model: the way of producing and consuming, transforming waste into value-added products, involving the entire supply chain (Bianchini et al., 2019b). There is also the need for new organizational competences (for example, team motivation, organizational culture, participation) for implementing circular business across different organizational functions. With regard to the technical challenges, Bianchini et al. (2019b) cite the need to adopt specific technologies (that is, recycling ones) for the redesign of circular products and production systems; the need to develop procedures for dissemination of innovation without excessive delay between design and diffusion phases; and, related to this, the need for qualified employees with technical and technological know-how and expertise. Implementing CE activities also implies financial challenges, since these are more complex practices that require costly management and planning processes, and high, long-term investments.

Note: R&C = resources and capabilities; * Enablers of CE.
Source: Adapted from Bianchini et al. (2019b) and Rosa et al. (2019).

Figure 2.2   Circular economy: challenges and enablers for SMEs

Focusing on external challenges, three challenges can be highlighted: institutional and regulatory, market and stakeholders' relationship issues (named 'supply chain' by Rosa et al., 2019). The institutional and regulatory issues have to do with a poor institutional framework with misaligned incentives and/or complexity of regulations, that is, the lack of a conducive legal system.

With regards to the market there might be issues with customer acceptance: specific restrictions, rigidity in customer behaviours and business routines (Bianchini et al., 2019b). Korhonen et al. (2018) also point to the existence of limits of social and cultural definitions of waste concept, which have a strong influence on its handling, management and utilization. They state that the concept is culturally and socially constructed in a temporal context and, therefore, is dynamic and changing. It can be expected that the climate emergency will ease this potential challenge.

Bianchini et al. (2019a) also point to challenges within the stakeholders' relationship: lack of compatibility with partners' business models; lack of supply network support; geographical dispersion, poor services and infrastructures, conflict of interest within companies and misaligned profit-share along supply chain. Korhonen et al. (2018) refer to this challenge as 'limits of governance and management', stating that intra-organizational and intra-sectoral management of interorganizational and intersectoral physical flows of materi-

Table 2.1   *Studies evidencing these challenges*

Resources and capabilities: organizational	Sousa-Zomer et al. (2018)
	De los Ríos and Charnley (2017)
	Accenture strategy (2014)
	Lüdeke-Freund and Dembek (2017)
	Smith-Gillespie (2017)
	de Lange and Rodić (2013)
	Guldmann and Jensen (2015)
Resources and capabilities: technical	Ritzén and Sandström (2017)
	Rizos et al. (2016)
	Van Buren et al. (2016)
	Linder and Williander (2017)
	Korhonen et al. (2018)
Resources and capabilities: financial	Rizos et al. (2016)
	Van Buren et al. (2016)
	Linder and Williander (2017)
Institutional and regulatory	Roos (2014)
Market	Rizos et al. (2016)
	Morlat and Pinto-Silva (2014)
Stakeholders' relationship (supply chain)	Geissdoerfer et al. (2018)
	Witjes and Lozano (2016)
	Rizos et al. (2016)
	Bianchini et al. (2019b)
	Chertow and Ehrenfeld (2012)
	Franco (2017)
ICT	Howell et al. (2018)
	Pagoropoulos et al. (2017)
	Planing (2017)
Lean thinking	Kurilova-Palisaitiene et al. (2018)
	Romero and Rossi (2017)

Source: Based on Bianchini et al. (2019b) and Rosa et al. (2019).

als and energy can be a serious concern when implementing circular economy activities.

With regard to enablers of CE, Rosa et al. (2019) point out studies that highlight two of them: ICT and digital technologies, and lean thinking. For example, ICT could help in the transition to new CE business models, and also help 'frugal innovation' through which companies can create high-quality products with limited resources, appealing to cost-conscious and environmentally aware consumers. For its part, lean production could be used to design processes reducing resources consumption, or remanufacturing ones, increasing value added for consumers by reducing lead times. Parida and

Wincent (2019) highlight that apart from a change from a linear to a circular model of production, there are two other business trends that are contributing to achieve sustainability-based competitive advantages: from a product-centric to a service-centric approach (servitization); and from an analogue to a digital focus (digitalization).

The following section shows the engagement of European firms in CE activities, and the challenges confronted with the information provided by the Flash Eurobarometer 441 published in 2016.

CIRCULAR ECONOMY WITHIN EUROPEAN SMES: MAIN CHALLENGES

In April 2016, the network TNS Political & Social carried out a survey in the 28 member states of the European Union, interviewing 10 618 companies amongst the small and medium-sized enterprises (SMEs) employing 1–250 employees in manufacturing (NACE category C), services (NACE categories G, H, I, J, K, M, N) and the industry sector (NACE categories B, D, E, F).

Fortunately, already in 2016, almost three-quarters of the firms surveyed pointed out that they were undertaking at least one activity related to the circular economy. However, there is considerable variation among the member states (see Figure 2.3). According to the European Commission (2016) companies are more likely to have undertaken at least one activity related to the circular economy, the larger they are (72 per cent of the smallest companies have done so, compared to 89 per cent of those with 50–250 employees), and the higher a company's turnover (69 per cent with the lowest turnover have done so, compared to 80 per cent of those with the highest turnover).

The survey considers five circular economy activities, which are (in order of relevance in terms of the EU28 average): (1) minimize waste by recycling or reusing waste, or selling it to another company (55 per cent); (2) replan energy usage to minimize consumption (38 per cent); (3) redesign products and services to minimize the use of materials, or use recycled materials (34 per cent); (4) replan the way water is used to minimize usage and maximize reusage (19 per cent); (5) use of renewable energy (16 per cent) (see Figure 2.4). The pattern of circular economy activities that are given more importance is similar to the average in the different countries, with just minor differences in this pattern: such as more emphasis on renewable energy (5) than on planning the use of water (4) in certain countries – Denmark, Germany, Malta, the Netherlands, Austria, Slovenia, Finland and Sweden; or more emphasis on minimizing energy (3) than on the use of less materials or recycled ones (2) in Bulgaria, Estonia, France, Luxembourg and Sweden. In general, it seems that firms still do not pay enough attention to using renewable energies or replanning the use of water.

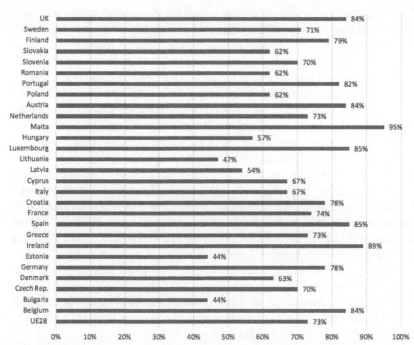

Source: Own elaboration with data from Flash Eurobarometer 441 – European SMEs and the Circular Economy.

Figure 2.3   SMEs undertaking some CE activities by country

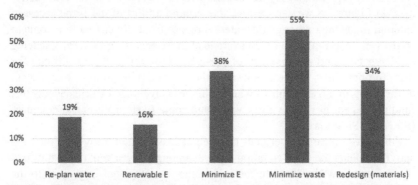

Source: Own elaboration with data from Flash Eurobarometer 441 – European SMEs and the Circular Economy.

Figure 2.4   Engagement in circular economy activities in EU28

More than half of the sample recognizes having confronted at least one difficulty when undertaking CE activities (see Figure 2.5). For those companies
that have undertaken activities related to the circular economy, the most
frequently mentioned issues encountered were: (1) complex administrative or
legal procedures (34 per cent); (2) the cost of meeting regulations or standards
(32 per cent); and (3) difficulties accessing finance (27 per cent); see Figure
2.6. There is considerable variation between member states in the issues
encountered, but the pattern is similar: institutional and regulatory challenges
(complexity of procedures and costs of regulation standards) seem to be the
hardest ones, which means that policy-makers have to take this into account to
facilitate firms' engagement in the CE. However, internal challenges in terms
of human capital and expertise, although mentioned, are not the greatest barrier
for these SMEs to engage in the CE. Also, firms that have not undertaken
any activities related to the circular economy were surveyed regarding the
potential difficulties encountered, these being: a lack of clear ideas about the
cost–benefit ratios of improved work processes (27 per cent), a lack of clear
ideas about the investment required (27 per cent) and a lack of expertise to
implement activities (26 per cent). Other difficulties (EU28 average) were:
lack of human resources (20 per cent), complex administrative or legal procedures (23 per cent), the cost of meeting regulations or standards (23 per cent),
financing (25 per cent), and 'other' (29 per cent).

Since financing the CE activities seems to be an important barrier, the
Eurobarometer has more specific questions about this issue. In Figure 2.7 we
focus on all the firms that undertake CE activities, and observing the EU28
average, we can highlight that the majority self-financed them (63 per cent, or
six of every ten firms): they did not use external sources to finance the activities. In Figure 2.8 we can observe that around a third of the firms accessed
external financing (although this interval ranges from 14 per cent in Estonia to
56 per cent in Malta). The EU28 average of those accessing external financing
is 31 per cent and the majority of these firms state that it was difficult for
them to obtain that funding. Normally there was a perception of easy access
to financing in those countries where a higher percentage of firms access this
funding, except in Greece and Cyprus and some Eastern European countries
(Slovenia, Slovakia).

From these firms, 59 per cent invested at least some turnover in such CE
activities, being the more common interval among 1–5 per cent of the turnover
(46 per cent). With regard to the information on financial incentives to the
circular economy through government programmes, a small proportion of the
firms were aware of them (35 per cent, and only 3 per cent have used them),
few say some or sufficient information is available (19 per cent) but most have
never searched for that information (48 per cent). In contrast to the scarce use
of public sources, almost one-third (32 per cent) have access to at least one of

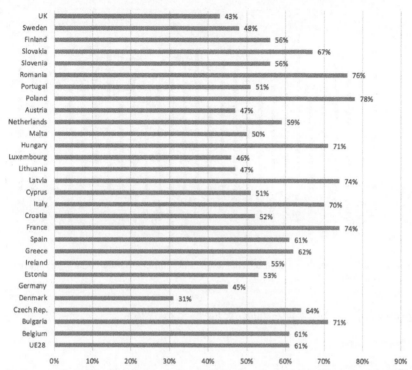

Source: Own elaboration with data from Flash Eurobarometer 441 – European SMEs and the Circular Economy.

Figure 2.5   *SMEs reporting problems when undertaking CE activities*

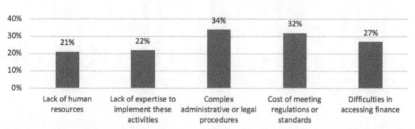

Source: Own elaboration with data from Flash Eurobarometer 441 – European SMEs and the Circular Economy.

Figure 2.6   *Issues encountered when undertaking CE activities, average EU28*

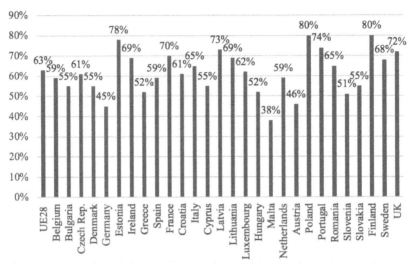

Source: Own elaboration with data from Flash Eurobarometer 441 – European SMEs and the Circular Economy.

Figure 2.7   SMEs self-financing their CE activities

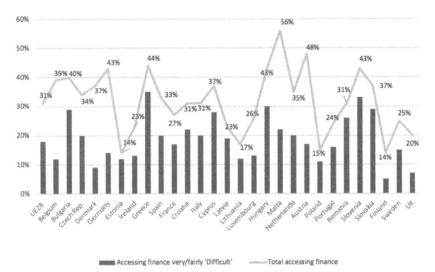

Source: Own elaboration with data from Flash Eurobarometer 441 – European SMEs and the Circular Economy.

Figure 2.8   SMEs financing CE activities: total using external sources and difficulty perceived

the 'alternative' sources of financing (that is, green banks, 17 per cent; and the capital market, 12 per cent).

CONCLUSIONS

The linear economy is unsustainable, surpassing the physical limits of the planet, and therefore a shift towards CE is inevitable. However, the speed of conversion is not rapid. In this sense, reviewing important issues regarding the CE concept and literature, and putting special emphasis on the challenges that SMEs confront, is a must.

Notwithstanding that ecological economics is a fruitful source of scientific and theoretical support for CE, the fact that the actual policy and business orientated concept of CE is so tightly related to changes in the way firms, especially SMEs, work and generate value (business models) means that entrepreneurship and strategic management theories are also crucial in contributing to improving firms' adoption of CE business models. Literature on CE business model design can be divided into different topics, the most relevant being: best practices, business model innovation frameworks for CE, decision-support tools for CE, and challenges confronted by firms. In this chapter we have focused on this last issue, aiming to understand how SMEs, most of the firms within the European Union, can be helped to confront the challenges related to circular economy activities.

Although almost three-quarters of the SMEs surveyed by the Eurobarometer point out that they were undertaking at least one activity related to the circular economy, this innovation in the business model is normally undertaken by larger firms in terms of employees and turnover. Only the focus on minimizing waste is considered by most firms; but replanning the use of water, or the use of renewable energy, are still areas in which much improvement can be achieved. Most of the firms report confronting barriers, of which institutional and regulatory barriers are the most important ones, followed by lack of financing; whereas lack of human resources and technical expertise seems to be more important for those companies which have not undergone any circular economy activity. So maybe different policies can be directed to these two groups of SMEs, with a special emphasis in facilitating complex administrative or legal procedures, reducing the cost of meeting regulations or standards, and facilitating lines of finance directed towards CE activities (although they are costly practices, the majority of the firms still self-finance them without searching for external funds). Incentives should be provided for companies to translate the concept of the circular economy into practical actions, and there should be enough diffusion among the business community.

In the academic realm, more effort must be made in emphasizing the economic and business perspective so that advantages for industries and SMEs are made explicit and implementation is facilitated. Also, in providing empirical evidence that increases public awareness of the potential of the circular economy.

ACKNOWLEDGEMENTS

The authors would like to acknowledge support from the Spanish Ministry of Science, Innovation and Universities, Research Grant RTI2018-101867-B-I00.

REFERENCES

Accenture strategy (2014), *Circular Advantage: Innovative Business Models and Technologies to Create Value in a World without Limits to Growth.* https://www.accenture.com/t20150523T053139__w__/us-en/_acnmedia/Accenture/Conversion-Assets/DotCom/Documents/Global/PDF/Strategy_6/Accenture-Circular-Advantage-Innovative-Business- Models-Technologies-Value-Growth.pdf (accessed 21 November 2019).
Bianchini, A., A. Benci, M. Pellegrini and J. Rossi (2019a), 'Supply chain redesign for lead-time reduction through Kraljic purchasing portfolio and AHP integration', *Benchmarking*, **26**, 1194–1209.
Bianchini, A., J. Rossi and M. Pellegrini (2019b), 'Overcoming the main barriers of circular economy implementation through a new visualization tool for circular business models', *Sustainability*, **11**, 6614–6647.
Brown, L. (2006), *Plan B 2.0: Rescuing a Planet Under Stress and a Civilization in Trouble*, Earth Policy Institute. www.earthpolicy.org/Books/PB2/Contents.htm, accessed 13 May 2020.
Chertow, M. and J. Ehrenfeld (2012), 'Organizing self-organizing systems: toward a theory of industrial symbiosis', *Journal of Industrial Ecology*, **16**(1), 13–27.
CIRAIG (Centre for the Life Cycle of Products, Processes and Services) (2015), *Circular Economy: A Critical Literature Review of Concepts*, Polytechnique Montréal, Canada.
COM (2014), *Towards a Circular Economy: A Zero-Waste Programme for Europe*, Communication from the Commission to the European Parliament, the Council, the European Economic and Social Committee and the Committee of the Regions, Brussels (EN).
COM (2015), *Closing the Loop – An EU Action Plan for the Circular Economy*, Communication from the Commission to the European Parliament, the Council, the European Economic and Social Committee and the Committee of the Regions.
de Lange, J. and L. Rodić (2013), *From Waste Handler to Resource Manager: New Roles for Solid Waste Management Companies in a Circular Economy.* Available in Researchgate: https://www.researchgate.net/publication/277954988_From_waste_handler_to_resource_manager_New_roles_for_solid_waste_management_companies_in_a_circular_economy, accessed 13 May 2020.
De los Ríos, I.C. and F.J.S. Charnley (2017), 'Skills and capabilities for a sustainable and circular economy: the changing role of design', *Journal of Cleaner Production*, **160**, 109–122.
EEA (2016), *Circular Economy in Europe: Developing the Knowledge Base*, EEA (European Environment Agency) Report No. 2/2016.

Ellen MacArthur Foundation (2015), *Towards a Circular Economy: Business Rationale for an Accelerated Transition.*

European Commission (2015), *Closing the Loop: An EU Action Plan for the Circular Economy.* Communication from the Commission to the European Parliament, the Council, the European Economic and Social Committee and the Committee of the Regions. https://eur-lex.europa.eu/resource.html?uri=cellar:8a8ef5e8-99a0-11e5-b3b7-01aa75ed71a1.0012.02/DOC_1&format=PDF (accessed 21 November 2019).

European Commission (2016), *Flash Eurobarometer 441 Report: European SMEs and the Circular Economy.* https://ec.europa.eu/commfrontoffice/publicopinion/index.cfm/Survey/getSurveyDetail/instruments/FLASH/surveyKy/2110 (accessed 22 December 2019).

Franco, M.A. (2017), 'Circular economy at the micro level: a dynamic view of incumbents' struggles and challenges in the textile industry', *Journal of Cleaner Production*, **168**, 833–845.

Geissdoerfer, M., S.N. Morioka, M.M. de Carvalho and S. Evans (2018), 'Business models and supply chains for the circular economy', *Journal of Cleaner Production*, **190**, 712–721.

Guldmann, E. and J.P. Jensen (2015), 'Implementation of circular economy in Danish companies', Global Cleaner Production and Sustainable Consumption Conference, Barcelona, Spain, pp. 1–2.

Howell, R., C. van Beers and N. Doorn (2018), 'Value capture and value creation: the role of information technology in business models for frugal innovations in Africa', *Technological Forecasting and Social Change*, **131**, 227–239.

Korhonen, J., A. Honkasalo and J. Seppälä (2018), 'Circular economics: the concept and its limitations', *Ecological Economics*, **143**, 37–46.

Kurilova-Palisaitiene, J., E. Sundin and B. Poksinska (2018), 'Remanufacturing challenges and possible lean improvements', *Journal of Cleaner Production*, **172**, 3225–3236.

Lahti, T., Wincent, J. Parida, V. (2018), 'A definition and theoretical review of the circular economy, value creation and sustainable business models: Where are we now and where should research move in the future?', *Sustainability*, **10** (8), 2799–2818.

Lieder, M. and A. Rashid (2016), 'Towards circular economy implementation: a comprehensive review in context of manufacturing industry', *Journal of Cleaner Production*, **115**, 36–51. https://doi.org/10.1016/j.jclepro.2015.12.042.

Linder, M. and M. Williander (2017), 'Circular business model innovation: inherent uncertainties: circular business model innovation', *Business Strategy and Environment*, **26** (2), 182–196.

Lüdeke-Freund, F. and K. Dembek (2017). 'Sustainable business model research and practice: emerging field or passing fancy?', *Journal of Cleaner Production*, **168**, 1668–1678.

Morlat, C. and K. Pinto-Silva (2014), 'Dynamic modelling of cost systems applied to energy efficiency', IAEE 2014 – 14th European Energy Conference – Sustainable Energy Policy and Strategies for Europe, Rome, Italy, pp. 1–2.

Osterwalder, A. and Y. Pigneur (2010), *Business Model Generation*, Hoboken, NJ: John Wiley & Sons. https://doi.org/10.1017/CBO9781107415324.

Pagoropoulos, A., D.C.A. Pigosso and T.C. McAloone (2017), 'The emergent role of digital technologies in the circular economy: a review', *Procedia CIRP*, **64**, 19–24.

Parida, V. and J. Wincent (2019), 'Why and how to compete through sustainability: a review and outline of trends influencing firm and network-level transformation', *International Entrepreneurship and Management Journal*, **15**, 1–19.

Planing, P. (2017), 'Will digital boost circular? Evaluating the impact of the digital transformation on the shift towards a circular economy', *International Journal of Management Cases*, **19**(1), 22–31.

Ritzén, S. and G.Ö. Sandström (2017), 'Barriers to the Circular Economy–Integration of perspectives and domains', *Procedia CIRP*, **64**, 7–12.

Rizos, V., A. Behrens, W. van der Gaast, E. Hofman, A. Ioannou, et al. (2016), 'Implementation of circular economy business models by small and medium-sized enterprises (SMEs): barriers and enablers', *Sustainability*, **8**, 1212.

Romero, D. and M. Rossi (2017), 'Towards circular lean product-service systems', *Procedia CIRP*, **64**, 13–18.

Roos, G. (2014), 'Business model innovation to create and capture resource value in future circular material chains', *Resources*, **3**, 248–274.

Rosa, P., C. Sassanelli and S. Terzi (2019), 'Towards circular business models: a systematic literature review on classification frameworks and archetypes', *Journal of Cleaner Production*, **236**, 117696.

Smith-Gillespie, A. (2017), *Defining the Concept of Circular Economy Business Model*. http://r2piproject.eu/wp-content/uploads/2017/04/Defining-the-Concept-of-Circular-Economy-Business-Model.pdf, accessed 13 May 2020.

Sousa-Zomer, T.T., L. Magalhães, E. Zancul and P.A. Cauchick-Miguel (2018), 'Exploring the challenges for circular business implementation in manufacturing companies: an empirical investigation of a pay-per-use service provider', *Resources, Conservation and Recycling*, **135**, 3–13.

Urbinati, A., D. Chiaroni and V. Chiesa (2017), 'Towards a new taxonomy of circular economy business models', *Journal of Cleaner Production*, **168**, 487–498.

Van Buren, N., M. Demmers, R. van der Heijden and F. Witlox (2016), 'Towards a circular economy: the role of Dutch logistics industries and governments', *Sustainability*, **8**, 647–664.

WCED (World Commission on Environment and Development) (1987), *Our Common Future*, New York: Oxford University Press.

Witjes, S. and R. Lozano (2016), 'Towards a more circular economy: proposing a framework linking sustainable public procurement and sustainable business models', *Resources, Conservation and Recycling*, **112**, 37–44.

3. Entrepreneurial cognition, sustainability and venture performance: a machine learning approach

Anna Vuorio and Kaisu Puumalainen

INTRODUCTION

Decision-making and action in a highly uncertain context are at the centre of the entrepreneurial process (Sarasvathy, 2001; McMullen and Shepherd, 2006). Although action characterizes the entrepreneurial process, it is often preceded by decision-making (Lerner et al., 2018). Two complementary decision-making logics, causation and effectuation, have been recognized in the prior literature to describe how entrepreneurs make decisions leading to opportunity recognition and exploitation (Sarasvathy, 2001). Regardless of the substantial amount of research on decision-making logics, effectuation theory and the concept of effectuation still need further development (Arend et al., 2015; Read et al., 2016). Especially, conditions under which effectuation and causation are applied and the type of benefits and disadvantages they generate under specific conditions need further examination (Sarasvathy, 2001; Read et al., 2016). Recently, some results (e.g., Welter and Kim, 2018; Jiang and Tornikoski, 2019) have been provided about the context in which entrepreneurs use the two different decision-making logics. However, to the best of our knowledge, it seems that the research on conditions for effectuation and causation has tended to focus on uncertainty and accuracy of prediction. In the contemporary economies, in which the pace of change and complexity are high, alternative approaches that rely on experimentation and provide flexibility are needed to generate diversity through entrepreneurial actions (Arend et al., 2015).

Sustainable entrepreneurship is a particular form of entrepreneurship, through which three types of value – social, environmental and economic value to an entrepreneur and others – are created (Dean and McMullen, 2007; Patzelt and Shepherd, 2011; Schaltegger and Wagner, 2011; Shepherd and

Patzelt, 2011). The focus on three types of value is the factor which makes sustainable entrepreneurs different from other types of entrepreneurs (Patzelt and Shepherd, 2011; Schaltegger and Wagner, 2011). Despite the decade of research, there is still a lack of understanding of how sustainable enterprises come into existence (Muñoz and Dimov, 2015; Muñoz and Cohen, 2018). Furthermore, the assumption about balancing three types of value has been found to be problematic, since these values seem to be conflicting (Hahn et al., 2010; Muñoz and Cohen, 2018). Instead, sustainable ventures have a step-by-step approach to developing value creation goals, rather than trying to manage all three types of goals at once (Belz and Binder, 2017). The aim to balance the three types of value associated with sustainability has been argued to constrain a company's willingness to fundamentally change core business practices and thus settle for solutions that do not radically change business practices (Hahn et al., 2010).

Since sustainable entrepreneurship centres on three types of value creation potentials, these value potentials should also characterize potential entrepreneurial opportunities. However, there is only limited evidence about the attributes of potential entrepreneurial opportunities that include sustainable value creation. Furthermore, although decision-making logics have gained considerable attention in the entrepreneurship literature (e.g., Chandler et al., 2011; Smolka et al., 2018; Welter and Kim, 2018; Jiang and Tornikoski, 2019), there seems to be a lack of studies that focus on decision-making in sustainable entrepreneurship (Muñoz, 2018). Additionally, there is only limited evidence about entrepreneurial opportunity recognition (e.g., Hanohov and Baldacchino, 2018) in sustainable entrepreneurship, and the literature seems to focus on factors that shape sustainable entrepreneurial opportunity recognition rather than dimensions of a perceived potential entrepreneurial opportunity.

This chapter thus attempts to shed light on how decision-making logics and perceptions of entrepreneurial opportunities shape venture performance. Although the impact of being sustainable has been studied in the prior literature, it remains unclear how perceptions of opportunities together with decision-making logics influence performance outcomes. Findings of the prior literature on impacts of effectuation and causation have been mixed and there is only limited evidence on how the two logics may be utilized in the context of sustainability incentives (e.g., Grimm and Amatucci, 2013). Furthermore, Muñoz and Cohen (2018) have put forward a call for an alternative methodological approach to study sustainable entrepreneurship, and this chapter thus applies a machine learning approach.

The results of the study provide new insights by, first, extending findings of the prior literature about the conditions under which effectuation and causation provide benefits and disadvantages. Second, the results extend our understanding of a connection between effectuation and causation. Third, the results provide new light on the decision-making in the context of potential sustainable entrepreneurial opportunities by including three types of value creation potentials. Lastly, a methodological approach that has been less conventional in entrepreneurship research is applied.

OPPORTUNITY RECOGNITION AS A COGNITIVE PROCESS

Entrepreneurial opportunity recognition, which is the first step towards entrepreneurial action, occurs through two cognitive processes: signal and pattern detection. Opportunity recognition is a cognitive process in which external market signals are interpreted through mental filters, through which an image of a potential entrepreneurial opportunity is formed (Renko et al., 2012). According to Baron and Ward (2004, p. 558), 'perhaps opportunities come into existence in the external world as a result of unrelated changes in technology, markets, demographics, and government policies or regulations; however, they remain merely a potential until one or more persons "connects the dots" and perceives a pattern among them'. Discrete external changes may only be considered as potential entrepreneurial opportunities when an individual or a group of individuals perceives a pattern among them. As a result, identifying a pattern of dispersed external changes resulting from subjective interpretation is described by recognition of a potential entrepreneurial opportunity.

According to signal detection theory, when an individual is attempting to define whether a signal exists or not, four different scenarios are present: correct identification, miss, false alarm and correct rejection (Baron, 2004). Correct identification occurs when a signal exists and an individual perceives it; while the false alarm is a situation in which an individual perceives a signal, although the signal does not exist. Similarly, a miss occurs when an individual does not perceive a signal, although it exists; and correct rejection is a situation in which a signal does not exist and an individual does not perceive it. Thus, two types of signals, 'real' signals and false signals, and two distinct signal-processing mechanisms, recognition and blocking, can be identified (Baron, 2004). However, perceiving different market signals is not enough for an individual to recognize a potential entrepreneurial opportunity; one must perceive a pattern among these signals. According to the pattern detection theory, individuals utilize experience-based cognitive frameworks to make decisions about connections between multiple discrete external signals (Baron, 2006). Individuals thus notice patterns among separate external events. This means that emergence of entrepreneurial opportunities requires that individuals recognize connections between changes in the surrounding environment, including technological, political, demographic or market development (Baron and Ward, 2004; Baron, 2006).

Key to entrepreneurial opportunity recognition are cognitive frameworks in the form of mental models (Barreto, 2012; Renko et al., 2012). These mental models are knowledge filters that process actual market signals, and as a result of this process, perceptions of a potential entrepreneurial opportunity are formed (Renko et al., 2012). Potential entrepreneurial opportunities thus are recognized by utilizing knowledge structures that act as perceptual filters to notice and interpret different market signals (Barreto, 2012; Renko et al., 2012). A match or a mismatch between perceptual filters and signals determines which signals are processed or blocked. In other words, decisions on whether something is perceived as a potential entrepreneurial opportunity or not are made based on these perceptual filters, which build on a person's prior experience.

There is only limited evidence about the characteristics of potential entrepreneurial opportunities or new venture ideas (Davidsson, 2019), which in this study are seen as the same phenomenon. The prior literature has included the following characteristics to describe entrepreneurial opportunities: novelty, economic value potential, growth and riskiness (e.g., Baron and Ensley, 2006; Haynie et al., 2009; Gruber et al., 2015; Santos et al., 2015). Out of these characteristics, innovativeness/novelty, economic value potential and riskiness/ uncertainty are inherently related to entrepreneurship. Despite the emergence of sustainable entrepreneurship, alternative value creation beyond economic value has not been included as a dimension of a potential entrepreneurial opportunity (with the exception of Shepherd et al., 2013). Simultaneously, entrepreneurship has been proposed as one way to alleviate poverty and others' suffering (Patzelt and Shepherd, 2011; Sutter et al., 2019). Alternative value creation potentials (social, environmental and sustainable value) thus should be included as a dimension of a potential entrepreneurial opportunity.

DECISION-MAKING LOGICS

Decision-making logics describe individual strategies towards opportunity recognition, development and exploitation. The prior literature has approached new venture creation from the perspective of two decision-making logics: causation and effectuation (Sarasvathy, 2001). Causation has been connected to planning, while effectuation is associated with controlling (Sarasvathy, 2001; Smolka et al., 2018). More precisely, causation is connected to predefined goals, competitive analysis, business planning, expected return maximization, capabilities and resources; while effectuation focuses on developing goals, environmental contingencies, pre-commitment, affordable loss and alliances (Chandler et al., 2011; Brettel et al., 2012).

Four key elements differentiate effectuation from causation (Sarasvathy, 2001). First, causation logic focuses on a particular goal as the basis for action and centres on gathering the needed resources to achieve that goal (Sarasvathy, 2001; Reymen et al., 2015). Thus the starting point of venture creation under causation logic is setting a specific goal (Reymen et al., 2015). Conversely, effectuation logic focuses on an individual's means (knowledge, resources, capabilities and social capital) and explores what kind of possible effects may be generated by combining those means (Sarasvathy, 2001; Reymen et al., 2015). Second, effectual decision-making relies on how much individuals are able to lose, and as a result, individuals using effectual logic tend to prefer those options that generate more options in the future. Conversely, decision-making under causation is based on expected returns, and thus those options that generate the largest possible returns from the decision-making are preferred. Third, while causation focuses on analysing competition in the market, effectuation relies on building alliances and pre-commitments to tackle uncertainty (Sarasvathy, 2001). Closing and protecting oneself from the competition is connected to causation, while effectuation is focusing more on coopetition. Fourth, effectuation acknowledges that the future is unpredictable, and thus the focus should be on those aspects that are controllable (Sarasvathy, 2001). As a result, effectual decision-making enables an entrepreneur to exploit events and conditions through flexibility (Chandler et al., 2011). Conversely, decision-making under causation associates unexpected events as interruptions to the current plan to achieve a particular goal, and thus an ability to predict and controllability of the future go hand in hand (Sarasvathy, 2001; Reymen et al., 2015). The two decision-making logics thus differ in fundamental ways in terms of outcome and the way to achieve it: under causation, the focus is on what is needed to create a particular effect; while effectuation centres on which kind of effect can be created with existing resources, capabilities and relationships.

Although these two decision-making logics are opposites, they are not substitutes for one another. For example, the prior research has found that causation together with experimentation has a positive impact on venture performance (Smolka et al., 2018). When experimentation is high, the impact of causation on venture performance is higher than when experimentation is low. Furthermore, similar results on the connection between effectuation and causation have been provided by Jiang and Tornikoski (2019), though they show that context matters.

Mental Models, Decision-Making and Performance Implications

The entrepreneurial decision-making process is connected to venture performance. However, results regarding the influence that causation and effectuation have on venture performance are mixed. First, a positive effect of planning on performance has been found; however, this relationship is contingent on the age of a company and its cultural context (Brinckmann et al., 2010). According to the results, established small companies gain more from planning than new ventures, and there are less benefits from planning in a cultural context with higher uncertainty avoidance compared to lower uncertainty avoidance. Furthermore, causation has been connected to venture viability (Greene and Hopp, 2017) and financial performance (Roach et al., 2016). Conversely, effectuation has been found to provide positive search performance outcomes over causation (Welter and Kim, 2018); and different elements of effectuation have been found to enhance different aspects of venture performance (Read et al., 2009), including financial performance, sales growth and cash flow, time of the first sale and profit (McKelvie et al., 2013). Additionally, the prior research (e.g. Smolka et al., 2018) has shown a connection between causation and effectuation, thus suggesting that these two decision-making logics may be complementary.

Entrepreneurial decision-making always is context-specific. Being essential to human reasoning, effectuation and causation are associated with different decision-making contexts and actions and thus they may be intertwined, overlapping and occur simultaneously (Sarasvathy, 2001). More recently, it has been proposed that effectuation could be beneficial under most conditions. However, applying both decision-making logics simultaneously, rather than separately, would seem likely to generate better results (Reymen et al., 2015; Welter and Kim, 2018). Sarasvathy (2001) proposed that effectuation is associated with uncertain contexts, while causation relates to risky contexts. Moreover, regardless of the type of uncertainty, effectuation becomes more prominent when uncertainty is present during the first phases of starting a venture; while when uncertainty is absent, the entrepreneurs seem to rely on causation (Jiang and Tornikoski, 2019). On the other hand, the findings of Welter and Kim (2018) show that effectuation provides better performance outcomes under conditions of both uncertainty and risk. Beyond uncertainty, the use of the two decision-making logics has been shown to depend on the degree of innovativeness of a research and development project (Brettel et al., 2012). The results show that in the context of high innovativeness, affordable loss and flexibility enhance process efficiency and project outcome. Conversely, in the context of low innovativeness most elements of causation had a positive impact on process efficiency and project outcome. This suggests that the degree of novelty or innovativeness may play a role in the use of decision-making logics. Additionally, such context-specific factors as the amount of resources available and the degree of external pressure have been proposed to influence the chosen decision-making logic through changes in venture scoping decisions (Reymen et al., 2015). However, these do not particularly relate to the perceived dimensions of a potential entrepreneurial opportunity.

Decision-making involving sustainability is contextual, includes balancing values and tends to focus on social actions (Martin, 2015). Furthermore, to create sustainable value through making sustainable decisions, a complex balance between cognitive factors is needed, since three types of objectives (economic, social and environmental) are combined in these decisions (Muñoz and Dimov, 2015). The prior social entrepreneurship literature has shown that the combination of effectuation and causation is present in the entrepreneurial opportunity development (Corner and Ho, 2010). This implies that there might be some context-specific differences in the use of causation and effectuation depending on the type of perceived value creation potential. However, it remains unclear whether or not being sustainable is beneficial for companies. Corporate social responsibility (CSR) activities have been found to both enhance and limit financial performance (Wang and Bansal, 2012; Dixon-Fowler et al., 2013); but the relationship between CSR activities and financial performance has been found to be strengthened by long-term orientation; that is, CSR activities decrease financial performance when long-term orientation is low, but the relationship is positive when long-term orientation is high (Wang and Bansal, 2012). This implies that new ventures which have a long-term plan for sustainable business practices tend to generate positive results from those activities. Additionally, small firms seem to generate more benefits from CSR activities than larger firms (Dixon-Fowler et al., 2013).

METHODOLOGY

A representative sample (N = 301) of Finnish small and medium-sized enterprises (SMEs) was collected via a survey in 2017. The survey was targeted at owner-managers of Finnish SMEs who preferably had also been involved in establishing the firm themselves. Three target regions were selected: the capital, the southeast (low entrepreneurship rate) and the Ostrobothnia (high entrepreneurship rate) region. To capture variability in perceptions of entrepreneurial opportunities, several (37) ISIC two-digit level industry categories were selected, among them manufacturing, water and waste management, electricity, trade, construction, business services, hospitality, information and social services. The aim of the multiple industries was to include different types of businesses and entrepreneurs, who have varying perceptions of entrepreneurial opportunities, in order to capture diversity in entrepreneurial opportunities. Additionally, the firms included had to fulfil the following criteria: (1) firms were young (three to five years old) and micro, small and medium-sized (5–250 employees); or (2) firms were older (over five years old) and small or medium-sized (10–250 employees). Through the above criteria, the aim was to reach firms whose direction for the company was already established and which had grown at different pace since their founding.

The survey was executed via computer-aided telephone interviews by a large market research company. A stratified sample contained 2386 companies from the Bisnode company register, which covers all Finnish enterprises, out of which 1625 firms (68 per cent of the sample) were contacted. Out of the contacted firms, 301 responded to the survey, resulting in a response rate of 18.5 per cent, which can be considered satisfactory given the length of the survey. Out of those 301 individuals, 204 had founded the firm either by themselves or together with others. The average age of the enterprises was 12, while the average age of the respondents was 51, and 73 per cent of the respondents were male. Over half of the respondents had an entrepreneurial background, and the average respondent had over 17 years of entrepreneurial experience. Additionally, the average respondent had over 23 years of industry-specific experience.

The survey contained measurement scales adopted from the literature, and one self-developed scale for entrepreneurial opportunity perceptions. The self-developed scale is derived from the prior entrepreneurship literature and covers the following dimensions: economic, social and environmental value potential (e.g., Baron and Ensley, 2006; Haynie et al., 2009; Shepherd and Patzelt, 2011), novelty (Haynie et al., 2009; Santos et al., 2015) and uncertainty (Baron and Ensley, 2006; Haynie et al., 2009; Gruber et al., 2015). Economic value potential consists of four items describing the value potential for the entrepreneur and in general. Sustainable value potential includes six

Table 3.1   Descriptive analysis

	Mean	St.d.	Cron	Cau	Exp	AL	Flex	PA	Nov	Eco	Sust	Unc
Cau	3.36	0.83	0.82									
Exp	2.45	1.00	0.72	-0.16*								
AL	3.49	1.22	0.82	0.06	-0.01							
Flex	4.11	0.74	0.65	0.08	-0.07	0.33*						
PA	3.12	0.81	0.75	0.35*	0.05	-0.00	0.10					
Nov	2.63	1.19	0.82	0.20*	0.06	-0.07	-0.07	0.13				
Eco	3.02	1.02	0.80	0.10	-0.03	0.03	0.07	-0.02	0.10			
Sust	3.09	0.89	0.77	0.38*	-0.12	0.12	0.03	0.16*	0.34*	0.17*		
Unc	1.94	0.55	0.45	0.31*	0.00	-0.19*	-0.05	0.13	0.17*	0.02	0.21*	
FP	2.39	0.69	-	0.11	-0.12	0.15*	0.10	0.02	-0.04	0.05	-0.04	-0.04

Notes:
* p < 0.05.
** St.d. = standard deviation. Cron = Cronbach's alpha, Cau = causation, Exp = experimentation, AL = affordable loss, Flex = flexibility, PA = pre-commitments and alliances, Nov = novelty of an opportunity, Eco = economic value of an opportunity, Sust = sustainable value of an opportunity, Unc = uncertainty of an opportunity, FP = financial performance.

items covering the social and environmental value creation potential to society and its importance to the entrepreneur. Novelty comprises of three items that focus on novelty in general and the degree of novelty; while uncertainty includes three items covering uncertainty caused by financial investment, risk of failure and time pressure. Decision-making logic was measured utilizing the scale developed by Chandler et al. (2011). Apart from causation, effectuation comprises of four dimensions: experimentation, affordable loss, flexibility and pre-commitments/alliances. Lastly, profitability was measured by asking the respondents to rate their companies' performance during the past few years relative to their closest competitors. The measure was dichotomized into three categories: higher, the same, and lower performance, compared to competitors. The variables were composed based on factor analyses (see Table 3A.1). The results show that the variables seem reliable, since the Cronbach's alphas are above 0.6, except for uncertainty. Descriptive analysis is presented in Table 3.1.

Machine Learning Methods

The data was analysed using artificial neural networks (ANN), which is inspired by the nervous system. ANN is a semi-parametric or non-parametric model, which means that coefficients cannot be used in a similar manner as, for example, in logistic regression (Dreiseitl and Ohno-Machado, 2002). ANN is used to model complex and non-linear relationships between attribute set X and the outcome (Kotu and Despande, 2015). It aims to create predictions by utilizing backpropagation to learn the relationship between an attribute set and an outcome. This is accomplished by using hidden layers and multiple nodes inside the hidden layer. X can be described as follows:

$$X = \{X_1, X_2, X_3, \dots, X_n\}$$

Information about the attribute set is assigned to nodes inside the hidden layer by using weights. It can be described as a linear function between the inputs and hidden layer as well as the hidden layer and the outputs (Dreiseitl and Ohno-Machado, 2002). The ANN model used in the study is presented in Figure 3.1.

The use of a hidden layer in the model transforms the model into a non-linear one since there is no linear relationship between inputs and outputs (Dreiseitl and Ohno-Machado, 2002). Furthermore, the ANN model's weights are optimized using maximum likelihood estimation. ANN models are flexible, which may create overfitting. The flexibility can be increased by adding hidden layers and hidden nodes.

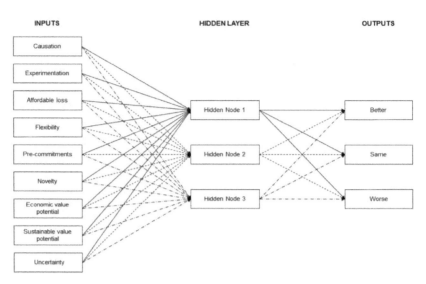

Figure 3.1   Illustration of ANN model

RESULTS

An ANN model was applied in order to examine connections between input and output variables. We used cross-validation to strengthen the reliability of the models. The sample was randomly divided into ten folds in a way that each fold contained a training set and a test set. Cross-validation was used to define the optimal number of hidden nodes in the hidden layer. Generally, one hidden layer is adequate for most datasets, which was also the case here. A training set was used to train the model, which predicted the outcomes in a test set. The results show that the ANN model (one hidden layer, three nodes) is able to predict 44.63 per cent of the outcomes correctly (accuracy). The confidence level in the model is 7.77 per cent, suggesting that the accuracy between ten alternative solutions generated during ANN varies between 36.86 and 52.40 per cent. Furthermore, class recall varies between 57.58 and 11.54 per cent, and class precision is between 51.35 and 27.27 per cent. This suggests that the model is able to predict correctly 57.6 per cent of those whose subjective financial performance is better than competitors' performance; while it was able to predict correctly 11.5 per cent of those whose subjective financial per-formance is worse than competitors' performance. In order for the model to be better than a random model, accuracy, recall and precision should be over 33.3 per cent. This applies to the ANN model for the most part; however, the model does not meet this criterion for class recall and precision when predicting those

Table 3.2   Results for ANN

Prediction accuracy

	True: same	True: better	True: worse	Class precision
Predicted: same	38	9	37	37.33%
Predicted: better	57	14	51	51.35%
Predicted: worse	4	3	27	27.27%
Class recall	38.58%	57.58%	11.54%	
Accuracy	44.63% (+/-7.77%)			

Effect of input layer factor on hidden layer nodes

	Node 1	Node 2	Node 3	Total contribution
Causation	-2.928	5.594	4.638	7.304
Experimentation	1.392	-5.315	-6.239	-10.162
Affordable loss	-7.891	3.765	-4.202	-8.328
Flexibility	-0.385	4.845	0.420	4.880
Pre-commitments	-1.291	-3.761	3.094	-1.958
Novelty	3.892	5.671	-1.809	7.754
Economic value	2.425	-6.111	8.618	4.932
Sustainable value	-4.875	2.054	-2.938	-5.759
Uncertainty	11.529	2.916	-4.918	9.527
Bias	-9.805	-12.368	-12.525	-34.698

Effect of hidden layer nodes on output variable (profitability)

	Better	Same	Worse	Total contribution
Node 1	-0.816	-4.664	5.419	-0.061
Node 2	2.012	-1.912	-5.943	-5.843
Node 3	5.045	-6.704	-5.041	-6.700
Bias	-0.360	0.009	-2.344	-2.695

who perceive their venture to perform worse than their competitors do. The ANN typology describing the connection between decision-making logics, dimensions of opportunity perceptions and perceived venture performance is presented in Table 3.2.

First, the effect of each input layer factor on the hidden layer was examined. The results of the ANN analysis show that the last factor of the input layer (the degree of uncertainty) has the highest total contribution of 9.527 to the three hidden nodes constituting the hidden layer. The second-highest contribution is generated by the degree of novelty (7.754), which is closely followed by causation with the total contribution of 7.304 on the three hidden nodes. The lowest total contribution of 4.880 to the hidden layer nodes is created by flexibility. Conversely, most of the elements of effectuation and the degree of sustainable value potential act as inhibitors, having a negative effect on the hidden layer. The highest inhibitory effect of -10.162 is generated by experimentation and the second-highest inhibitory effect is shown by affordable loss (-8.328). The lowest inhibitory effect of -1.958 is generated by pre-commitments and alliances.

Experimentation (1.392), as well as the degree of novelty (3.892), economic value potential (2.425) and uncertainty (11.529) of an opportunity, contribute to the first node, and thus the node 1 is labelled 'experimenter mindset'. Conversely, causation, the other elements of effectuation and the degree of sustainable value potential contribute negatively to the hidden layer node, having an inhibitory effect on the node. The largest negative weight of -7.891 on the node is generated by affordable loss, followed by the degree of sustainable value potential (-4.875). This suggests that when a perceived opportunity is high in uncertainty, novelty and economic value potential, and low in sustainable value potential, this type of opportunity perception is connected with experimentation. Furthermore, the results imply that perceived opportunities characterized by high uncertainty may direct entrepreneurs to experiment more, since there is so much unknown that experimentation is the only way to approach the opportunity. Conversely, considering how much a person can afford to lose, a more planning-oriented approach may not be beneficial in the case of perceived opportunities that are characterized by uncertainty and novelty.

The second node is labelled 'flexible planner mindset' since its contributory weight is derived from causation (5.594), affordable loss (3.765), flexibility (4.845), and the degree of novelty (5.671), sustainable value potential (2.054) and uncertainty (2.916) of an opportunity. Other elements of effectuation and the degree of the economic value potential have an inhibitory effect on the node (negative weight). The highest negative effect of -6.111 is generated by the degree of the economic value potential of an opportunity, followed by experimentation (-5.315). This suggests that perceived opportunities that are novel, uncertain and enable sustainable value creation are associated with planning and consideration of how much a person can lose combined with flexibility. Conversely, free experimentation may not provide benefits when combined with this type of perceived opportunity.

Causation (4.638), flexibility (0.420), pre-commitments and alliances (3.094), and the degree of economic value potential (8.618) contribute to the third node of the hidden layer, and thus the third node is labelled 'networking planner mindset'. Conversely, experimentation, affordable loss and the degree of novelty, sustainable value potential and uncertainty have an inhibitory effect on the node and thus contribute negatively to the node. The highest inhibitory effect of -6.239 is generated by experimentation, which is followed by the degree of uncertainty (-4.918). These results suggest that when the perception of an opportunity focuses on economic value potential, it seems that planning and utilizing personal networks may be a beneficial strategy, while experimenting and thinking how much one can afford to lose may not generate benefits.

Second, the impact of the hidden layer nodes on the output layer was examined. The output variable contained three categories: better, the same and worse profitability than competitors. The weights of each hidden layer node on the outcome level node are shown in Table 3.2. The results show that both the flexible planner mindset (node 2) and the networking planner mindset (node 3) contribute to the perception of better performance compared to competitors' performance (output node 2). The highest contributory weight of 5.045 is generated by the networking planner mindset, while the effect of 2.012 is shown by the flexible planner mindset. The experimenter mindset (node 1) has an inhibitory effect (albeit marginal, less than 1.0) of -0.816 on the perceived higher performance than competitors have. Conversely, none of the hidden layer nodes have a contributory effect on the perceived similar level of performance with competitors. However, the experimenter mindset contributes to the perception of worse performance compared to competitors' performance, with the weight of 5.419 (output node 3). On the other hand, the flexible planner mindset (node 2) and networking planner mindset (node 3) show an inhibitory effect on the perception of worse performance compared to competitors' performance (output node 3). Taking these results together, it seems that having a plan and utilizing one's social capital under specific circumstances may provide performance benefits; while not having a specific plan under a context of high uncertainty seems to generate undesirable performance implications.

DISCUSSION AND CONCLUSIONS

The goal of the study was to provide new insights on how decision-making logics and perceptions of entrepreneurial opportunities shape the venture performance. The recent results of the prior literature on effectuation and causation have provided some insights about the conditional differences related to uncertainty, under which these two logics have been utilized during the venture creation process (Jiang and Tornikoski, 2019). However, there is still only limited understanding of under which conditions effectuation and causation provide benefits and disadvantages, a call put forward by Sarasvathy (2001). By examining data collected from Finnish owner-entrepreneurs via the machine learning method, the contribution of this chapter is threefold. The findings of the study provide new understanding about: (1) the use of two different decision-making logics; (2) conditions under which those decision-making logics are used; and (3) the performance implications of the logics combined with certain conditions.

The results of the study extend and support the findings of the prior literature on effectuation and causation. First, the results of the study are in line with the results of the prior entrepreneurship research regarding the use of effectuation when the decision-making context is uncertain. Sarasvathy (2001) proposed that effectuation is associated with uncertain contexts, while causation relates more to risky contexts. More recently, it has been suggested that effectuation logic becomes more prominent when uncertainty is present during the first phases of starting a venture; while when uncertainty is absent, the entrepreneurs seem to rely on causation (Jiang and Tornikoski, 2019). The findings of this study also suggest that under conditions of perceived uncertainty and novelty in a potential opportunity, the experimenter mindset that includes the experimentation element from effectuation is the 'go-to' decision-making logic for the entrepreneurs. However, this decision-making logic combined with the context seems to generate disadvantages, since the experimenter mindset is linked to worse profitability compared to competitors. Similarly, the results regarding the degree of novelty of an opportunity differ somewhat from those of the prior literature (Brettel et al., 2012). The results show that both effectuation and causation are connected to perceptions of novelty. Furthermore, the findings of the study extend the prior research by taking into account additional dimensions of the perceived context via a perceived potential entrepreneurial opportunity.

The findings of the study provide evidence that instead of seeing effectuation and causation as opposites, they are complementary in nature. However, conversely to the results of Smolka et al. (2018), who found a positive interaction between experimentation and causation, the results of this study show that affordable loss, flexibility, and pre-commitments and alliances are linked to causation, while experimentation is not. Thus, this further highlights the importance of including perceptions of the conditions under which the individual is making the decisions beyond individual and venture characteristics. Additionally, the results show that better subjective performance is linked to mindsets that combine both causation and effectuation, while the mindset that only includes experimentation is connected to worse subjective performance. Thus, this renders further support for the findings of the prior literature suggesting that the optimal decision-making approach would be one that combines both causation and effectuation (Welter and Kim, 2018).

The findings of the study contribute to the sustainable entrepreneurship literature by showing that perceived sustainable value creation potential is connected to both effectuation and causation. The results of the prior social entrepreneurship research have indicated that social entrepreneurs use a combination of both causation and effectuation (Corner and Ho, 2010). However, the study also extends findings of the prior research by showing which particular elements – namely, flexibility and affordable loss – are linked to a particular type of perceived potential sustainable entrepreneurial opportunity. Furthermore, these results imply that decision-making in the context of potential sustainable entrepreneurial opportunities may differ from decision-making in the context of other types of potential opportunities. The findings of the study also generate new insight about the performance implications of being sustainable by showing that the flexible planner mindset, combined with a potential opportunity characterized by innovativeness, uncertainty and sustainable value creation, is linked to a perception of better performance than competitors have.

These results also have practical implications. The results suggest that particular decision-making logic combinations are linked to better subjective performance. The findings of the study show that the networking planner mindset and flexible planner mindset, which combine both effectuation and causation, are connected to better subjective performance; however, this is only under certain conditions. This implies two important considerations for entrepreneurs. First, combining elements of both decision-making logics may provide better performance outcomes in terms of profitability, but their effectiveness is contingent on the perceived potential opportunity. When uncertainty is moderate, a combination of the logics may provide the best performance outcomes. Conversely, when uncertainty is high, experimentation may be the best option to move forward, since the uncertainty may be so high that making any plans may seem impossible.

This chapter has limitations that also open up new avenues for research. First, the chapter is limited to the context of Finnish SMEs. Expanding and testing the models in a different national context would provide new insights about conditions under which decision-making logics provide benefits to ventures. Second, the chapter has focused on certain aspects of entrepreneurial cognition, namely decision-making logics and perceptions of entrepreneurial opportunities. Including additional variables, such as motivation, 'grit' or passion, would provide a more complex picture of entrepreneurial cognition. Lastly, the dependent variable in the study was a self-reported measure, and thus utilizing objective performance measures might provide different insights about the impact of decision-making logics and perceptions on performance. This has been also indicated by the prior literature, showing that the use of objective performance measurement over subjective performance measurement moderates the relationship between planning and performance (Brinckmann et al., 2010). Furthermore, having different aspects of performance besides profitability could provide a further understanding of how effectuation and causation under specific conditions shape performance.

REFERENCES

Arend, R.J., H. Sarooghi and A. Burkemper (2015), 'Effectuation as ineffectual? Applying the 3E theory-assessment framework to a proposed new theory of entrepreneurship', *Academy of Management Review*, **40** (4), 630–651.

Baron, R.A. (2004), 'The cognitive perspective: a valuable tool for answering entrepreneurship's basic "why" questions', *Journal of Business Venturing*, **19** (2), 221–239.

Baron, R.A. (2006), 'Opportunity recognition as pattern recognition: how entrepreneurs "connect the dots" to identify new business opportunities', *Academy of Management Perspectives*, **20** (1), 104–119.

Baron, R.A. and M.D. Ensley (2006), 'Opportunity recognition as the detection of meaningful patterns: evidence from comparisons of novice and experienced entrepreneurs', *Management Science*, **52** (9), 1331–1344.

Baron, R.A. and T.B. Ward (2004), 'Expanding entrepreneurial cognition's toolbox: potential contributions from the field of cognitive science', *Entrepreneurship: Theory and Practice*, **28** (6), 553–573.

Barreto, I. (2012), 'Solving the entrepreneurial puzzle: the role of entrepreneurial interpretation in opportunity formation and related processes', *Journal of Management Studies*, **49** (2), 356–380.

Belz, F.M. and J.K. Binder (2017), 'Sustainable entrepreneurship: a convergent process model', *Business Strategy and the Environment*, **26** (1), 1–17.

Brettel, M., R. Mauer, A. Engelen and D. Küpper (2012), 'Corporate effectuation: entrepreneurial action and its impact on RandD project performance', *Journal of Business Venturing*, **27** (2), 167–184.

Brinckmann, J., D. Gruchnik and D. Kapsa (2010), 'Should entrepreneurs plan or just storm the castle? A meta-analysis on contextual factors impacting the business planning–performance relationship in small firms', *Journal of Business Venturing*, **25** (1), 24–40.

Chandler, G.N., D.R. DeTienne, A. McKelvie and T.V. Mumford (2011), 'Causation and effectuation processes: a validation study', *Journal of Business Venturing*, **26** (3), 375–390.

Corner, P.D. and M. Ho (2010), 'How opportunities develop in social entrepreneurship', *Entrepreneurship Theory and Practice*, **34** (4), 635–659.

Davidsson, P. (2019), 'Opportunities re-conceptualized: updating the research agenda', Working Paper. Accessed 23 January 2019 at www.researchgate.net/profile/PerDavidsson/publication/330081102_Opportunities_Reconceptualized_Updating_the_Research_Agenda/links/5c2c6dcda6fdccfc70773517/Opportunities-Re-conceptualized-Updating-the-Research-Agenda.pdf.

Dean, T.J. and J.S. McMullen (2007), 'Toward a theory of sustainable entrepreneurship: reducing environmental degradation through entrepreneurial action', *Journal of Business Venturing*, **22** (1), 50–76.

Dixon-Fowler, H.R., D.J. Slater, J.L. Johnson, A.E. Ellstrand and A.M. Romi (2013), 'Beyond "Does it pay to be green?" A meta-analysis of moderators of the CEP–CFP relationship', *Journal of Business Ethics*, **112** (2), 353–366.

Dreiseitl, S. and L. Ohno-Machado (2002), 'Logistic regression and artificial neural network classification models: a methodology review', *Journal of Biomedical Informatics*, **35** (5–6), 352–359.

Greene, F.J. and C. Hopp (2017), 'Are formal planners more likely to achieve new venture viability? A counterfactual model and analysis', *Strategic Entrepreneurship Journal*, **11** (1), 36–60.

Grimm, R.C. and F.M. Amatucci (2013), 'Effectuation: an alternative approach for developing sustainability architecture in small business', *Journal of Small Business Strategy*, **23** (1), 55–69.

Gruber, M., S.M. Kim and J. Brinckmann (2015), 'What is an attractive business opportunity? An empirical study of opportunity evaluation decisions by technologists, managers, and entrepreneurs', *Strategic Entrepreneurship Journal*, **9** (3), 205–225.

Hahn, T., F. Figge, J. Pinkse and L. Preuss (2010), 'Editorial: Trade-offs in corporate sustainability: you can't have your cake and eat it', *Business Strategy and the Environment*, **19** (4), 217–229.

Hanohov, R. and L. Baldacchino (2018), 'Opportunity recognition in sustainable entrepreneurship: an exploratory study', *International Journal of Entrepreneurial Behavior and Research*, **24** (2), 333–358.

Haynie, J.M., D.A. Shepherd and J.S. McMullen (2009), 'An opportunity for me? The role of resources in opportunity evaluation decisions', *Journal of Management Studies*, **46** (3), 337–361.

Jiang, Y. and E.T. Tornikoski (2019), 'Perceived uncertainty and behavioral logic: temporality and unanticipated consequences in the new venture creation process', *Journal of Business Venturing*, **34** (1), 23–40.

Kotu, Vijay and Bala Despande (2015), *Predictive Analytics and Data Mining*, Waltham, MA: Elsevier.

Lerner, D.A., R.A. Hunt and D. Dimov (2018), 'Action! Moving beyond the intendedly-rational logics of entrepreneurship', *Journal of Business Venturing*, **33** (1), 52–69.

Martin, L. (2015), 'Incorporating values into sustainability decision-making', *Journal of Cleaner Production*, **105**, 146–156.

McKelvie, A., D.R. DeTienne and G.N. Chandler (2013), 'What is the appropriate dependent variable in effectuation research?', *Frontiers of Entrepreneurship Research*, **33** (4), 1–15.

McMullen, J.S. and D.A. Shepherd (2006), 'Entrepreneurial action and the role of uncertainty in the theory of the entrepreneur', *Academy of Management Review*, **31** (1), 132–152.

Muñoz, P. (2018), 'A cognitive map of sustainable decision-making in entrepreneurship: a configurational approach', *International Journal of Entrepreneurial Behavior and Research*, **24** (3), 787–813.

Muñoz, P. and B. Cohen (2018), 'Sustainable entrepreneurship research: taking stock and looking ahead', *Business Strategy and the Environment*, **27** (3), 300–322.

Muñoz, P. and D. Dimov (2015), 'The call of the whole in understanding the development of sustainable ventures', *Journal Business Venturing*, **30** (4), 632–654.

Patzelt, H. and D.A. Shepherd (2011), 'Recognizing opportunities for sustainable development', *Entrepreneurship Theory and Practice*, **35** (4), 631–652.

Read, S., S.D. Sarasvathy, N. Dew and R. Wiltbank (2016), 'Response to Arend, Sarooghi, and Burkemper (2015): cocreating effectual entrepreneurship research', *Academy of Management Review*, **41** (3), 528–556.

Read, S., M. Song and W. Smit (2009), 'A meta-analytic review of effectuation and venture performance', *Journal of Business Venturing*, **24** (6), 573–587.

Renko, M., R.C. Schrader and M. Simon (2012), 'Perception of entrepreneurial opportunity: a general framework', *Management Decision*, **50** (7), 1233–1251.

Reymen, I.M.M.J., P. Andries, H. Berends, R. Mauer, U. Stephan and E. van Burg (2015), 'Understanding dynamics of strategic decision making in venture creation: a process study of effectuation and causation', *Strategic Entrepreneurship Journal*, **9** (4), 351–379.

Roach, D.C., J.A. Ryman and J. Makani (2016), 'Effectuation, innovation and performance in SMEs: an empirical study', *European Journal of Innovation Management*, **19** (2), 214–238.

Santos, S.C., A. Caetano, R. Baron and L. Curral (2015), 'Prototype models of opportunity recognition and the decision to launch a new venture', *International Journal of Entrepreneurship Behavior and Research*, **21** (4), 510–538.

Sarasvathy, S.D. (2001), 'Causation and effectuation: toward a theoretical shift from economic inevitability to entrepreneurial contingency', *Academy of Management Review*, **26** (2), 243–263.

Schaltegger, S. and M. Wagner (2011), 'Sustainable entrepreneurship and sustainability innovation: categories and interactions', *Business Strategy and the Environment*, **20** (4), 222–237.

Shepherd, D.A. and H. Patzelt (2011), 'The new field of sustainable entrepreneurship: studying entrepreneurial action linking "what is to be sustained" with "what is to be developed"', *Entrepreneurship Theory and Practice*, **35** (1), 137–163.

Shepherd, D.A., H. Patzelt and R.A. Baron (2013), '"I Care about nature, but...": disengaging values in assessing opportunities that cause harm', *Academy of Management Journal*, **56** (5), 1251–1273.

Smolka, K.M., I. Verheul, K. Burmeister-Lamp and P.P.M.A.R. Heugens (2018), 'Get it together! Synergistic effects of causal and effectual decision-making logics on venture performance', *Entrepreneurship Theory and Practice*, **42** (4), 571–604.

Sutter, C., G.D. Bruton and J. Chen (2019), 'Entrepreneurship as a solution to extreme poverty: a review and future research directions', *Journal of Business Venturing*, **34** (1), 197–214.

Wang, T. and P. Bansal (2012), 'Social responsibility in new ventures: profiting from a long-term orientation', *Strategic Management Journal*, **33** (10), 1135–1153.

Welter, C. and S. Kim (2018), 'Effectuation under risk and uncertainty: a simulation model', *Journal of Business Venturing*, **33** (1), 100–116.

APPENDIX: RESULTS OF FACTOR ANALYSIS

Table 3A.1   Factor loadings for variables

Causation–effectuation	C	E	AL	F	PA
1. We analysed long-run opportunities and selected what we thought would provide the best returns.	0.60				
2.We developed a strategy to best take advantage of resources and capabilities.	0.69				
3.We designed and planned business strategies.	0.84				
4. We organized and implemented control processes to make sure we met objectives.	0.71				
5. We researched and selected target markets and did meaningful competitive analysis.	0.71				
6. We had a clear and consistent vision for where we wanted to end up.	0.55				
7. We designed and planned production and marketing efforts.	0.74				
8. We experimented with different products and/or business models.		0.66			
9. The product/service that we now provide is essentially the same as originally conceptualized.*		0.69			
10. The product/service that we now provide is substantially different than we first imagined.		0.72			
11. We tried a number of different approaches until we found a business model that worked.		0.78			
12. We were careful not to commit more resources than we could afford to lose.			0.83		
13. We were careful not to risk more money than we were willing to lose with our initial idea.			0.88		
14. We were careful not to risk so much money that the company would be in real trouble financially if things did not work out.			0.79		
15. We allowed the business to evolve as opportunities emerged.				0.71	
17. We were flexible and took advantage of opportunities as they arose.				0.81	
18. We avoided courses of action that restricted our flexibility and adaptability.				0.70	
19. We used a substantial number of agreements with customers, suppliers and other organizations and people to reduce the amount of uncertainty.					0.60
20. We used pre-commitments from customers and suppliers as often as possible.					0.62

Causation–effectuation	C	E	AL	F	PA
21. Network contacts provided low-cost resources.					0.63
22. By working closely with people/organizations external to our organization, we have been able to greatly expand our capabilities.					0.72
23. We have focused on developing alliances with other people and organizations.					0.72
24. Our partnerships with outside organizations and people play a key role in our ability to provide our product/service.					0.73
Entrepreneurial opportunity	N	E	S	U	
1. Our venture represents the most innovative idea.	0.79				
9. There is no similar way of doing business anywhere.	0.87				
17. Our business idea is new and original.	0.90				
3. The venture would provide me with nice profit.		0.97			
11. I can make a living with the income from the venture.		0.77			
19. With the help of the venture, I am able to generate wealth for myself in the future.		0.69			
22. The venture would generate economic added value.		0.81			
4. We would contribute to solving social problems.			0.69		
6. The venture operates in an environmentally friendly way.			0.61		
12. The venture helps to improve the state of the environment for its part.			0.70		
14. Social responsibility is self-evident to us.			0.64		
20. We would generate societal added value that cannot be measured in monetary terms.			0.69		
23. Our business idea enhances sustainable development.			0.71		
2. In order to start the venture, we would have to invest in it considerable resources.				0.77	
5.The opportunity would have passed us soon if would not have exploited it.				0.52	
10. This business would have a considerably high risk of failure.				0.69	

Note:
* Items were originally in Finnish. C = causation, E = experiments, AL = affordable loss, F = flexibility, PA = pre-commitments and alliances, N = the degree of novelty in an opportunity, E = the degree of economic value in an opportunity, S = the degree of sustainable value in an opportunity, U = the degree of uncertainty in an opportunity.

4. The way to be green: determinants of eco-process innovations in the food sector

María C. Cuerva, Ángela Triguero and Francisco José Sáez-Martínez

INTRODUCTION

In order to maintain or expand the market share and profitability in dynamic markets, innovation strategies have become crucial for the food sector (Lefebvre et al., 2015). Although empirical evidence supports that it is a low-tech industry, food firms are very aware of their market and the demands of customers and consumers, more concerned with the environmental impact of production, who increasingly require food products with technological processing characteristics such as quality, safety, ease of use and storability (Capitanio et al., 2010).

The food sector is characterized by its high environmental impact and level of emissions (Demirel and Kesidou, 2011). This fact is related to the inefficiency in the resources use and food distribution stage, and high rates of food waste, that require the transition towards more sustainable practices (Jurgilevich et al., 2016). Therefore, the sector is under pressure to face up to the eco-innovation challenge: the valorization and treatment of waste arising from food production and consumption; new or improved production processes increasing resource efficiency; innovative ways to treat wastewater; and new packaging solutions (European Commission, 2013).

Although the food sector has developed a range of different types of innovation, previous research illustrates the engagement of food firms especially in process innovation, and the incremental nature of innovation (Archibugi et al., 1991; Galizzi and Venturini, 1996; Grunert et al., 1997; Martinez and Briz, 2000; Capitanio et al., 2010; Baregheh et al., 2012). According to Caiazza et al. (2014), process innovation in the agro-food sector is defined as the implementation of a new or significantly improved method of producing or distributing a food product. These innovations are related to production methods, such as the techniques and equipment used in the production of goods and services, or in the delivery methods for inputs and final products. In the specific case of eco-innovation, practices oriented to reduce the consumption of materials and energy (water pollution abatement, waste management, solid waste collection, materials recycling or incineration and energy recovery) in the food industry are considered eco-process innovations.

Since eco-innovation depends on sectoral characteristics (Del Río et al., 2016) it is necessary that further research takes into account differences across sectors. Most of the literature analyses the adoption of eco-innovation in the manufacturing sector (Brunnermeier and Cohen, 2003; Wagner, 2007, 2008), high- tech sectors (Chen et al., 2006; Kammerer, 2009) or the most polluting sectors (Del Río, 2005; González-Moreno et al., 2013; Mondéjar-Jiménez et al., 2015). The economic importance of the food sector and its innovation behaviour has led to a body of research into innovation within the sector. Nevertheless, there has been little research about drivers of eco-innovation strategies (Cuerva et al., 2014; Bossle et al., 2016; Triguero et al., 2018; Cuerva, 2019; Triguero, 2019; Córcoles, 2019; González-Moreno et al., 2019). Thus, the analysis of the determinants of eco-process innovation in the food sector is under-researched or mainly based upon surveys not specifically designed to approach eco-innovation (for example, the Community Innovation Survey, CIS). In this regard, more reliable data from surveys specifically intended to gather information on eco-innovation are needed (Maçaneiro et al., 2013). On the other hand, most of the previous research analyses the influence of knowledge sources in eco-innovation without considering external knowledge explicitly oriented to the improvement of environmental performance (Ghisetti et al., 2015).

This chapter contributes to fill the gap in the literature about the study of the factors influencing the adoption of eco-process innovation in the food sector in Spain. The main contributions are twofold. First, the focus is on the drivers of eco-process innovations in food firms. Second, attention is placed on the influence of the external sources of knowledge on this type of eco-innovation and how the frequency and the diversity of these sources influence eco-process innovation.

The remainder of the chapter is structured as follows. First, the theoretical framework and hypotheses about the drivers of eco-innovation are considered. We then describe the dataset and method used, before discussing our findings. The final section presents our conclusions and the research limitations.

THEORETICAL FRAMEWORK: DRIVERS OF ECO-INNOVATION

The adoption of eco-innovation depends on the internal resources and knowledge of the firm. From this perspective, the resource-based view (RBV) theory serves as a theoretical framework to examine the link between companies' resources and innovation performance. In this sense, in order to gain a competitive advantage through eco-innovation strategies, the firm's internal characteristics and resources are decisive. These resources include intangible and tangible assets such as human and knowledge resources, information technology and capital (Sarkis et al., 2010; Hojnik and Ruzzier, 2016). On the other hand, the evolutionary perspective emphasizes not only the importance of internal factors influencing the innovation process, but also the characteristics of the innovation systems, the dynamic interaction between different actors, and other external factors (Jové-Llopis and Segarra-Blasco, 2018).

Hence, taking into account the RBV and evolutionary perspectives, Figure 4.1 shows the proposed theoretical framework, where internal and external factors influence the decision to eco-innovate. Internal factors refer to internal resources, preconditions and features of the firms that facilitate eco-innovation (Del Río et al., 2016). External drivers represent the interaction of the firms through cooperation or collaboration with institutional, market or social actors (Hojnik and Ruzzier, 2016).

Figure 4.1   Drivers of eco-process innovation

Among internal capabilities, size is used to assess the role of complementary assets of the firm and its internal capability to eco-innovate (Segarra-Oña et al., 2011). Most studies also highlight size as a main driver of eco-innovation (Cleff and Rennings, 1999; Rehfeld et al., 2007; Demirel and Kesidou, 2011; De Marchi, 2012; Le Bas and Poussing, 2013; Triguero et al., 2017), especially for eco-process innovations (Hojnik and Ruzzier, 2016). A high availability of financial resources is usually the reason given to explain a high environmental awareness of large firms in comparison with small and medium-sized enterprises (SMEs). Nevertheless, empirical evidence is not conclusive, and studies such as Horbach (2008) and Bernauer et al. (2007) do not confirm the positive relationship between eco-innovation and size. In the case of Spanish food firms, Cuerva et al. (2014) and Triguero et al. (2018) find that size is relevant for eco-innovation. In the latter study, the authors confirm that large food firms eco-innovate more than SMEs, both in eco-product and in eco-process innovations. Therefore, we hypothesize that:

H1: The size of the firm is positively associated with the adoption of eco-process innovation in the food sector.

The age of the firm is also a factor that could foster or discourage eco-innovation. However, the results are not conclusive and firm age could be a double-edged sword (Del Río et al., 2016). The older the firm, the higher the accumulation of internal capabilities which influence eco-innovation. Nevertheless, on the other hand, young firms are more prone to develop new competences required in the challenge of the adoption of eco-innovation processes (Díaz-García et al., 2015). The majority of studies confirm the positive effect of age on the probability of eco-innovating (Cleff and Rennings, 1999; De Marchi, 2012; Le Bas and Poussing, 2013; Demirel and Kesidou, 2011), although young firms seem to have a higher probability of undertaking eco-innovation for Ziegler and Rennings (2004) and Rehfeld et al. (2007). Innovation in food firms has also been associated with younger firms (Cabral and Traill, 2001), but in the case of eco-innovation the scarce empirical literature does not find a significant relationship with the age of the firm (Cuerva et al., 2014; Triguero et al., 2018). Following the majority of studies on eco-innovation, we hypothesize:

H2: The age of the firm is positively associated with the adoption of eco-process innovation in the food sector.

The probability of eco-innovating is also associated with the degree of export orientation of production (Cainelli et al., 2012). First, international customers exert stronger environmental pressures on innovative firms than national consumers do. Second, exporter firms develop eco-innovations to overcome the trade barriers imposed on non-sustainable companies. Third, the exposure to higher competition in global markets stimulates export-oriented firms to invest in environmentally friendly technologies. Brunnemeier and Cohen (2003) and Horbach (2008) highlight that firms more exposed to international competition are more engaged in environmental innovation. Nevertheless, the results are not conclusive. De Marchi (2012) finds a significant and negative relationship between exports and eco-innovation in Spanish firms. Analyses carried out for the food sector conclude that firms oriented towards international markets have a stronger innovation competence (Gellynck et al., 2007). In fact, the analyses show a positive relationship between export and innovation activities (product and process) in the food sector, as do previous studies in the manufacturing sector (Alarcón and Sánchez, 2016). In this study, it is assumed that firms operating in international markets direct a higher percentage of resources to eco-innovation. Therefore, we hypothesize:

H3: Export orientation of the firm is positively associated with the adoption of eco-process innovation in the food sector.

In dynamic markets, managers perceive rapid changes in the competitive environment and try to increase flexibility by renewing products and processes (Worren et al., 2002). According to the RBV, flexibility refers to the capability of the firm to rapidly relocate and reconfigure resources and processes (Sánchez, 1995). Flexibility is associated with a reduction in the resistance to change and in the operational complexity that facilitates attention to new challenges and opportunities (Bock et al., 2012), increasing technological capabilities of the firm and, thereby, innovation (Zhou and Wu, 2010). Since innovation integrates new products and processes, which imply new ideas and practices in the organization of the firm, innovation is influenced by the degree of flexibility of the firm. The food sector is a very dynamic industry, exposed to changes in the external environment (competitors, regulation, customers and resource scarcity). This calls for the ability to quickly adapt and change the organization of production in order to gain competitive advantages. Among factors encouraging process innovation in food firms, the empirical literature points out the operational flexibility in production, which can help in reducing costs or increasing benefits (Acosta et al., 2015). Flexibility provides food firms with a distinct competitive advantage facilitating the meeting of challenges related to the environment. Based on these arguments, we assume that:

H4: Flexibility in the productive process of the firm is positively associated with the adoption of eco-process innovation in the food sector.

The acquisition of embodied technology is also crucial for eco-process innovation (Marzucchi and Montresor, 2017). In the particular case of the food sector, studies confirm no association of research and development (R&D) intensity with process innovation (Traill and Meulenberg, 2002). In fact, several analyses highlight the important role of the acquisition of new machinery, software and hardware to increase the technological capabilities of low-tech sectors where R&D expenditure is not high (Santamaría et al., 2009; Hervas-Oliver et al., 2011). Since food firms are more oriented to eco-process innovation, the intensive use of embodied technology is one of the main characteristics of the food sector (Capitanio et al., 2010; Triguero et al., 2018), underlining the important contribution of the suppliers of machinery and equipment to the process of innovation in food firms. Therefore, we formulate the following hypothesis:

H5: Technological absorptive capacity (embodied technology) of the firm is positively associated with the adoption of eco-process innovation in the food sector.

In relation to the external factors, technology knowledge acquisition from external market (customer, providers, competitors) and non-market (universities, research institutes, consultants) sources of information may help firms to create, develop or improve their own innovations (Acosta et al., 2013). In the case of eco-innovation, this entails collaborating with external actors to a greater extent (Horbach et al., 2012), because the knowledge used in eco-innovation is more disciplinary than the knowledge needed in general innovation (Rennings and Rammer, 2011), requiring more interdependency between the firms, customers, providers and other organizations (Bossle et al., 2016). The knowledge and competences acquired from partners complement internal investments of the firm and could play a key role in the development of eco-innovations (De Marchi and Grandinetti, 2013). In fact, as Ghisetti et al. (2015) highlight, openness to external sources of knowledge could help firms to compensate for their internal barriers, such as the lack of capabilities and resources to develop or adopt environmental knowledge, that often hamper the gaining of competitive advantage based on eco-innovation. Testing the role of these sources of information in support of innovation in food firms is of great interest (Capitanio et al., 2009). Although there is a relatively low level of engagement in collaborating in the food sector (Baregheh et al., 2012), food firms take advantage of external sources of knowledge without the need to expend resources on internal R&D (Acosta et al., 2015). The scarce literature about eco-innovation in the food sector is not conclusive about the effect of collaboration with different stakeholders. On the one hand, Cuerva et al. (2014) do not find evidence for a significant effect of any type of collaboration on eco-innovation. On the other hand, Bossle et al. (2016), Triguero et al. (2018) and González-Moreno et al. (2019) show that cooperation is a key external factor which enables easier access to the necessary external knowledge to adopt eco-innovation.

Additionally, not only is cooperation important, but also the knowledge source diversity and frequency. The wider the partners' diversity, the greater the probability of developing eco-innovation. The empirical literature shows the positive effect exerted by the use of a variety of external sources of knowledge on eco-innovation in manufacturing firms (Cai and Zhou, 2014; Ghisetti et al., 2015; Marzucchi and Montresor, 2017; Jové-Llopis and Segarra-Blasco, 2018). In the case of food firms, recent literature confirms the essential role of intense and frequent interactions with partners for the development of eco-process innovation through the acquisition of more resources and information (González-Moreno et al., 2019). Taking into account previous results, we claim that:

H6a: External sources of knowledge of the firm are positively associated with the adoption of eco-process innovation in the food sector.

H6b: The frequency and the diversity of sources of knowledge of the firm are positively associated with the adoption of eco-process innovation in the food sector.

DATA AND METHOD

Data on specific environmental innovation strategies at the firm level are not usually available from published sources. To overcome this difficulty, we used an ad hoc questionnaire. Firm-relative information comes from a survey launched to a randomly chosen sample of food and beverage firms in Spain in 2017. It included several questions about the type of eco-innovation introduced in the last three years (2014–16) and the specific characteristics of the

Table 4.1   *Characteristics of eco-process innovators in the food industry in Spain (total sample = 279)*

	Total eco-innovators (178)	Eco-process innovators (151)
By size		
Micro	40 (22.5%)	34 (22.5%)
Small	71 (39.9%)	57 (37.8%)
Large	67 (37.6%)	60 (39.7%)
By type of innovation		
Only radical	18 (10.1%)	19 (12.6%)
Only incremental	125 (70.2%)	111 (73.5%)
Both	35 (19.7%)	20 (13.2%)
NA	-	1 (0.7%)
By collaboration		
Collaborate	64 (36.0%)	53 (35.1%)
No collaboration	112 (63.0%)	96 (63.6%)
NA	2 (1.0%)	2 (1.3%)

Source: Own elaboration based on survey data.

Table 4.2   *Dependent and explanatory variables: definition and measurement*

Dependent variable	
Eco-process	= 1 if the firm has developed in the last three years (2014–16) eco-process innovations (in the process of production, delivery or recovery of waste) = 0 otherwise
Explanatory variables	
Internal capabilities	
Size	Log value of the number of employees of the firm
Age	Log value of the number of years since the establishment of the firm
Age^2	Squared log value of the number of years since the establishment of the firm
Export	= 1 if the firm is engaged in international markets = 0 otherwise
Flexibility capacity	Categorical variable identifying the capacity of the firm to adjust their productive capacity. Three categories: = 1 if the firm reports low capacity flexibility = 2 if the firm reports medium capacity flexibility = 3 if the firm reports high capacity flexibility
Tech_absorp_cap	Tangible and intangible assets as a percentage of the sales of the firm (log of the average 2014–16)
External knowledge	
Collaboration	= 1 if the firm has collaborated with any type of external agents in the development or exploitation of eco-innovations = 0 otherwise
Vertical collaboration	= 1 if the firm has collaborated with customers and/or providers in the development or exploitation of eco-innovations = 0 otherwise
Other collaboration	= 1 if the firm has collaborated with universities, public research centres, consultants or other agents in the development or exploitation of eco-innovations = 0 otherwise
Collaboration_ frequency	Number of collaborations (frequency) with external agents in the development or exploitation of eco-innovations
Collaboration_ diversity	Variable ranging from 0 to 7 depending on the number of types of collaborators (diversity: firms of the group, customers, providers, competitors, universities, public research centres, consultants, other agents) in the development or exploitation of eco-innovations
Control variables	
Region	17 dummy variables for the different regions in Spain
Subsector	8 dummy variables for the different subsectors in the food industry

knowledge used and the type of eco-innovations carried out. Additionally, this information has been completed with data from the SABI database which contains financial information, characteristics of the firms (size, age, human capital, export) and other miscellaneous information at firm level in Spain. The final sample size is 279 firms (response rate of 27.9 per cent).

A binary measure distinguishes between eco-process innovators and non-eco-process innovators. In the sample, 178 of the firms are eco-innovators (two-thirds of the firms), with 151 of them being eco-process innovators (61 per cent of the total sample). Therefore, 85 per cent of eco-innovators carry out process innovations, most of them incremental rather than radical (Table 4.1). Regarding their size, 22.5 per cent of eco-process innovators have less than ten employees, 37.8 per cent are medium-sized firms, and 39.7 per cent are large firms. Another characteristic of the eco-process innovators in the food sector is that collaboration in the development or exploitation of this innovation is low. Only one-third of eco-process innovators report collaborating with external partners. This result confirms the incremental nature of process innovations and the low collaboration with external sources of knowledge in this sector.

We examine the factors influencing the adoption of eco-process innovation using probit regressions. The variables included distinguish among internal and external factors to the firm. Table 4.2 provides a complete list of variables and definitions used in this study (Table 4A.1 in the Appendix gives summary statistics of the variables and Table 4A.2 shows the correlation matrix). Among internal factors, we consider the internal capabilities and resources of the firms: size, age and squared age, internationalization (export) and flexibility in the production capacity. Finally, we introduce the technological absorptive capacity, measured as the embodied technology through the acquisition of tangible and intangible assets in relation to the sales, similar to other works such as Van Leeuwen and Klomp (2006).

Among external factors, we take into account the external networks in eco-innovation, in terms of the diversity of collaboration (competitors, customers, providers, universities, consultants, and so on) and frequency (number of collaborations). Finally, we introduce sector and regional dummies to capture the different regional innovation systems in Spain, similar to Acosta et al. (2015).

RESULTS

Table 4.3 shows the results of the probit models in terms of the average marginal effects. Given the correlation between the size and the export variable, we have estimated two separate models. In Model I we include the size and in Model II we consider if the firm exports. To test for multicollinearity among independent variables, the mean variance inflation factor (VIF) corresponding

Table 4.3   *Average marginal effects of probit models*

	Model I				Model II			
	(1)	(2)	(3)	(4)	(1)	(2)	(3)	(4)
Size	0.0535***	0.0614***	0.0548***	0.0535***				
	(0.0172)	(0.0162)	(0.0164)	(0.0167)				
Age	-0.519**	-0.557**	-0.581**	-0.562**	-0.555***	-0.615**	-0.639***	-0.622**
	(0.256)	(0.246)	(0.244)	(0.243)	(0.255)	(0.247)	(0.245)	(0.242)
Age^2	0.101**	0.106**	0.111***	0.108***	0.114***	0.123***	0.127***	0.124***
	(0.0435)	(0.0419)	(0.0418)	(0.0417)	(0.0435)	(0.0424)	(0.0422)	(0.0417)
Export					-0.00738	0.00714	0.00968	0.00842
					(0.0606)	(0.0598)	(0.0589)	(0.0590)
Flexibility capacity: medium (ref. low)	0.260***	0.263***	0.256***	0.257***	0.307***	0.311***	0.307***	0.306***
	(0.0991)	(0.0949)	(0.0954)	(0.0964)	(0.0958)	(0.0927)	(0.0923)	(0.0932)
Flexibility capacity: high (ref. low)	0.209**	0.210**	0.211**	0.210**	0.256***	0.265***	0.258***	0.257***
	(0.0915)	(0.0877)	(0.0861)	(0.0880)	(0.0860)	(0.0831)	(0.0813)	(0.0833)
Tech_absorp_cap	0.0907***	0.0913***	0.0897***	0.0917***	0.0999***	0.102***	0.101***	0.103***
	(0.0300)	(0.0287)	(0.0291)	(0.0288)	(0.0307)	(0.0294)	(0.0297)	(0.0292)
Collaboration	0.260***				0.345***			
	(0.0991)				(0.0668)			
Vertical collaboration		0.0751				0.172**		
		(0.0814)				(0.0815)		
Other collaboration		0.413***				0.471***		
		(0.125)				(0.119)		

	Model I				Model II			
	(1)	(2)	(3)	(4)	(1)	(2)	(3)	(4)
Collaboration_freq			0.151***				0.189***	
			(0.0339)				(0.0357)	
Collaboration_diver				0.243***				0.303***
				(0.0514)				(0.0500)
Region dummies	Yes	Yes	Yes	Yes	Yes	Yes	Yes	Yes
Sector dummies	Yes	Yes	Yes	Yes	Yes	Yes	Yes	Yes
Observa-tions	252	254	254	254	252	254	254	254
Mean VIF	1.56	1.53	1.53	1.53	1.54	1.52	1.53	1.54

Note: Standard errors in parentheses; *** $p < 0.01$, ** $p < 0.05$, * $p < 0.1$.

to the explanatory variables has been calculated in each estimation. In all of them, values are around 1.5, indicating no problems of multicollinearity given that values below 2.5 may not be the cause of concern in binary logistic regressions (Midi et al., 2010).

Regarding internal resources and capabilities, our findings confirm that larger firms in food sector have a higher probability of doing eco-process innovation than SMEs (H1), in line with those of Triguero et al. (2018), Cuerva (2019) and Córcoles (2019). One explanation could be that food SMEs are a little conservative in allocating resources for process innovation, impeding the exploitation of technological opportunities (Baregheh et al., 2012). Concerning age of the firm (H2), our results corroborate previous literature confirming the U-shaped relationship between the age and the probability to eco-innovate (Hojnik and Ruzzier, 2016) and in particular to carry out environmental process innovation (Ziegler and Rennings, 2004). This implies that when the food firm is young this has a negative impact on eco-process innovation. On the contrary, an advanced age triggers environmental process innovation. The reason could be that mature firms might have developed a broader base of internal knowledge, which leads them to develop more eco-innovations (Rehfeld et al., 2007).

We find evidence for the negative but not significant relationship between being an exporter and the probability of achieving eco-process innovations (H3 is not accepted). This could be explained by the fact that the internationalization strategy could be more closely linked to product innovation, or because the important question is not to be or not to be an exporter, just the effort or the degree of penetration in international markets.

The flexibility in production is positively associated with the adoption of eco-process innovation (H4). In this sense, firms reporting low flexibility to adjust their productive capacity have a lower probability to engage in eco-process innovation than medium- or high-capacity firms. In line with Acosta et al. (2015), we can conclude that flexibility encourages process innovation in food firms. Additionally, the technological absorptive capacity, measured as the embodied technology through the acquisition of tangible and intangible assets, influences positively the probability of carrying out eco-process innovation (H5). Therefore, the results underline the important contribution of the suppliers of machinery, software and hardware to promote eco-process innovation in Spanish food firms, and also corroborate previous findings for Spanish manufactures (Marzucchi and Montresor, 2017) and in particular for the food sector (Triguero et al., 2018).

Regarding the effect of external sources of environmental knowledge, our findings show that firms reporting collaboration have a higher probability to carry out eco-process innovation (H6a). We corroborate previous results obtained for eco-process innovative food firms (Triguero et al., 2018; Cuerva,

2019; González-Moreno et al., 2019) on the main role of the sources of knowledge. If we distinguish according to the type of external source, in Model I vertical cooperation (customers and suppliers) is not significantly associated with eco-process innovation, while collaboration with universities and public research centres, and consultants and other agents, is positively related. However, in Model II vertical cooperation seems to increase the probability of developing eco-process innovations, but the positive effect exerted is smaller than the effect of other types of collaboration. These results are in partly in line with those obtained by Gemünden et al. (1996) which show that collaboration with universities and consultants drives process innovation, while collaboration with supplier and customers seems to be more associated with product innovation. On the other hand, Maietta (2015) finds a significant and positive relation between innovation in the food sector and collaboration with institutional sources of knowledge, while Santamaría et al. (2009) conclude that consultants are very relevant for product and process innovations in low- and medium-tech firms.

Additionally, we find that the greater the frequency of this collaboration, the greater the propensity to develop eco-process innovation. In relation to the diversity, our findings highlight a positive relationship with process eco-innovations. Therefore, H6b is corroborated. In this respect, this result is consistent with the existing literature showing how the use of a variety of external sources of knowledge by manufacturing firms has a positive effect on eco-innovation (Cai and Zhou, 2014; Ghisetti et al., 2015, Marzucchi and Montresor, 2017; Jové-Llopis and Segarra-Blasco, 2018). In the particular case of the food sector, Triguero et al. (2018) and González-Moreno et al. (2019) find that the extensive (diversity of collaborators) and intensive (frequency of collaboration) use of external sources of knowledge increases the probability for Spanish firms to eco-innovate in products and processes. In this sense, our results confirm these previous ones.

CONCLUSIONS

This chapter contributes to the literature of innovation in the food sector by carrying out a more in-depth analysis regarding the factors associated with the adoption of environmental process innovations. Using data on a specific survey of Spanish firms, we analyse the effect of the internal capabilities and the external sources of knowledge in the probability to adopt process eco-innovations through probit models. We find that not only are internal firm resources and capabilities important, but also openness to external knowledge is associated with eco-innovation.

Among internal resources and capabilities, the size, the age, the productive flexibility and technological absorptive capacity of the firm are the main variables associated with the adoption of eco-process innovations. Our results confirm that large firms eco-innovate more than SMEs in processes. We also confirm the U-shaped relation found in previous literature between age and eco-process innovations. Technological capacity measured through the acquisition of technology embodied in the tangible and intangible assets of the firm also exerts a positive influence on eco-process innovation. The same occurs with flexibility, which helps food firms to pay attention to challenges related with the environment. On the contrary, export orientation is not decisive for eco-process innovations.

Regarding external sources of environmental knowledge, external collaboration has a key role in the development of eco-process innovation for food firms. In distinguishing by type of source, collaboration with institutions (universities and research centres) and consultants has a greater effect on the adoption of process eco-innovations than vertical cooperation (with suppliers and providers). Therefore, our results indicate that external sources are important, but their relevance depends on the type of collaborator. Although not all partners have the same impact on eco-process innovations, we find a greater influence of the diversity of external knowledge. The greater the array of collaborators (competitors, customers, providers, universities, research centres, consultants, others), the greater the probability to engage in eco-process innovation. In addition, the intensive use of this external collaboration is positively associated with eco-process innovation, confirming that it is important not only to have more extensive collaborative networks, but also to use them regularly.

Based upon our findings, some managerial and policy recommendations could be highlighted. The identification of the main factors associated with eco-process innovations helps food companies to define their innovation strategy. For this, it will be very important to have a high level of commitment to gathering the information on a large array of external knowledge sources. Collaboration with external sources will increase the knowledge base in order to move towards more environmentally friendly processes. Policy-makers should implement effective measures to promote a more environmentally friendly food sector in order to achieve environmental goals. In this task, government should assist the food sector to improve access to resources needed for innovation, and to engage in more collaborative innovative schemes.

One of the limitations of this study is the potential endogeneity problem derived from the use of cross-sectional data. One solution could be the use of instrumental variables. However, in this case it is not a feasible approach because of the limitations in the number of variables provided by the survey. In relation to further research, and in line with the limitations of the dataset, it could be interesting to expand the period of analysis to examine the direction of causality and capture the effect of the unobserved heterogeneity, alleviating the endogeneity problem. Regarding the necessity to meet the challenge of moving towards a sustainable ecosystem, the circular economy offers practical solutions to optimize processes and efficiency within the food sector. The adoption of such initiatives implies that food firms carry out different strategies leading to improvement of the circularity of the production system, necessarily based on the development of eco-innovation and, most of all, process innovations as a way to be green.

ACKNOWLEDGEMENTS

The authors gratefully acknowledge the financial support from the Spanish Ministry of Science, Innovation and Universities (RTI2018-101867-B-I00) and the University of Castilla-La Mancha (2019-GRIN-27081)

REFERENCES

Acosta, M., D. Coronado and E. Ferrándiz (2013), 'Trends in the acquisition of external knowledge for innovation in the food industry', in M.G. Martínez (ed.), *Open Innovation in the Food and Beverage Industry*, Cambridge: Elsevier, pp. 3–24.

Acosta, M., D. Coronado and C. Romero (2015), 'Linking public support, R&D, innovation and productivity: new evidence from the Spanish food industry', *Food Policy*, **57**, 50–61.

Alarcón, S. and M. Sánchez (2016), 'Is there a virtuous circle relationship between innovation activities and exports? A comparison of food and agricultural firms', *Food Policy*, **61**, 70–79.

Archibugi, D., S. Cesaratto and G. Sirilli (1991), 'Sources of innovative activities and industrial organization in Italy', *Research Policy*, **20** (4), 299–313.

Baregheh, A., J. Rowley, S. Sambrook and D. Davies (2012), 'Innovation in food sector SMEs', *Journal of Small Business and Enterprise Development*, **19** (2), 300–321.

Bernauer, T., S. Engels, D. Kammerer and J. Seijas (2007), 'Explaining green innovation: ten years after Porter's win–win proposition: how to study the effects of regulation on corporate environmental innovation?', Working Paper 17, ETH Zurich and University of Zurich.

Bock, A.J., T. Opsahl, G. George and D.M. Gann (2012), 'The effects of culture and structure on strategic flexibility during business model innovation', *Journal of Management Studies*, **49** (2), 279–305.

Bossle, M.B., M.D. De Barcellos and L.M. Vieira (2016), 'Why food companies go green? The determinant factors to adopt eco-innovations', *British Food Journal*, **118** (6), 1317–1333.

Brunnermeier, S.B. and M.A. Cohen (2003), 'Determinants of environmental innovation in US manufacturing industries', *Journal of Environmental Economics and Management*, **45** (2), 278–293.

Cabral, J. and W.B. Traill (2001), 'Determinants of a firm's likelihood to innovate and intensity of innovation in the Brazilian food industry', *Journal on Chain and Network Science*, **1** (1), 33–48.

Cai, W.G. and X.L. Zhou (2014), 'On the drivers of eco-innovation: empirical evidence from China', *Journal of Cleaner Production*, **79**, 239–248.

Caiazza, R., T. Volpe and D. Audretsch (2014), 'Innovation in agro-food chain: policies, actors and activities', *Journal of Enterprising Communities: People and Places in the Global Economy*, **8** (3), 180–187.

Cainelli, G., M. Mazzanti and S. Montresor (2012), 'Environmental innovations, local networks and internationalization', *Industry and Innovation*, **19** (8), 697–734.

Capitanio, F., A. Coppola and S. Pascucci (2009), 'Indications for drivers of innovation in the food sector', *British Food Journal*, **111** (8), 820–838.

Capitanio, F., A. Coppola and S. Pascucci (2010), 'Product and process innovation in the Italian food industry', *Agribusiness*, **26** (4), 503–518.

Chen, Y.S., S.B. Lai and C.T. Wen (2006), 'The influence of green innovation performance on corporate advantage in Taiwan', *Journal of Business Ethics*, **67** (4), 331–339.

Cleff, T. and K. Rennings (1999), 'Determinants of environmental product and process innovation', *European Environment*, **9** (5), 191–201.

Córcoles, D. (2019), 'The influence of collaboration with competitors on eco and non-eco-innovators: a study for the Spanish Food industry', in A. Triguero and A. González-Moreno (eds), *Research on Open-Innovation Strategies and Eco-Innovation in Agro-Food Industries*, Oxford: Chartridge Books Oxford, pp. 83–95.

Cuerva, M.C. (2019), 'Influence of suppliers and customers knowledge sources on product and process eco-innovations in the Food Industry', in A. Triguero and A. González-Moreno (eds), *Research on Open-Innovation Strategies and Eco-Innovation in Agro-Food Industries*, Oxford: Chartridge Books Oxford, pp. 73–82.

Cuerva, M.C., A. Triguero-Cano and D. Córcoles (2014), 'Drivers of green and non-green innovation: empirical evidence in low-tech SMEs', *Journal of Cleaner Production*, **68**, 104–113.

De Marchi, V. (2012), 'Environmental innovation and R&D cooperation: empirical evidence from Spanish manufacturing firms', *Research Policy*, **41** (3), 614–623.

De Marchi, V. and R. Grandinetti (2013), 'Knowledge strategies for environmental innovations: the case of Italian manufacturing firms', *Journal of Knowledge Management*, **17** (4), 569–582.

Del Río, P. (2005), 'Analysing the factors influencing clean technology adoption: a study of the Spanish pulp and paper industry', *Business Strategy and the Environment*, **14** (1), 20–37.

Del Río, P., C. Peñasco and D. Romero-Jordán (2016), 'What drives eco-innovators? A critical review of the empirical literature based on econometric methods', *Journal of Cleaner Production*, **112**, 2158–2170.

Demirel, P. and E. Kesidou (2011), 'Stimulating different types of eco-innovation in the UK: government policies and firm motivations', *Ecological Economics*, **70** (8), 1546–1557.

Díaz-García, C., A. González-Moreno and F.J. Sáez-Martínez (2015), 'Eco-innovation: insights from a literature review', *Innovation*, **17** (1), 6–23.

European Commission (2013), 'Eco-innovation: greener business through smart solutions', Luxembourg: Publications Office of the European Union.

Galizzi, G. and L. Venturini (1996), 'Product innovation in the food industry: nature, characteristics and determinants', in G. Galizzi and L. Venturini (eds), *Economics of Innovation: The Case of Food Industry*, Heidelberg: Physica-Verlag HD, pp. 133–153.

Gellynck, X., B. Vermeire and J. Viaene (2007), 'Innovation in food firms: contribution of regional networks within the international business context', *Entrepreneurship and Regional Development*, **19** (3), 209–226.

Gemünden, H.G., T. Ritter and P. Heydebreck (1996), 'Network configuration and innovation success: an empirical analysis in German high-tech industries', *International Journal of Research in Marketing*, **13** (5), 449–462.

Ghisetti, C., A. Marzucchi and S. Montresor (2015), 'The open eco-innovation mode: an empirical investigation of eleven European countries', *Research Policy*, **44** (5), 1080–1093.

González-Moreno, A., F.J. Sáez-Martínez and C. Díaz-García (2013), 'Drivers of eco-innovation in chemical industry', *Environmental Engineering and Management Journal*, **12** (10), 2001–2008.

González-Moreno, A., A. Triguero and F.J. Sáez-Martínez (2019), 'Many or trusted partners for eco-innovation? The influence of breadth and depth of firms' knowledge network in the food sector', *Technological Forecasting and Social Change*, **147**, 51–62.

Grunert, K.G., H. Harmsen, M. Meulenberg, E. Kuiper, T. Ottowitz, et al. (1997), 'A framework for analysing innovation in the food sector', in B. Trail and K.G. Grunert (eds), *Products and Process Innovation in the Food Industry*, Boston, MA: Springer, pp. 1–37.

Hervas-Oliver, J.L. J.A. Garrigos and I. Gil-Pechuan (2011), 'Making sense of innovation by R&D and non-R&D innovators in low technology contexts: a forgotten lesson for policymakers', *Technovation*, **31** (9), 427–446.

Hojnik, J. and M. Ruzzier (2016), 'What drives eco-innovation? A review of an emerging literature', *Environmental Innovation and Societal Transitions*, **19**, 31–41.

Horbach, J. (2008), 'Determinants of environmental innovation: new evidence from German panel data sources', *Research Policy*, **37** (1), 163–173.

Horbach, J., C. Rammer and K. Rennings (2012), 'Determinants of eco-innovations by type of environmental impact: the role of regulatory push/pull, technology push and market pull', *Ecological Economics*, **78**, 112–122.

Jové-Llopis, E. and A. Segarra-Blasco (2018), 'Eco-innovation strategies: a panel data analysis of Spanish manufacturing firms', *Business Strategy and the Environment*, **27** (8), 1209–1220.

Jurgilevich, A., T. Birge, J. Kentala-Lehtonen, K. Korhonen-Kurki, J. Pietikäinen, et al. (2016), 'Transition towards circular economy in the food system', *Sustainability*, **8** (1), 1–14.

Kammerer, D. (2009), 'The effects of customer benefit and regulation on environmental product innovation: empirical evidence from appliance manufacturers in Germany', *Ecological Economics*, **68** (8–9), 2285–2295.

Le Bas, C. and N. Poussing (2013), 'Firm voluntary measures for environmental changes, eco-innovations and CSR: empirical analyses based on data surveys', LISER Working Paper Series 2013-25.

Lefebvre, V.M., H. De Steur and X. Gellynck (2015), 'External sources for innovation in food SMEs', *British Food Journal*, **117** (1), 412–430.

Maçaneiro, M.B., S.K. da Cunha and Z. Balbinot (2013), 'Drivers of the adoption of eco-innovations in the pulp, paper, and paper products industry in Brazil', *Latin American Business Review*, **14** (3–4), 179–208.

Maietta, O.W. (2015), 'Determinants of university–firm R&D collaboration and its impact on innovation: a perspective from a low-tech industry', *Research Policy*, **44** (7), 1341–1359.

Martinez, M.G. and J. Briz (2000), 'Innovation in the Spanish food and drink industry', *International Food and Agribusiness Management Review*, **3** (2), 155–176.

Marzucchi, A. and S. Montresor (2017), 'Forms of knowledge and eco-innovation modes: evidence from Spanish manufacturing firms', *Ecological Economics*, **131**, 208–221.

Midi, H., S.K. Sarkar and S. Rana (2010), 'Collinearity diagnostics of binary logistic regression model', *Journal of Interdisciplinary Mathematics*, **13** (3), 253–267.

Mondéjar-Jiménez, J., M. Segarra-Oña, A. Peiró-Signes, A.M. Payá-Martínez and F.J. Sáez-Martínez (2015), 'Segmentation of the Spanish automotive industry with respect to the environmental orientation of firms: towards an ad-hoc vertical policy to promote eco-innovation', *Journal of Cleaner Production*, **86**, 238–244.

Rehfeld, K.M., K. Rennings and A. Ziegler (2007), 'Integrated product policy and environmental product innovations: an empirical analysis', *Ecological Economics*, **61** (1), 91–100.

Rennings, K. and C. Rammer (2011), 'The impact of regulation-driven environmental innovation on innovation success and firm performance', *Industry and Innovation*, **18** (3), 255–283.

Sánchez, R. (1995), 'Strategic flexibility in product competition', *Strategic Management Journal*, **16** (S1), 135–159.

Santamaría, L., M.J. Nieto and A. Barge-Gil (2009), 'Beyond formal R&D: taking advantage of other sources of innovation in low- and medium-technology industries', *Research Policy*, **38** (3), 507–517.

Sarkis, J., P. González-Torre and B. Adenso-Diaz (2010), 'Stakeholder pressure and the adoption of environmental practices: the mediating effect of training', *Journal of Operations Management*, **28** (2), 163–176.

Segarra-Oña, M.V., A. Peiró-Signes, J. Albors-Garrigós and P. Miret-Pastor (2011), 'Impact of innovative practices in environmentally focused firms: moderating factors', *International Journal of Environmental Research*, **5** (2), 425–434.

Traill, W.B. and M. Meulenberg (2002), 'Innovation in the food industry?', *Agribusiness: An International Journal*, **18** (1), 1–21.

Triguero, A. (2019), 'Does the sector matter? The role of open innovation in the adoption of eco-innovations in food versus non-food industries', in A. Triguero and A. González-Moreno (eds), *Research on Open-Innovation Strategies and Eco-Innovation in Agro-Food Industries*, Oxford: Chartridge Books Oxford, pp. 61–72.

Triguero, Á., M.C. Cuerva and C. Álvarez-Aledo (2017), 'Environmental innovation and employment: drivers and synergies', *Sustainability*, **9** (11), 1–22.

Triguero, A., S. Fernández and F.J. Sáez-Martinez (2018), 'Inbound open innovative strategies and eco-innovation in the Spanish food and beverage industry', *Sustainable Production and Consumption*, **15**, 49–64.

Van Leeuwen, G. and L. Klomp (2006), 'On the contribution of innovation to multi-factor productivity growth', *Economics of Innovation and New Technology*, **15** (4–5), 367–390.

Wagner, M. (2007), 'On the relationship between environmental management, environmental innovation and patenting: evidence from German manufacturing firms', *Research Policy*, **36** (10), 1587–1602.

Wagner, M. (2008), 'Empirical influence of environmental management on innovation: evidence from Europe', *Ecological Economics*, **66** (2–3), 392–402.

Worren, N., K. Moore and P. Cardona (2002), 'Modularity, strategic flexibility, and firm performance: a study of the home appliance industry', *Strategic Management Journal*, **23** (12), 1123–1140.

Zhou, K.Z. and F. Wu (2010), 'Technological capability, strategic flexibility, and product innovation', *Strategic Management Journal*, **31** (5), 547–561.

Ziegler, A. and K. Rennings (2004), 'Determinants of environmental innovations in Germany: Do organizational measures matter?', Discussion Paper No. 04-30, ZEW.

APPENDIX

Table 4A.1 Descriptive statistics

	Total sample (279)				Eco-innovators (178)				Eco-process innovators (151)			
	Mean	Std. dev.	Min.	Max.	Mean	Std. dev.	Min.	Max.	Mean	Std. dev.	Min.	Max.
Size	3.918	1.722	0	7.065	4.476	1.523	0	7.065	4.455	1.539	0	7.065
Age	3.170	0.656	0.693	4.663	3.262	0.681	0.693	4.663	3.264	0.688	0.693	4.663
Age^2	10.478	3.951	0.480	21.747	11.099	4.190	0.480	21.747	11.122	4.206	0.480	21.747
Export	0.595	0.492	0	1	0.674	0.470	0	1	0.649	0.479	0	1
Flexibility	2.602	0.675	1	3	2.697	0.580	1	3	2.709	0.549	1	3
Tech_absorp_cap	0.465	0.814	0	4.878	0.496	0.855	0	4.878	0.538	0.907	0	4.878
Collaboration	0.231	0.422	0	1	0.363	0.482	0	1	0.356	0.480	0	1
Vertical collaboration	0.139	0.347	0	1	0.219	0.415	0	1	0.199	0.400	0	1
Other collaboration	0.097	0.296	0	1	0.152	0.359	0	1	0.166	0.373	0	1
Collaboration_frequency	0.552	1.415	0	10	0.865	1.695	0	10	0.927	1.811	0	10
Collaboration_diversity	0.315	0.705	0	6	0.494	0.832	0	6	0.510	0.878	0	6

Table 4A.2 Correlation matrix of all variables of the model

	Eco-process	Size	Age	Export	Flexibility	Tech-absorp_cap	Collab.	Vertical collab.	Other collab.	Collab_ frequ	Collab_ divers
Eco-process	1.0										
Size	0.3394	1.0									
Age	0.1551	0.3017	1.0								
Export	0.1195	0.4886	0.2538	1.0							
Flexibility	0.1715	0.2784	0.1396	0.1304	1.0						
Tech-absorp_cap	0.0963	-0.0385	-0.1258	-0.0245	0.0044	1.0					
Collab.	0.3191	0.3790	0.1078	0.1413	0.1476	-0.0106	1.0				
Vertical collaboration	0.1845	0.3085	0.0976	0.1220	0.0846	-0.0075	0.7385	1.0			
Other collab.	0.2527	0.1966	0.0879	0.0972	0.0853	-0.0120	0.5995	0.0429	1.0		
Collab_freq	0.2884	0.1951	0.1252	0.0536	0.0574	0.0380	0.7156	0.6033	0.4813	1.0	
Collab_divers	0.3001	0.2368	0.1068	0.0689	0.0756	-0.0131	0.8210	0.6564	0.5595	0.8700	1.0

5. Emotion as an ethical compass in strategic sustainability decisions

Kirsi Snellman and Henri Hakala

Being ethical is about doing good deeds, and if you can generate revenues while doing good it is great. If there is a problem in the world, and you have the solution, it is your responsibility to tackle it. (Manager of Company 6, M6)

INTRODUCTION

Strategic sustainable decision-making is the process whereby entrepreneurs and/or managers make choices about business development while simultaneously considering its environmental, social and economic implications (Muñoz, 2017). When managers make sustainable decisions characterized by their strategic importance and the high stakes they entail for several stakeholders (Eisenhardt, 1989), they need to see beyond what already exists. In so doing, they often face ethical dilemmas, defined as 'situations in which the individual must reflect upon competing moral standards and/or stakeholder claims in determination of the ethically appropriate course of action among potential alternatives' (Schwartz, 2016, p. 757). While businesses have an opportunity and a responsibility to participate in setting the agenda for a more sustainable future (Markman et al., 2016), it is important to learn more about those factors that drive strategic sustainable decision-making. In this regard, trailblazer companies – those creating 'a path through new or unsettled terrain upon which others may follow' (Shepherd and Patzelt, 2017, p. 2) – are particularly interesting because they often set the new standards for sustainable businesses.

Prior research has approached strategic sustainability decisions mainly through applying hard measures and rational criteria (Feito-Cespon et al., 2016; Rezaee, 2017; Wenstøp and Seip, 2001). However, the impact of emotions is still not well understood. Hence, the objective of this study is to understand how emotion affects strategic sustainability decision-making. While emotion may be the enemy of good decisions for some (e.g., Callahan, 1988), we follow those who suggest that emotion and reason are complementary in good decisions (e.g., Dane and Pratt, 2007). We propose that emotion helps to navigate toward more sustainable ways of doing business and helps to resolve potential ethical dilemmas affecting strategic decisions (Markman et al., 2016; Rushton, 2002). Drawing on interviews with 23 small and medium-sized enterprise (SME) managers, we suggest that emotion carries important messages that complement rational information and reasoning. Based on our findings, we theorize a model in which sensitizing, sensing and selecting characterize emotion-imbued strategic sustainability decisions. We associate sensitizing with awareness of the ethical dilemma, sensing with establishing a sense of the whole, and selecting with the ultimate ethical choice. Through sensitizing the manager becomes more alert to potential ethical dilemmas related to compliance with an environmental and societal mission, priorities in short-term goal-setting, and conflicting interests with stakeholders. Sensing enables the manager to complement up-to-date knowledge derived from calculations and rational analysis, and use their own emotions in ethical evaluation. Treating emotion as an indicator of significance, the manager focuses on what feels important, and establishes a holistic picture of the situation. Finally, emotions can carry important messages when selecting the best ethical choice among potential alternatives in decision-making (Schwartz, 2016). Positive emotions can signal rightness/goodness, while negative emotions usually have opposite implications, and lack of emotion can signal that the dilemma itself is not that important after all. Through such capacity to balance environmental, social and financial goals, emotion helps managers to envision a better world where the natural environment is the foundation on which society sits and the economy operates (Markman et al., 2016).

The contribution of this chapter is threefold. First, we contribute to the literature of sustainability decision-making by adding emotion as an element that takes effect in multiple ways. While there are some exceptions (e.g., Chichilnisky, 2009; Wenstøp and Seip, 2001), thus far most sustainability decision models are based on rationality (Bolis et al., 2017; Feito-Cespon et al., 2016; Garcia et al., 2016). However, some studies (e.g., Chichilnisky, 2009; Wenstøp and Seip, 2001) have suggested that we need to move beyond rationality and add emotion to our multi-criteria decision models. To contribute to this goal, we introduce emotion as the sensitive compass that combines experience, observation and meaning (Brundin, 2002), and begin to acknowledge those important messages that emotions can carry to foster sustainability decisions.

Second, we add some nuanced insights to the theory of integrated ethical decision-making (Schwartz, 2016). Associating emotions not only with long-term strategic ethical goals but also with daily routines and sustainable practices, our empirical findings are aligned with the theoretical notion (Prinz, 2009) that moral facts are often associated with emotions. Letting emotions illuminate those aspects the manager considers important when making strategic sustainability decisions, our data suggest that managers pay attention to their emotions when judging something to be right or wrong. As such, we begin to treat emotion as an important tool that helps managers to decide how to compromise during the sustainable transformation process, thus addressing a call to investigate factors that enhance readiness to change in small innovative firms (Shevchenko et al., 2016).

Finally, our study supports the idea that we should allow emotions to play a larger role in business affairs (Lurie, 2004), because of their capacity to harmonize experience, observation and meaning (Brundin, 2002), and to recognize what really matters. Specifically, we find that we need to learn more about how emotions can influence ethical preferences in real-life organizational settings, because in those situations emotions do not represent a self-centred but a moral perspective (Kals and Maes, 2002), thus contributing to a positive change in the business world.

WHAT EMOTION CAN ADD TO ADDRESSING DILEMMAS IN SUSTAINABILITY DECISIONS

Strategic sustainability decisions are often ambiguous and risky (Martin, 2015), and involve a potential mismatch between business imperatives and stakeholder interests (Wright and Nyberg, 2017). Hence, they call for ethical sensitivity in weighing potential pros and cons under uncertainty (Trevino, 1986). To date, this uncertainty, and the risks involved in strategic sustainability decisions, have been tackled through hard measures and rational criteria (Feito-Cespon et al., 2016; Rezaee, 2017; Wenstøp and Seip, 2001). The rationality of production that affects the natural environment has been embraced through costs, system efficiencies and worker productivities (Elliot, 2004), and the key criteria of energy supply systems have been summarized from technical, economic, environmental and social aspects (Wang et al., 2009). Although very informative, these existing decision models largely disregard the role of emotions, thus indicating that a person facing an ethical dilemma arrives at a decision using rational reasoning alone (Callahan, 1988; Rest, 1986).

Adding the emotional perspective when investigating strategic sustainability decisions is important for at least three reasons. First, emotions can signal the presence of ethical challenges (Johnson, 2002). Strategic sustainability decisions are often made in the context of incomplete information, and emotions are suggested to help determine what information is important (Prinz, 2009). Discrete emotions (that is, excitement, joy, fear and anger) are 'intense prototypical affective experiences directed toward certain objects or situations' (Forgas, 1995; Russell, 2003; Seo and Barrett, 2007, p. 924), whereas feelings are more generic. When managers face a potential dilemma, the emotional system in the brain sends signals to the physical body to help them deal with an uncertain situation, and the looping interface between emotion and cognition can be associated with physical reactions (Smith and Semin, 2004). Our bodies also interpret other people's actions and emotions, and hence our emotions link with what we perceive as knowledge, even without conscious awareness (Dane and Pratt, 2007).

Second, given that what is right for one may not be right for another (Trevino, 1986), we acknowledge that each manager has different values, rules and approaches to ethical dilemmas related to sustainability. Although there may be almost universally accepted good goals such as addressing climate change through creating responsible products and services (Markman et al., 2016), each strategic decision-making situation is a unique puzzle. Embracing emotion as a compass when confronting an ethical dilemma (Schwartz, 2016), we acknowledge that for most sustainability decisions that involve ethical evaluation (right versus wrong), an intuitive process triggers an automatic gut sense of rightness and wrongness (Schwartz, 2016). For example, emotions can help a manager to tune in to what feels right, or act as ethical alarms when things are not right (Salvador and Folger, 2009). While positive emotions such as happiness, joy and fun can be associated with rightness/goodness, negative emotions such as pessimism and complacency can be associated with wrongness/badness (Johnson, 2002).

Third, although the aim would be to do what is right, just and fair, there is no machine into which the manager could feed the details of a situation and which would then deliver the one right and good ethical answer (Clarkeburn, 2002). Since organizational changes can challenge managers' extant cognitive lenses through which they interpret the world (Lockett et al., 2014; Moch and Bartunek, 1990), there can be a tendency to make choices grounded on dominant logic and old behaviour patterns. These behaviour patterns can be manifested through a company's extant strategic practices and approaches to competition (Prahalad and Bettis, 1986). Imposing severe demands upon managers' cognitive capabilities (Sadler-Smith and Shefy, 2004) and ethical sensitivity (Johnson, 2002), these judgements call for reason to be complemented with emotion in strategic decision-making (Dane and Pratt, 2007).

EMPIRICAL SETTING AND METHOD

Our empirical setting is 23 small and medium-sized trailblazer companies that 'make a path through new or unsettled terrain upon which others may follow' (Shepherd and Patzelt, 2017), and whose ethical foundation has sustainability embodied in the firm's strategy. Embracing sustainable business opportunities, these pioneering companies aim to develop responsible innovations that contribute to a better future than is currently foreseeable.

Sample Selection and Data Collection

Companies were identified using purposeful sampling (Smith and Osborn, 2003) to find a group of SMEs (following the EU definition) with 'trail-blazing' characteristics, active in the circular economy (see Appendix Table 5A.1). The sample consisted of 23 owner-managers from Finland, 20 men and three women, for whom the research problem was relevant and person-ally significant (Pietkiewicz and Smith, 2014). This provides an interesting context to examine how emotions can affect attempts to attain true sustaina-bility (Shevchenko et al., 2016), that is, to act ethically, and end reliance on non-renewable resources. Data were collected through interviews during 1 February 2018 to 30 March 2019. Interviews were recorded and transcribed to capture the interviewees' exact words for analysis (Sanders, 1982). The goal was to elicit first-person stories of how strategic decision-making unfolds in real life (Cardon and Glauser, 2011). Interviewees set the course of the dialogue and were free to express their views in whatever level of detail they wished (Cardon and Glauser, 2011). This approach brought the flexibility that permitted additional and unexpected issues to arise (Pietkiewicz and Smith, 2014), thus making each interview a unique dialogue between the interviewer and the interviewee. After this data collection phase, the 150 single-spaced pages of interview transcripts were coded to develop our model. We analysed the role of emotion in strategic sustainability decisions at the level of manag-ers' lived experiences.

Data Analysis

To analyse the data, we drew inspiration from the principles of phenome-nological data analysis (Kleiman, 2004; Smith and Osborn, 2003), which involves coding, categorizing and making sense of the essential meanings of the phenomenon. Our analysis began with a reading of the data to acquire a sense of the whole (Corbin and Strauss, 1990). A second reading enabled us to divide the data into meaningful sections or units (first-order codes) (Smith and Osborn, 2003), and to look for interview excerpts exemplifying the same underlying idea (Cardon and Glauser, 2011). Sections with a similar focus or content were grouped into higher-level categories (second-order themes) which highlighted the commonalities across the first-order codes. Finally, following Cacciotti et al. (2016), the second-order codes were clustered into high-level theoretical dimensions (third-order codes). This determined which units were essential for, and made up of, an identity for the phenomena.

FINDINGS

In our data, strategic sustainability decision-making is characterized by three interrelated but distinct elements: sensitizing, sensing and selecting. Sensitizing is associated with an initial awareness of the ethical dilemma, sensing with establishing a sense of the whole, and selecting with making the ultimate right/good ethical choice. These elements are presented below as they emerged in the data. The illustrative evidence of first-order codes, second-order themes and aggregate dimensions is reported in Table 5.1.

Sensitizing is the first element in our model. For our pool of managers, sensitizing appears to be associated with emotion-imbued awareness of the ethical dilemma. When emotion triggers ethical awareness in sustainability decision-making, the decision often involves some kind of dilemma. We identified three types of ethical dilemmas (second-order themes) from our data: dilemmas with environmental and social mission, dilemmas in goal-setting and dilemmas with conflicting interests.

Dilemmas with environmental and social mission were largely relating to switching to more ecological materials, health and safety issues, and attempting to establish true sustainability. When switching to more ecological alternatives, the problems were often associated with money. As M7 said: 'An ethical dilemma can emerge if we need to decide when to substitute our current packaging materials with more ecological but more expensive recycled materials.' Although most managers were inclined to choose the ecological alternative despite the cost, there were also problems with complying with the social mission. As M16 said: 'Current strategic decisions are linked with safety issues. Another reason for not entering a market can be associated rules and regulations that are not in line with our company values.' When approaching sustainability goals, some managers were more inclined to follow their company's code of ethics than others. As M6 said: 'Do we need to be very sustainable or is it OK to be somewhat sustainable? Is it acceptable to use 5% fossil ingredients in the product development, or should we instead try to eliminate non-renewable recources totally?'

Dilemmas in goal-setting were mostly attached to profits, quality demands and regulations. A typical dilemma in goal-setting was related to sacrificing profits in the short term to make a longer-term ethical impact. As M8 said: 'We make a lot of decisions that hamper our profits in the short run but will be more reasonable in the long run. There are not many companies that can sacrifice their profits in the short run because of an ethical impact in the long run.' Another typical dilemma in goal-setting was linked with quality expectations of the product in progress. As M12 emphasized: 'In our daily practices we try to make choices that are based on quality rather than costs. This leads to a cost

Table 5.1   Illustrative evidence, first-order codes, second-order themes and aggregate dimensions

Example quotations/first-order codes	Second-order themes	Aggregate dimensions
'An ethical dilemma can emerge if we need to decide when to substitute our current packaging materials with more ecological but more expensive recycled materials.' – M7 **Dilemma in switching to recycled materials** *'Current strategic decisions are linked with safety issues. Another reason for not entering a market can be associated rules and regulations that are not in line with our company values.' – M16* **Dilemma related to health and safety issues** *'Do we need to be very sustainable or is it OK to be somewhat sustainable? Is it acceptable to use 5% fossil ingredients in the product development, or should we instead try to eliminate non-renewable resources totally?' – M6* **Dilemma related to true sustainability**	Dilemmas with environmental and social mission	
'We make a lot of decisions that hamper our profits in the short run but will be more reasonable in the long run. There are not many companies that can sacrifice their profits in the short run because of ethical impact in the long run.' – M8 **Dilemma attached to sacrificing profits** *'In our daily practices we try to make choices that are based on quality rather than costs. This leads to a cost structure that is perhaps not so nice, but it is the way it goes.' – M12* **Dilemma attached to quality demands** *'Sometimes the progress is slower than expected. Technologies are not yet available to separate all the components of the waste. Even if we were tempted to do something radical, without the necessary permits we could not execute our plans.' – M13* **Dilemma attached to regulations**	Dilemmas in goal-setting	**Sensitizing** (awareness of ethical dilemma)
'Although we need to create a successful business, sometimes the willingness to help others feels more important than profit.' – M4 **Dilemma related to societal value** *'We are very careful when choosing collaboration partners and make sure that there are no value conflicts involved.' – M16* **Dilemma related to value conflicts with collaborators** *'How to solve the ethical dilemma in decision-making if a key stakeholder thinks that coal (cheaper, but harms the environment) is a better choice than wood (more expensive, but more ecological)?' – M3* **Dilemma related to different interests with key stakeholders**	Dilemmas with conflicting interests	

Example quotations/first-order codes	Second-order themes	Aggregate dimensions
'Feeling enhances your own understanding of the quality of the analysis conducted. The joy of success is a key driver in sustainable performance.' – M15 **Joy enhances understanding detailed analysis** *'You can feel good during decision-making if you are excited about the future possibilities or if you can validate facts. Afterwards it feels great if we know that we can accomplish those projects we have started.' – M18* **Excitement signals future possibilities** *'When your attitude toward the new possibility is positive, you sense excitement, and you see everything more clearly.' – M23* **Excitement enhances clarity in holistic evaluation**	Positive emotion	
'Although we could do it technically, but if there is no feeling involved, would it be wise to do it after all? Feeling is the final element in validation.' – M5 **Without feeling there is no willingness to change** *'I think that those people who can make their decisions without feeling are in some way mentally ill. Most skilful managers base their decisions on intuition when there is not enough information available.' – M14* **Without feeling incomplete information stays incomplete** *'Without feeling there are no results. Nobody works for the money. People will not commit to decisions that do not involve emotions.' – M9* **Without feeling there is no real commitment**	Lack of emotion	**Sensing** (establishing a sense of the whole)
'When there were lot of obstacles on our way, we decided to use the "frustration as a resource" slogan, because anger triggers action, and we are very good at justifying why there is no need for change.' – M7 **Frustration and anger accelerates the willingness to change** *'Strategic decision-making is about risk-taking, believing in success, and evaluating whether you can perform or not. I sense fear if I make a promise and can't keep it.' – M14* **Fear indicates risks regarding expected performance** *'Feeling shows the direction, helps in identifying risks, facing uncertainty and confronting fear.' – M22* **Gut feeling that shows optimal direction overrides fear**	Negative emotion	

Example quotations/first-order codes	Second-order themes	Aggregate dimensions
'Although in the middle of the decision-making process you can have some feelings, later when you know that you are making the right choice comes the best feeling.' – M10 **Best feeling signals rightness of the choice**		
'Mixing different criteria in decision-making can guide you to choose the best possible option. However, it is not only about an ecstatic feeling reflecting the way things should be ideally. Rather, the rightness can also be related to not following the crowd.' – M3 **Ecstatic feeling and rightness triggered by not following the crowd**	Signals related to goodness/rightness	
'When you are on the brink of making the commitment decision, you know that you are about to do the right thing if you feel excited.' – M4 **Excitement signals doing the right thing**		**Selecting** (emotion-imbued right/good choice)
'If you feel that the decision you are about to make is wrong, there will be no decision.' – M9 **Feeling signalling wrongness blocks making a decision**		
'In decision-making, feeling is related to uncertainty indicating that now we are betting on the wrong horse.' – M21 **Feeling signalling uncertainty is a warning**	Signals related to badness/wrongness	
'In our company people can show their feelings to their fellow co-workers even in those situations when something fails. Such an attitude brings life to our company and unleashes our creative energy.' – M12 **Bad feelings triggered by wrong decisions unleash creative energy**		

structure that is perhaps not so nice, but it is the way it goes.' Dilemmas in goal-setting were also surprisingly often associated with regulative issues. As M13 said: 'Sometimes the progress is slower than expected. Technologies are yet not available to separate all the components of the waste. Even if we were tempted to do something radical, without the necessary [regulatory] permits we could not execute our plans.'

Dilemmas with conflicting interests were often related to different view-points regarding societal contribution and common good, as well as company values. As M4 said: 'Although we need to create a successful business, sometimes the willingness to help others feels more important than profit.' Conflicting interests also emerged when choosing collaboration partners. As M16 said: 'We are very careful when choosing collaboration partners, and make sure that there are no value conflicts involved.' Conflicting interests were also recognized when key stakeholders had differing priorities. As

M3 asked: 'How to solve the ethical dilemma in decision-making if a key stakeholder thinks that coal (which is cheaper, but harms the environment) is a better choice than wood (more expensive, but more ecological)?' However, even if a manager were aware of the ethical dilemma through sensitizing, there will be no strategic sustainability decision unless that manager obtains a sense of the whole through sensing.

Sensing is the second element in our model. To establish a sense of the whole, managers use up-to-date knowledge derived from calculations and rational analysis as an important element in their ethical evaluation. However, sensing emotions and their implications is paramount. As such, emotions can be positive or negative. Lack of emotion also appears to have specific implications.

Positive emotion, such as excitement, was often associated with enhanced cognitive capacities. As M15 said: 'Feeling enhances your own understanding of the quality of the analysis conducted. Joy of success is a key driver in sustainable performance.' Excitement appeared to enhance clarity in holistic evaluation. As M23 stated: 'When your attitude toward the new possibility is positive, you sense excitement, and you see everything more clearly.' Excitement also enhanced creativity. As M18 pointed out: 'You can feel good during decision-making if you are excited about the future possibilities or if you can validate facts. Afterwards it feels great if we know that we can accomplish those projects we have started.'

Negative emotion such as fear was often associated with identifying the most essential risks. As M14 said: 'Strategic decision-making is about risk-taking, believing in success, and evaluating whether you can perform or not. I sense fear if I make a promise and can't keep it.' However, sometimes generic feeling carried the capacity to override fear. As M22 said: 'Feeling shows the direction, helps in identifying risks, facing uncertainty and confronting fear.' Negative emotion such as frustration and anger were often interpreted as drivers for sustainable transformation activity. As M7 stated: 'When there were lot of obstacles on our way, we decided to use the "frustration as a resource" slogan, because anger triggers action, and we are very good at justifying why there is no need for change'.

Lack of emotion was mostly linked with unwillingness to change or make the commitment. As M5 said: 'Although we could do it technically, but if there is no feeling involved, would it be wise to do it after all?' There were also many managers who felt that emotion might substitute and complement for incomplete information. As M14 stated: 'I think that those people who can make their decisions without feeling are in some way mentally ill. Most skilful managers base their decisions on intuition when there is not enough information available.' In turn, emotional disengagement was seen as a reason for poor performance. As M9 said: 'Without feeling there are no results. Nobody works for the money. People will not commit to decisions that do not involve emotions.' Although emotion makes the manager realize that there is an ethical dilemma, and obtain a sense of the whole by complementing rational thinking with emotions and feelings, one element is still missing. There is no strategic sustainability decision unless the managers use their hearts to establish their sense of rightness and wrongness of the available paths and select the ultimate emotion-imbued ethical choice.

Selecting is the third element in our model. When on the brink of selecting the best emotion-imbued ethical choice, both an emotion-imbued awareness of the ethical dilemma (sensitizing) and an emotion-imbued sense of the whole (sensing) plays a role. Evaluation of the rightness or wrongness of the chosen direction (at the intersection of thinking and feeling) involved both emotional and rational components.

Signals related to goodness/rightness were related to how it feels when making the decision. As M10 said: 'Although in the middle of the decision-making process you can have some feelings, later when you know that you have made the right choice comes the best feeling.' An ecstatic feeling was also associated with somewhat surprising implications: it caused the manager to avoid those things that everybody else does, and opt for a unique solution. As M3 emphasized: 'Mixing different criteria in decision-making can guide you to choose the best possible option. However, it is not only about an ecstatic feeling reflecting the way things should ideally be; rather, the rightness can also be related to not following the crowd.' Excitement was also associated with knowing that the chosen option is right. As M4 said: 'When you are on the brink of making the decision, you know that you are about to do the right thing if you feel excited.'

Signals related to badness/wrongness were mostly related to uncertainty and suspicions regarding the option at hand. As M21 pointed out: 'During decision-making, feeling is related to uncertainty indicating that now we are betting on the wrong horse.' Sometimes bad feelings triggered by wrong decisions also had positive implications. As M12 said: 'In our company, people can show their feelings to their fellow co-workers even when something fails. This attitude brings life to our company and unleashes our creative energy.' Signals related to wrongness had the capacity to terminate the ethical considerations. As M9 said: 'If you feel that the decision you are about to make is wrong, there will be no decision.'

Taken together, these ideas suggest that strategic sustainability decision-making requires three conditions. First, managers establish their initial emotion-imbued awareness of the potential ethical dilemma through sensitizing. Second, managers use their emotion-imbued perceptions to establish a sense of the whole through sensing. Third, managers make the ultimate emotion-imbued right/good choice through selecting.

DISCUSSION

The analysis of our data allowed us to capture three interrelated but distinct elements that fuel emotion-imbued strategic sustainability decision-making: sensitizing, sensing and selecting. Sensitizing is associated with an emotion-imbued initial awareness of the ethical dilemma, sensing with using emotion-imbued perceptions to establish sense of the whole, and selecting with making the ultimate emotion-imbued right/good choice. Although emotion can have both advantageous and disadvantageous implications for decision-making (Damasio et al., 1991; Callahan, 1988), our findings suggest that at the very least, emotion carries important messages that leaders observe and evaluate while they make decisions (Lerner et al., 2015). A more generic feeling can also have an effect (Guzak, 2015). Emotion is a mixture of experience, observation and meaning (Brundin, 2002) and has the capacity to serve as a sort of ethical compass that complements reason in strategic sustainability decision-making, in at least three ways (see Figure 5.1).

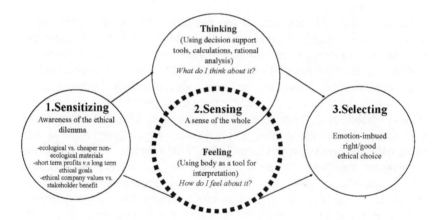

Figure 5.1   *Emotion as an ethical compass in strategic sustainability decisions*

Emotions affect decision-making through sensitizing the mind to ethical dilemmas and complementing rational awareness. Our data suggest that in sustainability decisions, sensitizing is linked with issues such as: (1) problems in complying with an environmental mission; (2) difficulties in short-term goal-setting; and (3) conflicting interests among key actors. Typically, there are no perfect or ideal practical solutions to deliver sustainability, but only compromises that are a little more sustainable than the currently available solutions. In the 'trailblazer' firms of our sample, the tendency to do good is often incorporated in company values and strategies, yet the ability to sensitize is very much dependent on the alertness and personal capacities of the manager (Schwartz, 2016). Traditionally a person's moral value system and company's ethical long-term goals are considered to be part of the reasoning process (Trevino, 1986; Trevino and Brown, 2004). Nevertheless, emotion also has the capacity to help interpret and ethically evaluate a situation. We also find that the human body, through its ability to feel emotion, serves as a sensor that scans the environment and recognizes the ethical issue that demands attention. Feelings can be treated as information (Schwarz, 2011), and anxiousness, for example, can signal the presence of a pressing ethical dilemma (Johnson, 2002). Of course, emotions can also have disadvantages (Damasio, 1994), especially if bodily reactions are so strong that they take over and lead to reflexive responses. While emotion helps in sensitizing and obtaining a first impression of the dilemma, our data do not suggest that it should substitute for reason; instead, the value comes from letting emotion enhance the openness to new discoveries.

Emotion also adds meaning to the evaluation of decision alternatives. Through sensing, managers acquire a sense of the whole. Rational models are informative in capturing moral reasoning in situations where the decision-maker is subject to multiple forces (Bommer et al., 1987). However; a more holistic understanding of why something feels important calls for acknowledging emotions as well. Such an extension adds creativity to product development processes (Amabile et al., 1996; Fredrickson, 2004), and is more in tune with the way humans behave (Bolis et al., 2017). In other words, things make perfect sense only after we begin to merge feeling with thinking. As such, emotion can help the manager to address the unknown and imagine alternative futures (Dunne and Martin, 2006). Our findings also suggest that without emotions, there is no readiness to change, nor willingness to move forward in the decision process. Positive emotions such as excitement, the joy of success and a more generic feeling of doing the right thing are associated with creative insights (Fredrickson, 2004). Negative emotions can also unleash creative energy (To et al., 2015) and spur people to make necessary changes. Within our pool of managers, especially frustration and anger appeared to trigger willingness to transform. We also find that positive emotions such as excitement or joy serve as important ethical assets that enhance not only holistic understanding, but also the understanding of the quality of detailed analysis. This is interesting, since research has previously suggested that positive emotions help in generating a sense of the whole (Fredrickson, 2004; Sadler-Smith and Shefy, 2004), while negative emotion enhance deliberative and detail-focused analysis (Delgado-García et al., 2015). Negative emotions such as fear, frustration or anger also help to identify problems by drawing attention to those factors that feel wrong or misplaced in the current situation.

We argue that emotion serves as an ethical compass through its capacity to recognize what really matters. Emotions assist in selecting the most appropriate ethical choice, especially in the presence of uncertainty, when rational thinking and analysis are not enough. Although we agree that cognition is important (Steiner, 1982), it is also important to allow emotion to play its role in strategic sustainability decisions. Positive emotions can signal the goodness/rightness of the chosen direction; negative emotions can have the opposite effects; and lack of emotion can signal that the dilemma itself is not that important after all. Bommer et al. (1987) argue that in the event of conflict between organizational and personal values, the emphasis will be on organizational and group values. The last point was manifested in our findings: many managers were ready to work long hours for the company at the cost of their private life, if this sacrifice contributed to solving global issues such as climate change. Interestingly, and possibly because of our sample of sustainability-driven informants, when the trade-off involved choosing between fast profit for the company or long-term ethical implications for society, the latter was often preferred.

As such, the ethical mission had the capacity to override business imperatives and made modest revenues acceptable (although most would have liked to have better business performance too). For some managers, being at the cutting edge of ecological business development was a great motivator, and most managers use their own excitement as an important signal of the validity of a certain path. In contrast, negative emotions served as warnings that prevented incorrect decisions. This is in concert with those who suggest that emotions carry important messages for ethical decision-making (Johnson, 2002; Schwartz, 2016).

Overall, emotion and reason can be mutually reinforcing when overcoming ethical dilemmas in strategic sustainability decision-making. Our findings contribute to theory in at least three ways. First, we extend the rational sustainability decision-making models by identifying three different elements of how emotions interact with rational reasoning. The model introduces emotion as a compass that helps the manager to sensitize to the ethical dilemma, to sense what really matters in ethical evaluation, and finally, to select the best possible ethical choice. This is essential, since rational processes tend to evaluate the novelty of sustainable technologies, materials and practices based only on previous experiences and memories (Rezaee, 2017). Although emotion carries important messages related to prior experience as well, it also embraces observation and meaning (Brundin, 2002). As such, emotion combines details with the big picture, and deliberative considerations with ad hoc thinking, when trying to imagine a better future that does not yet exist.

Second, we add empirical nuances to Schwartz's (2016) integrated ethical decision-making model. Our model identifies typical ethical dilemmas in the context of sustainable transformation: expensive ecological materials versus cheaper non-ecological materials, short-term profits versus long-term ethical goals, ethical company values versus stakeholder benefits. Schwartz (2016) has paid scant attention to this dimension. Moving beyond moral negative emotions such as anger and disgust (Johnson, 2002), we suggest that positive emotions such as excitement, joy and fun can also play a role in ethical decisions. While emotions can be positive, neutral or negative, they can also have diverse implications in establishing the rightness or wrongness of the available alternatives during evaluations. An important nuance is also that feeling has some physical attributes in addition to mental and brain-related attributes. While the embodiment of emotional experience is not new in the discussion on emotions as such (Prinz and Nichols, 2010), prior work on emotion-imbued ethical decision-making has only captured emotion as a process within the brain, thus neglecting its physical manifestations.

Third, we contribute to the knowledge on how managers of trailblazing companies make decisions in general. We have captured them as sensitive change agents who utilize their emotions in navigating toward a more sustainable future in the presence of ethical dilemmas. Our findings support those notions, affirming that emotions should be allowed a larger role in business (Lurie, 2004) because of their capacity to harmonize experience, observation and meaning (Brundin, 2002), and because they can contribute to replacing unsustainable practices with more sustainable alternatives (Huppatz, 2015). In addition, our findings suggest that when utilized as a strategic tool to support distinguishing right from wrong, emotions may improve the ethical quality of strategic decision-making. Although extant frameworks (Bolis et al., 2017; Hallstedt et al., 2010; Subramanian et al., 2010; Wang et al., 2009) on sustainability decision-making are informative, they fail to acknowledge the nuanced role of emotion in distinguishing the right/good from the wrong/bad in the context of a judgement. Emotions do not necessarily only represent self-centred feelings, but also reflect a moral perspective (Kals and Maes, 2002); although the excessive use of emotions can result in clouded decision-making (Damasio, 1994), for our pool of managers mixing rational criteria with emotions and feelings appears to be an important element in making sustainability decisions.

Finally, in terms of its practical contribution, the identification of emotional influences on decisions can be beneficial not only for company managers, but also for those stakeholders and governmental financing bodies who aim to contribute to worldwide sustainable development. To help managers and policy-makers address the challenges involved in the intelligent use of emotions, our findings could be synthesized to offer some practical, albeit metaphorical, advice as implied in the title of this chapter. One could consider emotions a compass for decision-making, with the caveat that the compass in question only shows the direction to north. North will not always be the right way to go; nevertheless, when combined with an appropriate map (in the form of knowledge), emotions can help the manager to make more ethical and sustainable decisions. However, if those managers are working with inaccurate maps, emotion alone can only help to distinguish what feels right or wrong, and push the strategic decisions toward whatever feels right.

LIMITATIONS

Our empirical setting is limited in the sense that we focus on 23 small and medium-sized 'trailblazer' companies in Finland, whose ethical foundation includes sustainability as embodied in their strategy. Hence, our results are valid and reliable only within the purview of our current sample. However, we embrace ethics mostly as a decision-making skill (Clarkeburn, 2002; Surie and Ashley, 2008), and hence do not highlight any specific school of thought on what is right or wrong. We follow Trevino (1986), who invites us to take account of individual differences in the context of ethical considerations, and accept that what is right for one may not be right for another. Therefore, culturally bound morality should not be an issue for the generalization of our findings. Given that collecting data through interviews is about retrospective interpretations, we acknowledge that the process involves the rationalization of past events (Schwartz, 2016). However, this is not a major issue for our research, on the grounds that if an emotion can be recalled after a period of time, it can be treated as meaningful (Brundin, 2002). Although calculations and rational analysis are critical elements in ethical judgement (Trevino, 1986; Rest, 1986), they are beyond the scope of this study. Moreover, we do not mean to suggest that in demanding situations managers would not benefit from decision-support tools, sophisticated computer programs, or utilizing artificial intelligence.

CONCLUSIONS

Overall, this chapter has illuminated an important link between research on the ethical aspects of strategic sustainability decisions (Blockley, 2015; Rushton, 2002; Wenstøp and Seip, 2001), and the real-life experiences of owner-managers. Merging the oral interpretations of owner-managers with theoretical insights concerning ethical decision-making (Trevino, 1986; Schwartz, 2016), we link these theoretical extensions with the emerging context of sustainable transformation (Markman et al., 2016). In doing so, we portray these managers as change agents, whose emotions can inspire them to realize their ethical images in strategic sustainability decision-making (Shepherd and Patzelt, 2017; Venkataraman et al., 2012), and to acknowledge the planet, its people and company profits simultaneously (Elkington, 1999). Through their capacity to direct attention to what feels important, emotions take effect through three interrelated but distinct elements: sensitizing, sensing and selecting. As such, emotion serves as an ethical compass when managers attempt to make strategic sustainability decisions. These decisions reflect their commitment not only to the sustainable goals of their business, but also to more universal goals such as addressing climate change. This is considered significant in that it supports the view that business success depends on sustainability (Rushton, 2002).

ACKNOWLEDGEMENT

This study is part of the research project "Reasons & Emotions – Taking the leap across the rationale gap: the role of emotions in making the transition to more sustainable materials" (Academy of Finland, grant no: 317570).

REFERENCES

Amabile, T.M., R. Conti, H. Coon, J. Lazenby and M. Herron (1996), 'Assessing the work environment for creativity', *Academy of Management Journal*, **39**(5), 1154–1184.

Blockley, D. (2015), 'Finding resilience through practical wisdom', *Civil Engineering and Environmental Systems*, **32**(1–2), 18–30.

Bolis, I., S.N. Morioka and L.I. Sznelwar (2017), 'Are we making decisions in a sustainable way? A comprehensive literature review about rationalities for sustainable development', *Journal of Cleaner Production*, **145**, 310–322.

Bommer, M., C. Gratto, J. Gravander and M. Tuttle (1987), 'A behavioral model of ethical and unethical decision making', *Journal of Business Ethics*, **6**(4), 265–280.

Brundin, E. (2002), 'Emotions in motion: the strategic leader in a radical change process', Doctoral dissertation, Jönköping International Business School.

Cacciotti, G., J.C. Hayton, J.R. Mitchell and A. Giazitzoglu (2016), 'A reconceptualization of fear of failure in entrepreneurship', *Journal of Business Venturing*, **31**(3), 302–325.

Callahan, S. (1988), 'The role of emotion in ethical decision making', *Hastings Center Report*, **18**(3), 9–14.

Cardon, M.S. and M. Glauser (2011), 'Entrepreneurial passion: sources and sustenance', Wilson Center for Social Entrepreneurship, Paper 3. http://digitalcommons .pace.edu/wilson/3.

Chichilnisky, G. (2009), 'The topology of fear', *Journal of Mathematical Economics*, **45**(12), 807–816.

Clarkeburn, H. (2002), 'The aims and practice of ethics education in an undergraduate curriculum: reasons for choosing a skills approach', *Journal of Further and Higher Education*, **26**(4), 307–315.

Corbin, J.M. and A. Strauss (1990), 'Grounded theory research: procedures, canons, and evaluative criteria', *Qualitative Sociology*, **13**(1), 3–21.
Damasio, A. (1994), *Descartes' Error: Emotion, Reason, and the Human Brain*, New York: Putnam.
Damasio, A.R., T. Daniel and H. Damasio (1991), 'Somatic markers and the guidance of behaviour: theory and preliminary testing', in H.S. Levin, H.M. Eisenberg and A.L. Benton (eds), *Frontal Lobe Function and Dysfunction*, New York: Oxford University Press, pp. 217–229.
Dane, E. and M.G. Pratt (2007), 'Exploring intuition and its role in managerial decision-making', *Academy of Management Review*, **32**(1), 33–54.
Delgado-García, J.B., E. De Quevedo Puente and V. Blanco Mazagatos (2015), 'How affect relates to entrepreneurship: a systematic review of the literature and research agenda', *International Journal of Management Reviews*, **17**(2), 191–211.
Dunne, D. and R. Martin (2006), 'Design thinking and how it will change management education: an interview and discussion', *Academy of Management Learning and Education*, **5**(4), 512–523.
Eisenhardt, K.M. (1989), 'Agency theory: an assessment and review', *Academy of Management Review*, **14**(1), 57–74.
Elkington, J. (1999), 'Triple bottom-line reporting: looking for balance', *Australian CPA*, **69**, 18–21.
Elliott, D. (2004), *Energy, Society and Environment*, London: Routledge.
Feito-Cespon, M., W. Sarache, F. Piedra-Jimenez and R. Cespon-Castro (2016), 'Redesign of a sustainable reverse supply chain under uncertainty: a case study', *Journal of Cleaner Production*, **151**, 206–217.
Forgas, J.P. (1995), 'Mood and judgment: the affect infusion model (AIM)', *Psychological Bulletin*, **117**(1), 39–66.
Fredrickson, B.L. (2004), 'The broaden-and-build theory of positive emotions', *Philosophical Transactions: Royal Society of London Series B Biological Sciences*, **359**(1449), 1367–1378.
Garcia, S., Cintra, Y., Rita de Cássia, S. R., and Lima, F. G. (2016), 'Corporate sustainability management: a proposed multi-criteria model to support balanced decision-making'. *Journal of Cleaner Production*, **136**, 181–196.
Guzak, J.R. (2015), 'Affect in ethical decision-making: mood matters', *Ethics and Behavior*, **25**(5), 386–399.
Hallstedt, S., H. Ny, K.H. Robèrt and G. Broman (2010), 'An approach to assessing sustainability integration in strategic decision systems for product development', *Journal of Cleaner Production*, **18**(8), 703–712.
Huppatz, D.J. (2015), 'Revisiting Herbert Simon's "science of design"', *Design Issues*, **31**(2), 29–40.
Johnson, C.E. (2002), 'Ethical decision-making and behavior', in *Meeting the Ethical Challenge of Leadership: Casting Light or Shadow*, Thousand Oaks, CA: SAGE Publications, pp. 235–269.
Kals, E. and J. Maes (2002), 'Sustainable development and emotions', in P. Schmuck and W.P. Schultz (eds), *Psychology of Sustainable Development*, Boston, MA: Springer, pp. 97–122.
Kleiman, S. (2004), 'Phenomenology: to wonder and search for meanings', *Nurse Researcher*, **11**(4), 7–19.
Lerner, J.S., Y. Li, P. Valdesolo and K.S. Kassam (2015), 'Emotion and decision-making', *Psychology*, **66**, 799–823.

88 *Sustainable entrepreneurship and entrepreneurial ecosystems*

Lockett, A., G. Currie, R. Finn, G. Martin and J. Waring (2014), 'The influence of social position on sensemaking about organizational change', *Academy of Management Journal*, **57**(4), 1102–1129.

Lurie, Y. (2004), 'Humanizing business through emotions: on the role of emotions in ethics', *Journal of Business Ethics*, **49**(1), 1–11.

Markman, G.D., M. Russo, G.T. Lumpkin, P.D. Jennings and J. Mair (2016), 'Entrepreneurship as a platform for pursuing multiple goals: a special issue on sustainability, ethics, and entrepreneurship', *Journal of Management Studies*, **53**, 673–694.

Martin, L. (2015), 'Incorporating values into sustainability decision-making', *Journal of Cleaner Production*, **105**, 146–156.

Moch, M.K. and J.M. Bartunek (1990), *Creating Alternative Realities at Work: The Quality of Work Life Experiment at FoodCom*, New York: HarperBusiness.

Muñoz, P. (2017), 'A cognitive map of sustainable decision-making in entrepreneurship: a configurational approach', *International Journal of Entrepreneurial Behavior and Research*, **24**(3), 787–813.

Pietkiewicz, I. and J.A. Smith (2014), 'A practical guide to using interpretative phenomenological analysis in qualitative research psychology', *Psychological Journal*, **20**(1), 7–14.

Prahalad, C.K. and R.A. Bettis (1986), 'The dominant logic: a new linkage between diversity and performance', *Strategic Management Journal*, **7**(6), 485–501.

Prinz, J.J. (2009), *The Emotional Construction of Morals*, New York: Oxford University Press.

Prinz, J.J. and S. Nichols (2010), 'Moral emotions', in J. M. Doris and The Moral Psychology Research Group (eds), *The Moral Psychology Handbook*, Oxford: Oxford University Press, pp. 111–146.

Rest, J.R. (1986), *Moral Development: Advances in Research and Theory*, New York: Praeger.

Rezaee, Z. (2017), 'Corporate sustainability: theoretical and integrated strategic imperative and pragmatic approach', *Journal of Business Inquiry: Research, Education and Application*, **16**(1). Available at SSRN: https://ssrn.com/abstract=3148705.

Rushton, K. (2002), 'Business ethics: a sustainable approach', *Business Ethics: A European Review*, **11**(2), 137–139.

Russell, J.A. (2003), 'Core affect and the psychological construction of emotion', *Psychological Review*, **110**(1), 145–172.

Sadler-Smith, E. and E. Shefy (2004), 'The intuitive executive: understanding and applying "gut feeling" decision-making', *Academy of Management Executive*, **18**(4), 76–91.

Salvador, R. and R.G. Folger (2009), 'Business ethics and the brain', *Business Ethics Quarterly*, **19**(1), 1–31.

Sanders, P. (1982), 'Phenomenology: a new way of viewing organizational research', *Academy of Management Review*, **7**(3), 353–360.

Schwartz, M.S. (2016), 'Ethical decision-making theory: an integrated approach', *Journal of Business Ethics*, **139**(4), 755–776.

Schwarz, N. (2011), 'Feelings-as-information theory', in P. Van Lange, A.W. Kruglanski and E.T. Higgins (eds), *Handbook of Theories of Social Psychology*, Vol. 1, London: SAGE Publications, 289–308.

Seo, M.G. and L.F. Barrett (2007), 'Being emotional during decision-making – good or bad? An empirical investigation', *Academy of Management Journal*, **50**(4), 923–940.

Shepherd, D.A. and H. Patzelt (2017), 'Researching entrepreneurships' role in sustainable development', in *Trailblazing in Entrepreneurship*, Cham: Palgrave Macmillan, pp. 149–179.
Shevchenko, A., M. Levesque and M. Pagell (2016), 'Why firms delay reaching true sustainability', *Journal of Management Studies*, **53**(5), 911–935.
Smith, E.R. and G.R. Semin (2004), 'Socially situated cognition: cognition in its social context', *Advances in Experimental Social Psychology*, **36**, 57–121.
Smith, J. and M. Osborn (2003), 'Interpretative phenomenological analysis', in J.A. Smith (ed.), *Qualitative Psychology: A Practical Guide to Methods*, London: SAGE, pp. 53–80.
Steiner, I.D. (1982), 'Heuristic models of groupthink', in H. Brandstatter, J.H. Davis and G. Stocker-Kreichgauer (eds), *Group Decision Making*, New York: Academic Press, pp. 503–524.
Subramanian, R., B. Talbot and S. Gupta (2010), 'An approach to integrating environmental considerations within managerial decision-making', *Journal of Industrial Ecology*, **14**(3), 378–398.
Surie, G. and A. Ashley (2008), 'Integrating pragmatism and ethics in entrepreneurial leadership for sustainable value creation', *Journal of Business Ethics*, **81**(1), 235–246.
To, M.L., C.D. Fisher and N.M. Ashkanasy (2015), 'Unleashing angst: negative mood, learning goal orientation, psychological empowerment and creative behaviour', *Human Relations*, **68**(10), 1601–1622.
Trevino, L.K. (1986), 'Ethical decision-making in organizations: a person–situation interactionist model', *Academy of Management Review*, **11**(3), 601–617.
Trevino, L.K. and M.E. Brown (2004), 'Managing to be ethical: debunking five business ethics myths', *Academy of Management Perspectives*, **18**(2), 69–81.
Venkataraman, S., S.D. Sarasvathy, N. Dew and W.R. Forster (2012), 'Reflections on the 2010 AMR Decade Award: whither the promise? Moving forward with entrepreneurship as a science of the artificial', *Academy of Management Review*, **37**, 21–33.
Wang, J.J., Y.Y. Jing, C.F. Zhang and J.H. Zhao (2009), 'Review on multi-criteria decision analysis aid in sustainable energy decision-making', *Renewable and Sustainable Energy Reviews*, **13**(9), 2263–2278.
Wenstøp, F. and K. Seip (2001), 'Legitimacy and quality of multi-criteria environmental policy analysis: a meta-analysis of five MCE studies in Norway', *Journal of Multi-Criteria Decision Analysis*, **10**(2), 53–64.
Wright, C. and D. Nyberg (2017), 'An inconvenient truth: how organizations translate climate change into business as usual', *Academy of Management Journal*, **60**(5), 1633–1661.

APPENDIX

Table 5A.1   Company descriptions

Core purpose of the company	No. of employees	Turnover 2017
1. Natural, resin-based pharmaceuticals	3	€0.9 million
2. Technological innovation for food production	8	€0.14 million
3. Electricity production, solar panels, etc.	4	€0.19 million
4. Waste management, circular economy	1	€0
5. Wastewater treatment processes	2	€3.8 million
6. Reuse leftover materials for design products	3	€0.1 million
7. Ecological materials	12	€0.1 million
8. Responsible practices, recycling	17	€3.7 million
9. Micronutrient fertilizers, technology innovations	3	€0
10. Fly ash as an effective forest fertilizer	5	€1.8 million
11. Surface material containing recycled post-industrial plastic	18	€1.9 million
12. Biodegradable composites for mechanical and technical industries	30	€0.1 million
13. Waste recycling system	16	€7.8 million
14. Ecological fertilizers, circular economy	13	€3.5 million
15. Biofuels	4	€0.2 million
16. Environmental friendly warming systems	67	€7.8 million
17. Lighting innovations, reducing electricity consumption	93	€40 million
18. Vertical farming innovations	25	€2.7 million
19. Mushroom-growing innovations	2	€0.1 million
20. Environment-friendly, oil-free lubricant for agricultural machinery	10	€1.8 million
21. Technological innovation for drying materials	3	€0.12 million
22. Treatment of stormwater, nutrient recycling, efficient organic algriculture	2	€0.12 million
23. Produce products that are based on biocoal	29	€10 million

PART II

Entrepreneurial ecosystems

6. Understanding the emergence of the university-based entrepreneurial ecosystem: comparing the university and company actors' perspectives

Katja Lahikainen

INTRODUCTION

Entrepreneurial ecosystems promote entrepreneurship within specific regional boundaries. They consist of a set of interdependent actors that aim for new value creation, the creation of spin-offs and start-ups, as well as new jobs through entrepreneurial activities (Spigel, 2017; Stam, 2015). The distinctive feature of entrepreneurial ecosystems is that they enable entrepreneurs to identify market opportunities and offer local resources, support and financing to grow new high-growth ventures (Spigel and Harrison, 2018).

Recently, universities have been identified as important contributors in entrepreneurial ecosystems (Belitski and Heron, 2017; Isenberg, 2010; Stam, 2015). Universities can provide a large variety of resources to entrepreneurial ecosystems: new technologies that create entrepreneurial opportunities (Lawton Smith et al., 2014), human capital (teaching activities), knowledge capital (technology and research) and entrepreneurship capital (creation of spin-offs and an entrepreneurial mindset) (Audretsch, 2014; Guerrero et al., 2016; Huang-Saad et al., 2018). Additionally, universities may play an important role in creating and connecting entrepreneurs in their networks, thereby enabling entrepreneurs to acquire resources, knowledge and support from the actors of the entrepreneurial ecosystem (Spigel and Harrison, 2018). University-based entrepreneurial ecosystems can be researched as sub-systems of larger regional or local entrepreneurial ecosystems (Cavallo et al., 2018; Fuster et al., 2019) or as ecosystems on their own (Greene et al., 2010; Miller and Acs, 2017). This study focuses on investigating a university-based entrepreneurial ecosystem on its own. This chapter defines the university-based entrepreneurial ecosystem (U-BEE), in accordance with Hayter (2016), as the strategic and collective actions of various organizational components in order to maximize both the entrepreneurial and innovative contributions of universities.

Research on U-BEEs is still in a nascent stage and tends to focus on a narrow view of entrepreneurship that is limited to studies on new venture creation (Bischoff et al., 2018). The current research has focused on investigating organizational structures, curricular and extra-curricular study programmes and support services, such as technology transfer offices (TTOs), from the university point of view (Belitski and Heron, 2017; Greene et al., 2010; Hayter, 2016). Previous studies have acknowledged the importance of non-academic contacts of academics, diverse governance, openness and decentralization of activities as factors that enhance university-based entrepreneurship (Hayter, 2016; Miller and Acs, 2017). Spigel and Harrison (2018) posit that university knowledge spillovers are important in entrepreneurial ecosystems, yet still less important than the universities' role as producers of skilled entrepreneurs and workers. This study addresses this statement by investigating university and company actors' perspectives on the different roles of the university in promoting entrepreneurship in the region.

The objective of this chapter is to provide new insights on the immature theory of university-based entrepreneurial ecosystems. The specific aim of the study is to compare the different perspectives of the university and company actors towards the university as a producer of new knowledge and start-ups, and as a producer of skilled entrepreneurs and workforce. The research questions are: How do university and company actors perceive the university's role as a catalyst for entrepreneurship? Which factors constrain and reinforce the interaction between the companies and universities in the university-based entrepreneurial ecosystem? This chapter brings out the factors that enhance and hinder the emergence of U-BEE. It presents the findings of an inductive case analysis of the university-based entrepreneurial ecosystem that is formed around a Finnish university campus.

This chapter is structured as follows. After this brief introduction, the literature on entrepreneurial ecosystems is reviewed. The following section presents the research method, including a short description of the case, and provides detailed information on the data collection and data analysis process. The findings of the study are then presented, focusing on four themes that emerged during the data analysis process. The chapter ends by discussing the main conclusions and implications of the study.

UNIVERSITY-BASED ENTREPRENEURIAL ECOSYSTEMS (U-BEES)

In entrepreneurial ecosystems, entrepreneurs form the core of the ecosystem (Stam, 2015). The entrepreneurial ecosystems consist of social, material and cultural attributes. The success of entrepreneurial ecosystems is based on the interaction of these attributes which provide benefits and resources to entrepreneurs (Spigel, 2017). In regional entrepreneurial ecosystems, universities can be considered as one of the key material attributes (Isenberg, 2010; Spigel, 2017). The main social attributes include networks, investment capital, mentors and deal-makers, and worker talent. The cultural attributes consist of attitudes and histories of entrepreneurship (Spigel, 2017).

In a similar vein, U-BEEs consist of similar attributes as entrepreneurial ecosystems in general. According to Brush (2014), the key dimensions of U-BEEs are stakeholders, resources, infrastructure and culture. The stakeholders include internal and external stakeholders that have different needs, connections and motivations. Resources include, for example, intellectual knowledge and research capabilities, physical facilities, and monetary and human resources. The infrastructure includes elements related to connectivity; for example, technological platforms as well as formal and informal networks. Culture includes the symbolic aspect, norms, values and traditions (Brush, 2014). A distinctive feature of U-BEEs is that entrepreneurship activities revolve around curricular, co-curricular and research activities, and that they can be implemented by university staff, students or specific organizational structures of universities, such as TTOs or incubators (Greene et al., 2010; Brush, 2014).

A U-BEE can emerge as a proactive or reactive response to the internal or external needs of a university (Lahikainen et al., 2018). In a proactive development, the university creates, for example, new educational or economic initiatives, whereas in a reactive development the university may address the unfulfilled needs of students or local entrepreneurs (Rice et al., 2014).

The academics tend to collaborate with their like-minded social networks. In order to increase market-oriented motivations, values and practices, academics need to bridge the gap between the traditional academic networks and more entrepreneurial market-oriented entrepreneurial networks (Hayter, 2016). The engagement of faculty members and students with the outside world is crucial for developing a U-BEE, since the U-BEE can be attractive for the local companies because of the academic freedom that its students and faculty members enjoy (Miller and Acs, 2017). However, the development of a U-BEE is not an endeavour of a single active and engaged individual; instead, it requires a team of people and the involvement of all stakeholders to be successful (Rice et al., 2014). Additionally, some of the faculty would rather focus on research and teaching, which are the traditional tasks of universities (Lahikainen et al., 2018), than participate in entrepreneurial activity. This means that universities need to complement the faculty staff with staff members who excel in both traditional tasks and entrepreneurship (Rice et al., 2014).

The entrepreneurs and company representatives are the most frequently involved external stakeholder groups in U-BEEs. Moreover, the collaborative partners tend to be small and medium-sized companies. Collaboration with large companies is favoured where SMEs are underrepresented in the region (Bischoff et al., 2018). University spin-offs can have an important role in a U-BEE by acting as a knowledge hub that transfers the knowledge and connects the U-BEE to wider business ecosystems. In order to reinforce these interactions, the universities should develop a proactive strategy to support university-based spin-offs, for example through the intermediate functions such as a TTO and university-focused venture capital (UVC) (Fuster et al., 2019).

Empirical research highlights the need for a coordinated stakeholder management approach to strengthen the university-based entrepreneurial ecosystem through strong and focused stakeholder networks and collaboration (Bischoff et al., 2018). The universities have a potentially important role to play in the promotion of regional entrepreneurship, but they face challenges in societal interaction, especially in the commercialization of research outcomes (Lahikainen et al., 2018), and not all faculty want to be entrepreneurs (Huang-Saad et al., 2018). Additionally, the identified challenges usually relate to the orientation of universities and the transactions involved in, for example, conflicts over intellectual property rights (IPRs) and dealing with university administration. Trustful long-term relationships can lower these barriers, whereas increased scrutiny and formalized relationships can increase the transaction-related barriers (Bruneel et al., 2010). Universities can have a strong influence on the specialization of regions. The successful reorientation of industry depends on different factors; for example, organizational and incentive structures of universities, as well as the universities' capacity to establish external links with their regional stakeholders (Braunerhjelm, 2008).

METHOD

This chapter presents the findings from the case analysis of the U-BEE that is formed around Lappeenranta University of Technology (LUT). LUT, established in 1969, is located outside the capital region in southeast Finland. The region is by tradition dominated by large industry, but due to the industrial restructuring in recent years the company base has become more diverse. Even so, the region is still lacking in start-ups and small and medium-sized enterprises (SMEs).

Since its establishment, LUT has had extensive collaboration with industrial partners. LUT is strongly focused on seeking high-tech solutions that combine technology and business in the field of cleantech. In 2015, the *Times Higher Education* World University Rankings awarded LUT a high ranking for business interaction. LUT's latest strategy, launched in 2014, includes entrepreneurship in its mission, stating that LUT will be the first Finnish entrepreneurial university and emphasizing the broad scope of entrepreneurial actions. In actions related to new business creation, LUT collaborates closely with Saimaa University of Applied Sciences (Saimaa UAS), located in the same campus area. The role of Saimaa UAS is to provide, amongst others, practical applications for the inventions originating from LUT research. The campus formed by LUT and Saimaa UAS has centralized support services for research and innovation services, including a TTO and an investment company. The campus has a leading role in the region in promoting entrepreneurship and establishing new knowledge-intensive start-up companies.

This study is based on an exploratory qualitative research approach with the aim of developing a more comprehensive and nuanced understanding of the university campus as an entrepreneurial ecosystem, and the factors that constrain and reinforce the interaction between the university and local companies within the university-based entrepreneurial ecosystem.

Data Collection

In order to gain a more comprehensive and nuanced understanding of the phenomenon that is the emergence of the U-BEE, conversational thematic interviews were conducted. The interviews had a duration of 20–60 minutes each and they were conducted between February and August 2016. The purposive sampling technique was used (Saunders et al., 2016), and the interviewees were selected based on the previous knowledge of the persons who are active members in the U-BEE. The dataset comprises 22 in-depth interviews consisting of ten interviews made among company actors, and 12 interviews of academic and administrative staff members of LUT and Saimaa UAS. The titles and organizations of the interviewees are described in Table 6.1. All six university-based spin-offs and start-ups are high-tech growth companies whose expertise is based on the university research. The informants from the companies are either managing directors of the companies or experts who regularly collaborate with the university. The selected informants from LUT are researchers who have been active in research commercialization projects of the university. The informants from Saimaa UAS have been actively involved in the commercialization projects that are based on university research. Administrative staff from both higher education institutions (HEIs), who are involved in innovation and commercialization actions, were also selected for the interviews.

The aim of the interviews was to shed light on and recognize the factors that foster or hinder entrepreneurship in the U-BEE. The university interviewees were encouraged to talk about their perceptions of the entrepreneurial and

Table 6.1   Titles and organizations of the interviewees

Firm			University		
#	Title	Firm type and size	#	Title	University type
1	Managing director	University spin-off, small	11	Associate professor, technology	University
2	Research and development director	Process industry, large	12	Research associate, technology	University
3	Chief technical officer	University-based start-up, medium	13	Senior lecturer, business	UAS
4	Managing director	Software industry, medium	14	Professor, technology	University
5	Managing director	Software industry, medium	15	Associate professor, business	University
6	Managing director	University-based start-up, small	16	Professor, technology	University
7	Managing director	University spin-off, micro	17	Senior lecturer, technology	UAS
8	Managing director	University spin-off, micro	18	Professor, technology	University
9	Managing director	University-based start-up, medium	19	Research director	UAS
10	Managing director	Engineering, medium	20	Manager, Innovation Services	University
			21	Vice-rector	University
			22	Vice-rector	UAS

Note: Used measures of firm sizes: large > 250 employees, medium < 250 employees, small < 50 employees, and micro < 10 employees.

commercial activities as a part of their work. Similarly, the company representatives were asked to describe the methods of interaction with the university, emphasizing the university's role in fostering entrepreneurship in the region. All the interviews were recorded and transcribed. Confidentiality was guaranteed to all the interviewees, and hence the interview quotations here – which are free translations from Finnish – are anonymous.

Each interview followed its own path. However, the interviews covered three main themes, namely networking and collaboration, governance and leadership, and barriers and support. First, regarding networking and collaboration, the interviewees were asked to name the most central actors in the ecosystem, describe the kind of interaction and collaboration they had, name the most important means of collaboration, and finally, give examples of the successful and less successful outcomes of entrepreneurial actions. The second theme, governance and leadership, covered topics related to the strategic support of the university to enhance entrepreneurship in the region. Lastly, the interviewees were requested to provide information about organizational barriers and support.

Data Analysis

The data analysis followed the inductive thematic data analysis method introduced by Gioia et al. (2013). The analysis method was chosen because it is suitable especially for elaborating new concepts and ideas (Gioia et al., 2013). The data analysis followed the approach of composing first-order and second-order analysis; the approach that enables making the links between data and concepts visible (Gioia et al., 2013).

The analysis was started by using NVivo software. Very thorough coding was done of all the aspects (phares and sentences) that seemed relevant concerning the research questions. After a closer look of the codes, 75 codes were selected for further study and exported to an Excel file. In the Excel file, each code was marked in such a way that all the excerpts that belonged to different codes could be traced back to their original sources.

Furthermore, the codes were organized in the Excel file by grouping and deleting the codes and excerpts that began to seem irrelevant in terms of the research questions of this study. The grouping was continued by looking for similarities and differences among the codes. This resulted in 20 codes for describing company perspectives and 17 codes describing the perspectives of the HEIs. As suggested by Gioia et al. (2013), the informant-centric wording was used when naming the codes. As a result, these categories were given phrasal descriptions that became the first-order concepts.

At the second level of analysis, similarities and differences were looked for among the first-order concepts. Within this, group comparisons were made among company and university informants, as well as inter-group comparisons between the company and university informants. Altogether, four second-order themes were created by using the research-centric terminology in naming the themes. At the third level of analysis, the emergent second-order themes were further distilled into three aggregate dimensions that together form the preliminary data structure of this research (Figure 6.1).

During the data analysis process, already-existing theoretical frameworks were sought, to be ignored in order to avoid a potential guiding effect of the existing theories in data analysis (Gioia et al., 2013). However, the data analysis process was an iterative process that consisted of moving among data, emerging patterns and the literature until the final dataset structure was settled (Eisenhardt, 1989).

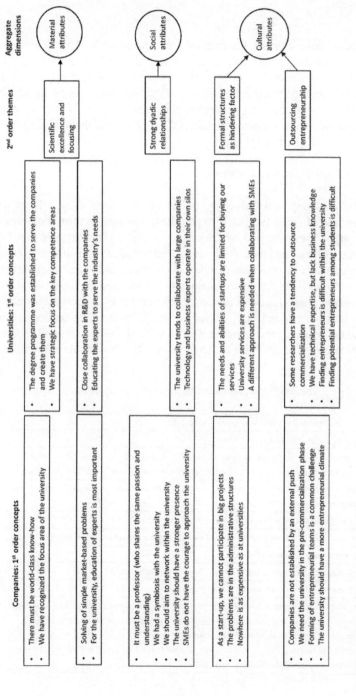

Figure 6.1 Data structure

FINDINGS

This section describes the findings of the data analysis. The findings are structured according to the themes that emerged based on the second level coding. The constructed second-order themes are: (1) scientific excellence and focusing; (2) strong dyadic relationships; (3) formal structures as a hindering factor; and (4) outsourcing entrepreneurship (see Figure 6.1). The numbers in brackets after each quotation in Tables 6.2–6.9 refer to the number of each informant as indicated in Table 6.1.

Scientific Excellence and Focusing

From the company and university points of view, the most critical and important task of the university is to educate the experts to meet the needs of the industry. In research and education, successful collaboration is based on scientific excellence and clear focus areas. Both company and university actors emphasized these success factors. Clear focus areas and research quality are the key preconditions for the companies to get the best possible workforce. The university graduates act as important intermediaries in knowledge transfer from the university to industry. Tables 6.2 and 6.3 present the first-order concepts and the selected representative data on scientific excellence and focusing from the company actor (Table 6.2) and university actor (Table 6.3) points of view.

Table 6.2   Scientific excellence and focusing: companies

First-order concepts and the selected representative data
There must be world-class know-how
One case led to the creation of a new company that was also funded by the university's investment company. Another notable example is that the problems of companies can be solved by top expertise. (4)
The university has top knowledge. We have top knowledge. We have built a team around these top experts. When these people start to work it leads to success. However, it is hard work. (6)
We have recognized the focus area of the university
We have recognized it as a focus area of LUT and we want to focus our efforts in this field. (2)
Solving of simple market-based problems
…simpler, clearer, market-based research for companies. No pipe dreams. (7)
For the university, education of experts is most important
A critical factor is how successful university is in recruiting? Had the research assistant who wrote the master's thesis not succeeded in getting good results, or had the collaboration otherwise failed, this company might not have been established. This is a notable thing. (7)
Nowhere can I find experts in this specific field as well-educated as those taught by Prof. N.N. Even our customers notice how they differ from the others. (9)

Table 6.3   Scientific excellence and focusing: university

First-order concepts and the selected representative data
The degree programme was established to serve the companies and create them
When we established this degree programme, we defined in our strategy that, because we lacked industrial customers, our mission would be to try to promote the establishment of new companies in the region that would later employ us, as well as serve the existing companies. (16)
We have strategic focus on the key competence areas
We have the ability and a sufficiently large research group. This inevitably leads to the accumulation of knowledge and focusing. We do not try to do everything, but we concentrate on the areas that are defined in our strategy. (16)
We have targets and we select the persons who implement them based on their competences. They must be scientifically qualified, as well as otherwise right-minded in order to fit in. (14)
Close collaboration in R&D with the companies
The university-based inventions are often still raw and not ready to be delivered to the end-user. Often the end-users are SMEs, with whom we begin the R&D project. (20)
We conduct research cooperation in the product development interphase. Then the knowledge is transferred by the persons and the IPRs. (14)
Educating the experts to serve the industry's needs
We produce the greatest impact by educating engineers and doctors to serve the Finnish industry. These persons are the ones who transfer the research knowledge to the markets. (14)
Five or six doctors went to work there [a company] during one day. However, some of these doctors were still employed by the university. (16)

Company actors perceive that the most important task of the university is to educate the experts to meet the demands of the industry. In terms of research collaboration, the university is expected to be a problem-solver of very concrete challenges of the companies; the kinds of problems that offer intellectual challenges for the professors and their students. Research as well as education must be based on the world-class knowledge that is competitive on global markets. The university must provide top knowledge that can be combined with the top expertise that companies have. The university has managed to make its focus areas known, since the companies have recognized them. They have also concentrated the collaborative actions and built the teams around those areas.

Correspondingly, university actors emphasized combining practical relevance and scientific excellence in all their actions. This applies especially to the School of Energy Technology at LUT that has practical relevance within scientific rigour as a guiding rule. The school is very focused in its actions. The research groups are formed based on the selected focus areas, and team members are selected based on their academic competences as well as their abilities to collaborate with other team members and industry. Like their industrial counterparts, the university actors emphasized the students as the key actors to transfer the research knowledge to the markets. One of the degree programmes of the School of Technology was even established to serve the existing companies, and with the aim of creating new companies in the region. One of the founding members of the degree programme mentioned that they had considered stopping the programme a number of times during its existence, since the collaboration with the industry was very limited at certain points, and they concentrated solely on scientific work without practical relevance.

Strong Dyadic Relationships

The collaborative actions between the companies and university are based on tight personal relationships between the company actors and senior professors or researchers. The company actors emphasize tight relationships with professors and experts in their field. However, at the same time they acknowledge that wider networking would bring benefits both to companies and to the university. The university actors highlight the collaboration with large companies and seek more collaboration with SMEs and interdisciplinary collaboration among their colleagues. The emerged concepts and representative data are presented in Tables 6.4 and 6.5.

The company actors have established tight dyadic relationships with the professors or senior experts in their field. They highlighted the symbiosis that was created by people – not by any intentional process – based on strong personal relationships. The symbiosis had blurred organizational boundaries, with staff members working simultaneously for the benefit of the university and company with or without an official employment contract.

Despite the benefits of having close dyadic relationships, the company actors acknowledge that wider networking would be beneficial for the university and companies as well as the surrounding region. Collaboration is easy and smooth for the company actors, who have managed to form close personal contacts with the university experts. According to the informants, the university has traditionally concentrated on large companies. However, it was noted that during recent years the university has become a more active actor in the region and approached SMEs in a more active and regular manner. However, the university was still expected to be more active and easily approachable for the SMEs that do not have personal contacts with the university professors and researchers.

The university actors acknowledge that they prefer to collaborate with large companies due to the persevering nature of the university research. Large companies have more capacity to invest and commit their time for the university projects compared to SMEs. Additionally, university actors feel that business and technology experts work in their own silos within the university. More collaboration would be needed, especially in the projects that aim to develop new business from the research outcomes.

Table 6.4   Strong dyadic relationships: companies

First-order concepts and the selected representative data
It must be a professor (who shares the same passion and understanding)
It must be the professor who shares the same passion, will and understanding. They know whether they have a PhD student who has the right attitude and background for us . . . I do not like very much what they offer [university administration], but I do like what the professors do. (9)
For me it is easy, since I know everyone personally. I contend that every company should aim for developing a relationship with the professor or senior researcher. (9)
In practice, we are in direct contact with the professors, always. (3)
We had a symbiosis with the university
We had a symbiosis with the university. It was personal relationships, not any process, that created it. We wrote many theses and conducted recruitments. (5)
We had the kind of research collaboration where I sometimes did not know whether it was the university's meeting or our company's meeting. It worked. We conducted research and so forth. (5)
He [PhD student] worked half the time for us and the other half as a research assistant. The university was very flexible. Double contracting was very beneficial for the university and for us. (7)
We should aim to network within the university
We should aim to network further within the university, not just within our own team. (6)
The university should have a stronger presence
The university should be a stronger and more visible actor in Lappeenranta. (4)
LUT overlooks this place a bit. It looks further to the world and to other regions in Finland – especially at the capital region. Large companies and so forth. (8)
SMEs do not have the courage to approach the university
The problem is how SMEs could better utilize the university – they do not even have the courage to go there. (10)

Table 6.5   Strong dyadic relationships: university

First-order concepts and the selected representative data
The university tends to collaborate with large companies
The university tends to collaborate with large companies because of the persevering nature of our work. (20)
The companies in the region are anaemic in welcoming our expertise, with only few expectations. (16)
Technology and business experts operate in their own silos
The technology experts are somewhat alone, and the business experts are absent. (16)
To a large extent, everyone here tends to concentrate on their own expertise area. However, when developing business ideas you should have broader expertise. (15)

Formal Structures as Hindering Factor

Despite the fact that the case university is rather small and considered to be agile, the bureaucracy typical for universities cannot be avoided. Bureaucracy increases the participation costs of projects, which particularly hinders SMEs' participation in the university projects. Additionally, finalizing formal agreements even in smaller projects can be time-consuming and complicated. Company and university perspectives on administrative challenges are described in Tables 6.6 and 6.7.

Participating in the projects initiated by the university is challenging, especially for the SMEs, which are seldom able to contribute to the projects financially. Instead, they tend to contribute in kind by working for the project without asking for compensation. However, SMEs have a willingness to participate in project work, since it provides them with an avenue for new research knowledge and the possibility for networking.

Almost all interviewees emphasized that the problems related to bureaucracy stem from the centralized university administration structures. The professors are the ones who act as buffers and intermediaries between the administration and companies. The interviewees stated that bureaucracy mainly manifests in delays in schedules. While large companies are less vulnerable, delays in university outputs can have a severe impact on the business operations of newly established start-ups.

Table 6.6   Formal structures as hindering factor: companies

First-order concepts and the selected representative data
As a start-up, we cannot participate in big projects
We are asked [by the university] to participate in projects in which we should provide a notable amount of our own funding. We cannot do that – or we could, if we were sure that we would get it back. For this reason, we mainly participate in projects by offering work contribution. We have a very limited role – we just want to be able to follow what is happening. (8)
The problems are in the administrative structures
Our needs are usually of the kind that cannot be solved by any bureaucracy. If we cannot get help when we need it, we get it from somewhere else. We usually cannot wait for a week. (3)
With the professors, I have not had the slightest problem – not even one. Instead, I have had problems with the administration and laboratory services of the university. (6)
The administration cannot help us, not at all. It does not work if the university establishes some kind of bigger support structures. (9)
Nowhere is as expensive as at universities
A specific feature of the university is that if you have an assignment to be completed, nowhere is as expensive. (10)

Table 6.7   Formal structures as hindering factor: university

First-order concepts and the selected representative data
The needs and abilities of start-ups are limited for buying our services
It is sad that we have a bright future behind us with these spin-offs. They now have a very limited ability and needs to buy expertise from us. (16)
University services are expensive
. . . and the biggest catastrophe is our pricing policy for SMEs. (12)
We have tried something, some small cases, but it has been problematic that they are small with a short duration and without large sums of money. It is very problematic for us to be on board, because even a small amount of work will be very expensive to commission. (15)
A different approach is needed when collaborating with SMEs
In some companies, requirements are higher and timetables are faster. These cases are problematic, since researchers are not used to respond by 2 p.m., for example. (19)
Our approach of being tough does not work with SMEs. (12)

Similarly, university actors also recognize the problem areas of bureaucracy and high costs of university services. They know that SMEs are unable to participate in bigger projects that require their own funding. Additionally, they acknowledge that the university should change the pricing policy and lighten the administrative burden especially when SMEs are involved. Lighter administrative processes would enable the university itself to participate in smaller assignments initiated by the companies and vice versa, which in turn would give SMEs better possibilities to participate in university projects.

Outsourcing Entrepreneurship

The university's role as a locus of new spin-offs and start-ups is seen as a challenging one. Company actors emphasized that commercialization of research outcomes is difficult due to their very technical nature and low readiness level for the markets. Additionally, company actors share the view that professors and researchers lack the passion that is needed for new business creation. In a similar vein, university actors recognized that they lack the needed business expertise. Moreover, the commonly shared concern is that there are not enough potential entrepreneurs, neither at the university nor in the surrounding region. Concepts and selected representative data related to these challenges are highlighted in Tables 6.8 and 6.9.

In general, the company actors had doubts about the overarching goal that has been set on the university to foster regional entrepreneurship. In their opinion, it should not be solely the university's responsibility for several reasons. First, companies are not established by an external push. As one interviewee put it: 'things do not happen they are done'. Professors seldom have the

Table 6.8   *Outsourcing entrepreneurship: companies*

First-order concepts and the selected representative data
Companies are not established by an external push
Most importantly there must be someone who really has the will, heart and soul. Not a single company is established by an external push. In general, professors with great ideas do not establish them. It requires you to put yourself out there and start acting. (9)
We need the university in the pre-commercialization phase
Start-ups are a hot topic at the national and ministerial levels. However, many inventions would have created new businesses and new jobs in existing companies had they been offered to them. However, I understand the researcher who thinks that the idea could become a new business and a start-up could be established. (5)
In all honesty, many of the inventions are technically okay, but when they need to be put into commercial use, they cannot be applied since it would be too expensive, or they have features that cannot be applied. (3)
Forming of entrepreneurial teams is a common challenge
Finding the right people for the start-ups is the challenge. It just needs to be acknowledged that a new type of knowledge is needed to secure the growth, but how to find the needed experts when the ready-made concept does not exist? (2)
The university should have a more entrepreneurial climate
The university should add more entrepreneurship to their curricula. They should have it in almost every course. Of course, not every student will become an entrepreneur, but there could be more of those who will. (10)
I would see that there should be a more entrepreneurial climate, especially from the point of view that students, especially the ones who continue their academic careers, would have higher intentions to commercialize the top-quality research. (4)

entrepreneurial passion and will to act. Second, university-based inventions are very technical and difficult to commercialize. In many cases, a more sensible solution would be to offer the invention to the existing companies rather than trying to commercialize them within the university. Third, the university could have a more entrepreneurial culture. There are many concrete ways to foster entrepreneurship, for example including entrepreneurship in curricula as much as possible in the most concrete manner. Lastly, entrepreneurship is also about changing attitudes, and that does not happen only through university teaching but also through upbringing at home and through informal activities.

The main concern of the university actors was finding potential entrepreneurs, especially finding them among the students. Since the researchers lack the passion and needed competences for starting up a business, they would like to outsource the commercialization activities and concentrate on the research. The professors are looking for mechanisms that would help in finding the potential entrepreneurs. They also acknowledge that even if students are eager and have the right attitude in commercialization projects, they lack the deeper

Table 6.9   Outsourcing entrepreneurship: university

First-order concepts and the selected representative data
Some researchers have a tendency to outsource commercialization
Researchers expect that more things should be done for their behalf. From the opposite perspective, the researchers should take more responsibility for themselves. Evidently, we need to have clearer roles. (20) Eventually, it is about people. Reports won't commercialize by themselves. We should speak in an active, not passive, form. (21)
We have technical expertise, but lack business knowledge
I cannot do the marketing. My students and I invent all kinds of things, but it is not that extraordinary that someone would come and take it from us. We should be able to sell our inventions by ourselves. There is no clear path on how to do it. (16)
Finding entrepreneurs is difficult within the university
We could not find entrepreneurs within the university, though we did find strong technological knowledge. (12)
The research teams have good technical preparedness, but we cannot always find business experts. (20)
Finding potential entrepreneurs among students is difficult
During the old days, when we had all kinds of collaboration and especially exercises, I could go and ask whether there was someone who stands out. Now I feel that no one stands out. Students are just faces who come and go. (18)
They were ordinary degree students. They wrote their master's thesis. They had a very good attitude and still have it. We were very pleased that we found these two people. (18)

understanding of the specific business area and the different application areas of the technology in question.

CONCLUSIONS

The objective of this study was to provide new insights on the emerging literature on U-BEEs. Based on the thematic analysis, four themes were constructed and analysed in the findings section. These themes can be further distilled to three aggregate dimensions, which are material, social and cultural attributes (Spigel, 2017).

This study confirms the statement that, in the entrepreneurial ecosystem, university spillovers are less important than the university's role as a provider of entrepreneurs and qualified workforce (Spigel and Harrison, 2018). According to the findings, the most important task of the university from the company and university actors' perspective is to educate the experts to meet the demands of the industry. However, this case shows that education of the workforce is expected to be based on scientific excellence that is competitive on global markets, meaning that strong material attributes form the firm ground for the emergence of a U-BEE. The transfer of technology and human talent is supported by flexible ways of working, for example by blurring organizational boundaries, as well as by increasing double contracting and internships between the university and companies.

Social interaction between the companies and the university takes place mainly through strong dyadic relationships between the senior academics and company representatives. This case proves that the university's tendency to scrutinize and formalize the relationships increases transaction-related challenges (Bruneel et al., 2010). These transaction-related challenges can become severe problems for SMEs in cases where they are treated in the same manner as larger companies. The company actors are of the opinion that the university administration creates additional bureaucracy, which can be avoided by having trustful dyadic relations with the senior academics in the faculties. This finding contradicts the earlier study, suggesting that a coordinated stakeholder management approach is needed to strengthen the U-BEE (Bischoff et al., 2018).

The importance of scientific excellence and educating a high-quality workforce is unquestionable, but the university's role as a promoter of regional entrepreneurship is more debatable. The basic elements of entrepreneurial culture – the attitudes and histories of entrepreneurship (Brush, 2014; Spigel, 2017) – seem to be in place. However, both company and university actors have concerns regarding the university as a locus of new start-ups and spin-offs, and they tend to share the view that new venture creation should be outsourced from the university. The reasoning behind this opinion is twofold. First, university-based inventions and their applications were seen as being excessively technology-focused and difficult to commercialize, and they would be better utilized if they were offered to existing companies in the first place instead of having the university try to commercialize them. Second, it was emphasized that new business creation requires genuine commitment and passion from the potential entrepreneurs. Academics often lack the needed will to become entrepreneurs (Huang-Saad et al., 2018), meaning that potential entrepreneurs need to be found outside the university. Similarly, the university actors are also dubious about the university's role as a catalyst for start-ups and spin-offs. They believe that the most efficient interaction mode is joint projects with existing companies, in which the resulting IPR is to be transferred to the companies. The professors see that they lack the needed expertise for commercialization actions and that the mechanisms by which, for example, students could be involved in the commercialization projects do not exist. The professors consider the creation of start-ups to be important, but the focus on start-ups might diminish the importance of knowledge transfer through research and education in the form of IPRs and a high-quality workforce.

In sum, this case confirms that a close and trustful relationship with non-academic contacts (Hayter, 2016; Miller and Acs, 2017) is an important factor that reinforces the interaction in the U-BEE. However, the close dyadic relationships hinder further networking within the university and among companies, especially among SMEs that are not active members in the U-BEE. This reinforces the interaction vertically but hinders horizontal networking across different disciplines and different fields of industry. This case confirms that the selection of a clear focus area enhances the university's role in the reorientation of the commercial sector in regions (Braunerhjelm, 2008). However, focusing enhances the special industrial cluster to be developed but neglects the entrepreneurs in other sectors and hinders them from acquiring resources and support from the university (Spigel and Harrison, 2018).

Finally, it should be noted that this study has some limitations. First, the company and university actors that were selected for the interviews are all active members in the emerging U-BEE. This fact may result in biased research results. Second, the U-BEE of this study is located in southeast Finland, with its specific regional characteristics. Additionally, the U-BEE analysed in this study has a strong technological focus, specializing in cleantech. For this reason, the results of the study might not reflect the reality in U-BEEs in other contexts. To address these gaps, future research could investigate the perceptions of non-active members of U-BEEs and select different types of U-BEEs in different regions for further investigation. Moreover, as the education of future entrepreneurs and a high-quality workforce seems to be the most important task of the university in U-BEEs, future research could focus on investigating how students are engaged in U-BEEs as active and engaged members through teaching and research.

IMPLICATIONS

This study brings new insights to the immature theory of U-BEEs by bringing out the factors that constrain and reinforce the emergence of U-BEEs. The current literature on U-BEEs has focused on investigating organizational structures and support services such as TTOs (Belitski and Heron, 2017; Greene et al., 2010). This study goes beyond investigating organizations and curricular and extra-curricular study programmes, but it gives voice to individuals: faculty, entrepreneurs and other company actors. The study highlights that entrepreneurship promotion in U-BEEs is not only about technology transfer and the creation of high-growth companies. The findings of this study pinpoint the importance of entrepreneurial culture and social relations, which do not receive enough attention in current empirical models and theories that emphasize formal structures and support mechanisms. Additionally, the current theories tend to neglect the students as important intermediaries and stakeholders in U-BEEs.

For the practitioners, policy-makers and higher education management, this study provides evidence about the importance of considering U-BEEs as a wider phenomenon than technology transfer and new business creation. Expectations for the universities in creating new businesses should not be set too high; rather, they should strengthen their role as educators of entrepreneurs and the workforce, as well as providers of scientific solutions to practical problems that stem from the needs of industry. This can be done by increasing awareness of entrepreneurship education among teachers, involving students in research commercialization projects and company assignments in a more systematic manner, and by minimizing the bureaucracy when collaborating with SMEs. Additionally, double contracting and internships of academics in the industry could be further enhanced.

Universities tend to centralize innovation and entrepreneurship-related functions. These centralized functions might have their role, but they cannot replace the dyadic relationships between companies and faculty. As the interaction in the entrepreneurial ecosystem is mainly based on informal social relationships between the faculty members and company actors, universities should avoid centralizing all entrepreneurship-related functions. Instead, they should decentralize them and their coordination. Certain senior academics enjoy a strong position among their company partners, and they have created trustful relationships with each other. Therefore, the companies prefer to collaborate with their academic counterparts directly, rather than involving administrative structures in collaboration.

REFERENCES

Audretsch, D. (2014), 'From the entrepreneurial university to the university for the entrepreneurial society', *Journal of Technology Transfer*, **39** (3), 313–321.
Belitski, M. and K. Heron (2017), 'Expanding entrepreneurship education ecosystems', *Journal of Management Development*, **36** (2), 163–177.
Bischoff, K., C.K. Volkmann and D.B. Audretsch (2018), 'Stakeholder collaboration in entrepreneurship education: an analysis of the entrepreneurial ecosystems of European higher educational institutions', *Journal of Technology Transfer*, **43**, 20–46.
Braunerhjelm, P. (2008), 'Specialization of regions and universities: the new versus the old', *Industry and Innovation*, **15** (3), 253–275.
Bruneel, J., P. D'Este and A. Salter (2010), 'Investigating the factors that diminish the barriers to university–industry collaboration', *Research Policy*, **39** (7), 858–868.
Brush, Candida G. (2014), 'Exploring the concept of an entrepreneurship education ecosystem', in S. Hoskinson and D.F. Kuratko (eds), *Innovative Pathways for University Entrepreneurship in the 21st Century*, Bingley, UK: Emerald Group Publishing, pp. 25–39.
Cavallo, A., A. Ghezzi and R. Balocco (2018), 'Entrepreneurial ecosystem research: present debates and future directions', *International Entrepreneurship and Management Journal*. https://doi.org/10.1007/s11365-018-0526-3.
Eisenhardt, K.M. (1989), 'Building theories from case study research', *Academy of Management Review*, **14** (4), 532–550.

Fuster, E., A. Padilla-Meléndez, N. Lockett and A.R. del-Águila-Obra (2019), 'The emerging role of university spin-off companies in developing regional entrepreneurial university ecosystems: the case of Andalusia', *Technological Forecasting and Social Change*, **141**, 219–231.

Gioia, D.A., K.G. Corley and A.L. Hamilton (2013), 'Seeking qualitative rigor in inductive research', *Organizational Research Methods*, **16** (1), 15–31.

Greene, P.G., M.P. Rice and M.L. Fetters (2010), 'University-based entrepreneurship ecosystems: framing the discussion', in M.L. Fetters, P.M. Greene, M.P. Rice and J.S. Butler (eds), *The Development of University-Based Entrepreneurship Ecosystems: Global Practices*, Cheltenham, UK and Northampton, MA, USA: Edward Elgar Publishing, pp. 1–11.

Guerrero, M., D. Urbano, A. Fayolle, M. Klofsten and S. Mian (2016), 'Entrepreneurial universities: emerging models in the new social and economic landscape', *Small Business Economics*, **47** (3), 551–563.

Hayter, C. (2016), 'A trajectory of early-stage spinoff success: the role of knowledge intermediaries within an entrepreneurial university ecosystem', *Small Business Economics*, **47** (3), 633–656.

Huang-Saad, A., N. Duval-Couetil and J. Park (2018), 'Technology and talent: capturing the role of universities in regional entrepreneurial ecosystems', *Journal of Enterprising Communities: People and Places in the Global Economy*, **12** (2), 92–116.

Isenberg, D. (2010), 'The big idea: how to start an entrepreneurial revolution', *Harvard Business Review*, **88** (6), 40–50.

Lahikainen, K., J. Kolhinen, E. Ruskovaara and T. Pihkala (2018), 'Challenges to the development of an entrepreneurial university ecosystem: the case of a Finnish university campus', *Industry and Higher Education*. https://doi.org/10.1177/0950422218815806.

Lawton Smith, H., D. Chapman, P. Wood, T. Barnes and S. Romeo (2014), 'Entrepreneurial academics and regional innovation systems: the case of spin-offs from London's universities', *Environment and Planning C: Government and Policy*, **32** (2), 341–359.

Miller, D.J. and Z.J. Acs (2017), 'The campus as entrepreneurial ecosystem: the University of Chicago', *Small Business Economics*, **49** (1), 75–95.

Rice, M.P., M.L. Fetters and P.G. Greene (2014), 'University-based entrepreneurship ecosystems: a global study of six educational institutions', *International Journal of Entrepreneurship and Innovation Management*, **18** (5–6), 481–501.

Saunders, M., P. Lewis and A. Thornhill (2016), *Research Methods for Business Students*, Harlow, UK and New York, USA: Pearson.

Spigel, B. (2017), 'The relational organization of entrepreneurial ecosystems', *Entrepreneurship Theory and Practice*, **41** (1), 49–72.

Spigel, B. and R. Harrison (2018), 'Toward a process theory of entrepreneurial ecosystems', *Strategic Entrepreneurship Journal*, **12** (1), 151–168.

Stam, E. (2015), 'Entrepreneurial ecosystems and regional policy: a sympathetic critique', *European Planning Studies*, **23** (9), 1759–1769.

7. Under the surface of the agricultural entrepreneurial support ecosystems: through the lens of complexity leadership theory

Jennie Cederholm Björklund and Jeaneth Johansson

INTRODUCTION

> For some time, there has been perceived dissatisfaction with the agricultural advice. While farmers have been critical, it has not been possible to concretize the dissatisfaction, especially beyond that the advisors know too little.[1]

> Many people see the support system as something negative and ironically call it support while meaning hindrance.[2]

There is an urgent call among practitioners and scholars to open up the black box of the agricultural entrepreneurial support ecosystem to take agricultural entrepreneurship one step further. There is a need to acquire more knowledge on hidden aspects of the agricultural support ecosystem. Agricultural entrepreneurs globally face the pressure to transform into entrepreneurial models to improve innovativeness and survive in the highly competitive landscape (Phillipson et al., 2004). Agricultural entrepreneurs, as innovators, constantly seek new opportunities and new ways of doing things, and they need advisors' support to accomplish this. Entrepreneurs and the ecosystem surrounding them are about to change.

Although rural development programmes are continuously evaluated (e.g., Hörnsten, 2017) and parts of the agricultural support ecosystem are studied from different perspectives, there is no overall picture and understanding of the roles played and the challenges faced by advisors in the ecosystem. Scholars note that knowledge about what is actually going on is scarce (Cederholm Björklund, 2018; Höckert, 2017). Previous studies highlight the challenges faced by advisors in the business support system (Johansson et al., 2019), but little is known about the agricultural support system. Much is known outside the entrepreneurship literature on the agricultural ecosystem at a meta level, while the social constructions and actions taking place at a micro level remain neglected both in general and in the entrepreneurship literature (Korsgaard, Müller and Tanvig, 2015; OECD, 2018). The agricultural entrepreneurial ecosystem operates much in the shadow of what reflects 'real' entrepreneurship and is often neglected in traditional entrepreneurship literature, causing a knowledge gap (Phillipson et al., 2004). This occurs even though the sector is one of the largest worldwide, accounting for 3 per cent of the global gross domestic product (FAO, 2016) and employing 1 billion people. Only in Sweden, the agricultural sector involved 131 571 registered businesses and constituted the primary business activity of 108 886 companies[3] in 2016 (Swedish Board of Agriculture, 2018a), making the Swedish case highly relevant for study. Also highlighting the relevance of the sector, the European Union (EU) has allocated €351.8 billion for the Common Agricultural Policy (CAP) 2014–20, of which approximately €2.1 billion are allocated to Sweden (Government Offices of Sweden, 2018). It is no longer possible for the agricultural entrepreneurship ecosystem, with its unique political, cultural and cognitive embeddedness, to be ignored in the entrepreneurship literature (Denzau and North, 1994; Dias et al., 2018; Fitz-Koch et al., 2018; Korsgaard, Müller and Tanvig, 2015; Zukin and DiMaggio, 1990). This chapter primarily focuses on the Swedish context, which is highly embedded in the European system. However, the agricultural support systems in all G20 countries are criticized for insufficient governance. They share a common need to establish long-term strategies, involve stakeholders throughout processes, clarify actors' roles, improve research and development coordination, and implement useful evaluation systems (OECD, 2019).

The current chapter answers the call to further contextualize agricultural entrepreneurship research by highlighting the specific context of the entrepreneurial agricultural support system in general and the advisory support system in particular. We explore the roles and challenges of advisors in the support system through the lens of complexity leadership theory (CLT). We look into advisors' relational leadership and connectedness in the agriculture entrepreneurial support ecosystem (Ospina and Foldy, 2010). This enables us to explore advisors' leadership in coordinating formal and informal work when operating in dynamic agricultural entrepreneurship environments where innovation is expected (cf. Allen, 2001; Cilliers, 1998; Stacey et al., 2000). The theory enables the exploration of advisors' formal and informal social interactions when dealing with new conditions. It provides a basis for exploring behaviours in the specific context of the complex adaptive system of agricultural entrepreneurship (Gartner et al., 2006; Welter, 2011; Welter et al., 2017; Zahra, 2007).

This chapter seeks to contribute to the entrepreneurship literature by exploring the environment surrounding advisors in agricultural entrepreneurship in several ways. First, we identify the roles played and challenges faced by advisors in the support ecosystem that affect advisor behaviour. We identify a strong path-dependency guiding everyday practice among the actors (Nee, 1998, p. 86). Many of these challenges remain tacit, and the study aims to contribute to making the ecosystem more transparent in order to enable change (Cederholm Björklund, 2018). We identify formal and informal interaction patterns between key actors in the support ecosystem – for example, governmental actors, agricultural advisory organizations, agricultural member organizations and rural societies – that impact upon the advice provided. We further observe the norms and values governing behaviour and fostering 'leadership practices', or collective action within and across the organizations in the system (Ospina and Foldy, 2010). This exercise may contribute knowledge for the development of advisory practices and support for agricultural entrepreneurs (Phillipson et al., 2004). Second, we contribute to the conceptualization of the advisor leadership practice in agricultural entrepreneurial support systems, and how everyday practice hinders the adoption of the innovation practices demanded by environmental pressure. We suggest that informal adaptive practices be adopted in order to develop the creativity and the formal administrative systems needed to develop goals and routines for challenging established practices (cf. Welter, 2011). Finally, we meet the need for qualitative methods in the research on agricultural entrepreneurship and advisory practice, which allows us to capture the richness and diversity of the agricultural entrepreneurial support ecosystem (Welter, 2011).

CONTEXTUALIZING THE SWEDISH AGRICULTURAL ENTREPRENEURSHIP SUPPORT ECOSYSTEM

To understand the actions taking place among advisors in the agricultural entrepreneurship support ecosystem, the contextual aspects of the ecosystem, such as the nature of the actor organizations and the political and cultural embeddedness, must be outlined (Denzau and North, 1994; Jack and Anderson, 2002; Korsgaard, Ferguson and Gaddefors, 2015). This chapter acknowledges the situational boundaries embedded in the context of the Swedish agricultural entrepreneurial support ecosystem. These boundaries are connected to the historical context of the industry as a whole, strong path-dependency, and changes in the conditions and the nature of modern agriculture, and push towards a higher degree of market and business orientation, greater competition, technology changes and digitalization.

Swedish agriculture has changed from being highly regulated by the government, when the state coordinated price levels, to being market-driven, when Sweden joined the EU in 1995. The EU opened up a market-driven agricultural sector based on free trade both within the EU and across the world. This change occurred in many other countries as well. To address the new market conditions, management became of critical importance for agricultural entrepreneurship. Agricultural entrepreneurs need support to guide their activities in the highly competitive market and their adjustment to the continuous changes in the market (OECD, 2018; Swedish Board of Agriculture, 2018b). Advisors in the agricultural entrepreneurship support ecosystem expect to be prepared to guide and facilitate these changes. Accomplishing change appears to be a challenging task, as agricultural entrepreneurs find it hard to obtain the help needed from those whose aim is to support their entrepreneurship. The highly institutionalized Swedish agricultural support ecosystem, with its 200-year-old traditions, is criticized for adapting poorly to support the development of sustainable agricultural business, for example because of limited advisory knowledge, agricultural entrepreneurship knowledge, and work methods (Höckert, 2017). This chapter aims to explore the challenges faced by agricultural advisors in their work of providing guidance to agricultural entrepreneurs.

The key actors in the Swedish agricultural entrepreneurial support ecosystem consist of governmental actors, agricultural advisory organizations, agricultural member organizations and rural societies, among others. The agricultural entrepreneurship support ecosystem may at a macro level be divided into a governmental system and an advisory system. The governmental system outlines the boundary of the support system. Funding and regulations governing the Swedish support ecosystem mainly derive from the EU and the CAP. Reform is implemented by the CAP every seventh year to cover a set period, such as 2014–20. The governmental system channels EU funds and government-level directives via the Swedish Board of Agriculture to county administrative boards and other organizations. The value of the EU cohesion policy in the 2014–20 programme period is €351.8 billion, almost one-third of the EU budget, and approximately €2.1 billion of this sum has been allocated to Sweden (Government Offices of Sweden, 2018). The programmes are currently under the close supervision of the European Commission (EC), but the Commission has signalled reform and greater opportunities for member states to control their own programmes in the future. The agricultural support ecosystem is nationally governed by the Swedish Rural Development Programme (RDP). The recently developed Swedish food strategy also guides and regulates activities in the agricultural support ecosystem at the national level.

The advisory system involves advisory organizations, such as governmental actors, associations and private organizations, which are merging into larger units. A large part of the advisory system consists of individual companies linked to a joint federation, which acts as coordinator and fosters development.

The federations have no mandates for deciding for or governing the member organizations, which are all independent legal units. Actors in the agricultural support ecosystem have a common vision of contributing to agricultural entrepreneurship and sustainable rural areas; but at the same time, most of the actors are competitors. The governmental advisory organizations are as such competitors of the non-governmental organizations. This competitive structure limits the willingness and ability of agricultural advisory support organizations to collaborate, and all organizations try to gain access to the limited resources allocated to the agricultural support system. There are governmental incentives for collaboration and knowledge-sharing, but most resources are allocated towards individual activities within organizations, contradictory to the desired development (Höckert, 2017; OECD, 2018).

Scholars point to various challenges in agricultural support organizations, and severe problems in advisor guidance have been observed in practice and in the literature (Höckert, 2017; OECD, 2019). The agricultural support ecosystem is criticized for being based on subject-based knowledge and non-systematic models, and the challenges of agriculture are considered systemic (Höckert, 2017). Höckert highlights the lack of space for reflection corresponding to higher loops of learning at all levels in the system. She outlines a control paradox where advisors are specialized and seldom collaborate, such that there is neither reflection nor learning within organizations. She notes the need for a broadened epistemological perspective in the advisory organizations, an extension of knowledge-sharing and interplay, the creation of a collaborative culture and, more broadly, a change from individual-based knowledge to knowledge that unites the knower and the knowing. The actors within the system have not managed to thoroughly describe the problems and their systemic boundaries, and the system has not reflected what is needed to enact the change from an individual to a collaborative culture. This chapter takes a further look under the surface of the agricultural entrepreneurial support ecosystem.

COMPLEXITY LEADERSHIP THEORY

To explore beyond the surface of the complex agricultural entrepreneurship support system and the advisors' roles and challenges, we apply complexity leadership theory (CLT). This framework allows us to explore the coordination and control structures of the support system. According to CLT, leadership is considered a social phenomenon involving much social interaction that causes a shift from emphasizing the human capital of the advisor and the entrepreneurs in the system, to emphasizing social capital (Arena and Uhl-Bien, 2016). The agricultural entrepreneurship support ecosystem is complex and involves many types of interdependent actors, such as agricultural entrepreneurs, financiers, policy-makers and scholars. The advisors expect to take the central role in the network of these key actors, who cooperate dynamically, seeking common goals (Uhl-Bien et al., 2007). Leadership reaches beyond the mere leadership position and authority to encompass the management of knowledge flows within and between organizations. In line with Fleming et al. (2007), we argue that understanding the leadership in such complex adaptive systems requires a thorough understanding of the interplay within and between the key groups acting in the ecosystem.

The agricultural entrepreneurship advisory ecosystem outlines a complex adaptive system, a promising arena for key actors to meet, problem-solve, learn and adopt new behaviours and ways of working (Carley and Hill, 2001). Organizational adaptability, taking place in the key actors' everyday life, is a critical component for reaching goals and bringing forth new and innovative contributions to collaborative interactions (Uhl-Bien and Marion, 2009). Advisors in the agricultural entrepreneurship system are considered facilitators or brokers in the system and are expected to have an active role in producing new behaviour and new ways of working (Uhl-Bien et al., 2007). Previous studies outline the broker role as involving interactive and dynamic actions, bridging meaning by different cohesive groups and ensuring trust and information-sharing (Arena and Uhl-Bien, 2016).

Formal and informal control are considered as coordinating the interdependent structures and activities in the dynamic ecosystem. In the conceptualization of advisors' roles and challenges in the social agricultural entrepreneurship system, we depart from the three closely intertwined modes of leadership outlined in CLT; that is, administrative, adaptive and enabling leadership (Kontopoulos, 2006; Uhl-Bien et al., 2007). The administrative modes of leadership characterize formal and bureaucratic leadership involving dynamic relationships of a hierarchical top-down character. Individuals and groups plan, coordinate and expect to act effectively to reach their stated goals. The bureaucratic functions of the administrative leadership focus on aligning and controlling actions for the collective purpose, establishing structures and allocating resources to reach the stated targets and managing conflicts (Mumford et al., 2008).

Enabling leadership conceptualizes the dynamic, non-hierarchical and informal interrelations between individuals and groups of actors. The informal mode is an enabler, facilitating actors in the support system to bridge the administrative and adaptive leadership functions. This mode of leadership serves as an adaptive emergent force that creates and facilitates organizational conditions to foster adaptive leadership, and provides guidance in situations that require transition and innovation. The focus of this mode is on adaption, creativity and learning. In this way, the administrative forces and the adaptive forces may either help or oppose one another. Enabling leadership assures the transfer of knowledge and creativity from the adaptive structures to the administrative structures. The key aim is to accomplish effective adaptive leadership through enabling leadership to bridge the two types of leadership without eliminating them (Ospina and Foldy, 2010).

The concept of adaptive space is a critical concept in this. Adaptive space arises between the creative adoptive system and the bureaucratic administrative system, and serves as an enabler in collaborative networks, bridging the formal and informal systems (Arena and Uhl-Bien, 2016; Uhl-Bien et al., 2007). The framework of CLT sets an overarching boundary for exploring and contextualizing organizational leadership in the agricultural entrepreneurial support system.

APPROACH AND METHOD

This study involves six types of loosely and moderated coupled national and regional key organizations in the agricultural entrepreneurship support ecosystem in Sweden. The organizations cooperate across borders to reach the common goal of nurturing agricultural entrepreneurship and the rural ecosystem. One federated organization is a joint union that includes 17 independent regional organizations. The federation coordinates and develops member organizations but cannot make decisions for or govern the members.

We used a research design triangulating data sources to understand the structures below the surface of the support ecosystem and to discern the behaviour and actions of individuals and organizations. This research design enabled us to explore the tacit structures of advisor roles and challenges, making the agricultural ecosystem more transparent. We collected data through in situ observations and interviews to provide the rich contextualized data based on qualitative methods called for in the literature (Welter, 2011). We observed meetings where key actors in support organizations at the regional and national levels discussed management and policy problems and challenges. In total, we observed 16 meetings involving the participation of 34 key actor organizations from the agricultural entrepreneurship support system. Fourteen of those meetings involved up to 50 participants, and two of the meetings were major meetings with between 50 and a couple of hundred participants. The data were collected over a period of eight months during 2018. Deeper knowledge of the organizations was provided through one researcher's insider access to key organizations and to native knowledge of the work processes in these organizations. This researcher collected data, attended the meetings, recorded what was said and took notes, but did not take an active role in any of the observed meetings. The observations were complemented with semi-structured interviews with key actors for follow-up, and further exploration of the advisors' roles and challenges in the complex agricultural ecosystem. In total, 54 hours

Table 7.1   *Categorizing representative statements and first-order concepts*

First-order concepts	Representative statement
Lack of trust/ uncertainty between actors	'It's complex and creates some uncertainty. The hardest thing, it's this checking, lion of…as it's called when you create fear. So, the Commission is afraid of the auditors, and Sweden is afraid of the Commission, and the Swedish government and all the way down to the County Administrative Board…and finally it ends up on the farmer.'
Lack of trust/ uncertainty between individuals	'It's the officers, the staff who are careful while the management had the idea that they would not be really careful, but it did not really work out.'
Lack of flexibility and sensitivity	'We are not responsive…so maybe we could have been a bit more responsive, but I think the members want us to be fairly uncompromising.'
Lack of understanding of different needs and roles	'The County Administrative Board is living its own little life. They think they… it will be very exciting to see…we will ask them how they handle the new management act. They have not even followed the current…'
	'It's very hard between our professional categories, and it has affected our investment applications in a negative way, and our customers.'
Fruitless collaboration efforts	'We're working together all the time, but then we should see…there would not be such problems with gravel in the machines. Then it would be much better. They probably collaborate de facto, but not…that's the result that counts.'
Lack of overall perspective	'You have to go all the way…from the time you leave until things come out at the other end. It has not worked all the way here. It's an important lesson for the whole system.'
Lack of collaborative intentions	'When there is an emergency situation, you can also add resources. But when the sun shines there is no need to collaborate.'
Old working methods and structure	'Since ancient times it has been said that we should do this way.'
Inherited roles	'We still have that tradition left…'
Discourse reinforces the importance of traditions	'What is revolutionary is that we will not have the governor as president next year…after 203 years, it feels strange.'
Focus on natural science	'It's a production specialist who manages marketing, not an educated communicator – that is the problem.'
	'We have a new business development in progress…focusing on plant cultivation.'
Innovations create more bureaucracy	'New solutions or innovations create almost exclusively more bureaucracy.'
Complicated procedures	'It was not so easy to do what we had planned – it did not work out according to EU regulations'.

Duplicate application procedures	'It's unnecessarily complicated. We know we've got this money to deal with, but we still have to apply for it.'
Individual (advisor) limitations	'We've learned the hard way that experience groups work better than advice.'
Interpretation of individuals in the system	'This with assessments…one tries to make them transparent, but it's not easy.'
	'Authorities interpret political decisions.'
Effects of individuals in the system (lobbies)	'So, we'll see what's happening, who they'll find as successor to him, and if it's still a good team of co-operation.'
Individual culture, who am I here for?	'You think of yourself in the first place and do not help a colleague or help someone. Nor do you share customers or work, and you don't look for the customer's best – what the customer would need for advice, but you look at your individual budget and yourself in the first place.'
Individual mindset	'The Swedish Board of Agriculture, they bring in new employees who ask a lot of new questions.'
	'It is building relations that gives effect.'
Rural Development Programme and National Food Strategy rules	'Our foundation is the Rural Development Programme.'
	'The strategic goals control…but we are affected by the National Food Strategy.'
The actors have different target groups and assignments	'I think we should not forget why we are applying for money…what goals we have…instead of running at all balls.'
	'It's not only agriculture in this region, it's everything that has to do with living and existing at the countryside.'
	'Our members are mainly farmers.'
Most of the actors are competitors	'This old question. It's a good time to have a small talk about it. If they do this… then we must actually have planned structured return fire.'
	'That's a sensitive question. We have old relationships.'
	'Still, they put too much energy inwards, so they will get even more outward and are a competitor to us in many contexts, but at the same time they are very open to cooperation. They are really very, very professional.'

of effective meeting and discussion time were observed, and three hours of interviews were recorded. In total, four key actors in the support system participated in longer semi-structured interviews, and another 28 individuals from the actor organizations participated in shorter interviews.

We base the results on the data from the observations and interviews that are recorded, transcribed, inductively analysed and coded into concepts, themes and dimensions using the Gioia methodology (Gioia et al., 2012). Table

7.1 presents the coding structure and the resulting categories. We started by individually reading the transcriptions, making a broad initial coding, and briefly noting ideas. Then, through a more thorough reading, we individually identified statements, discussions and frames. The researchers compared their coding and proposed first-order concepts. After discussing the findings and concepts, we identified seven overarching themes among the first-order categories, and developed second-order themes. The second-order themes identified are the lack of mutual understanding and trust, lack of collaboration, old traditions and culture, bureaucracy, individual impact/influence, coopetition and goal congruence, and lack of strategic management and leadership. The last-mentioned theme was developed during the analysis as a result of the discussions.

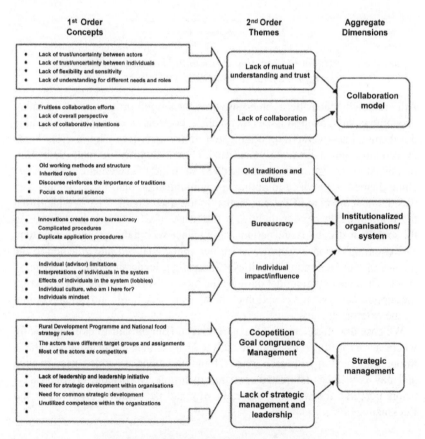

Figure 7.1   Conceptualizing challenges in the agricultural entrepreneurship support system

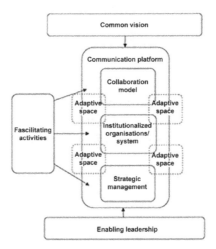

Figure 7.2   Model for enabling innovation in a sustainable rural entrepreneurial support ecosystem

After reviewing the patterns emerging from the second-order themes, we found phenomena and common issues that made it possible to connect and assemble the themes into overarching aggregated dimensions (see Figure 7.1). Three overarching dimensions were identified: (1) collaborative model; (2) institutionalized organizations/systems; and (3) strategic management. The overarching themes were coded to outline a communication platform. The next step was the development of the conceptual model (see Figure 7.2). We identified the value of exploring our findings with the use of CLT to gain knowledge on the social constructions and actions taking place within the support ecosystem. The communication platform was further conceptualized and attached to the themes of: (1) facilitating activities; (2) enabling leadership; and (3) adaptive space. The conceptual model outlines the mechanisms fostering and hindering the support ecosystem's adoption of the new practices and innovation required by the external society.

We base our study on social constructivism (Berger and Luckmann, 1966), where actors in the ecosystem socially construct their knowledge structures through interaction with each other. The implications are constructed in time and may as such be manifested or change over time. Knowledge arises because actors perceive the world in a certain way and act accordingly (Berger and Luckmann, 1966).

EMPIRICAL FINDINGS AND ANALYSIS

The agricultural entrepreneurial support ecosystem in Sweden has a common vision of contributing to a sustainable, prosperous rural society and a sustainable use of the land. However, the support organizations target different groups: the authorities work for the countryside, and some organizations work for their members, others for customers, and still others for a mix of members and customers. The members of organizations may be, for instance, agricultural entrepreneurs. Support organizations are managed and operated in different ways, with different intentions and missions. The organizations are often managed to fulfil requirements of the food strategy, RDP and other funding organizations rather than to fulfil agriculture entrepreneurs' expressed needs. The goals and funding are typically governed by the Ministry for Rural Affairs and interpreted by officials at the Swedish Board of Agriculture at different levels. The support organizations receive income through their provision of advisory services. The main part of the organizations' funding derives from the Swedish Board of Agriculture and County and Regional Administrative Boards. The organizations that aim to collaborate in the support system also compete for the same source of funding.

The funding that governs the Swedish support ecosystem derives largely from the EU. However, new directives propose greater national self-determination, and representatives from different organizations have gathered to discuss possibilities and common challenges. They try to interpret the future by discussing potential scenarios:

> A re-nationalization, moving the system to the Member States, is challenging. What will happen? There are opportunities.

> The idea is to set targets at the EU level. It is up to the Member States to find solutions. The question is how Sweden manages to handle it, given how detailed everything was before. Can you get rid of the administration we have today? Meanwhile, it is positive that there is such an input [required] instead of the details [required] at the EU level because we do not like it. There is a great opportunity for Sweden to do something good about this if they/we have capacity.

Policies and guidelines for work with environmental, economic and social sustainability are largely implemented and followed up by the support actors in the ecosystem. They agree that a prerequisite for sustainability and a functioning support system is to simplify and ensure the feasibility of the relevant policies, measures, and so on. The ability to simplify is vital. This is exemplified through the following statements:

> It should be as simple as possible. We do not want it to be a barrier for the farmer. It is sometimes, and it is sad. It's a bit complex with support systems and rules, but there's not much we can do there more than talking about it upwards, and we've done that. We know how difficult it is, we are very humble.

> New solutions or innovations create almost exclusively more bureaucracy. That's the dilemma. What would have to be more innovative is the simplification. It could be more innovative. Therefore, we are looking for simpler solutions. It's the innovation we want.

> What would be more innovative is the simplification. This is where we need to invest in innovation within the support system.

> A bit of lean production for bureaucracy. How can we make this work smoother?

A need for the development of a common collaboration model is identified based on observations and interviews. Uncertainty and lack of confidence exist between individuals and organizations, and sensitivity to and the understanding of different needs and roles in the ecosystem are lacking. While some collaboration efforts have been tested, the actors suggest a lack of overall perspective and collaborative intentions as reasons for the failure of these attempts at collaboration.

The observation and interviews outline the old traditions and culture, bureaucracy and individual influence that create a highly institutionalized ecosystem. The advisory organizations are more than 200 years old. The strong culture and the associated structures, methods and discourse make procedures complicated and bureaucratic. The individualistic culture is another problem identified within the system and has been confirmed by previous studies of Swedish agricultural advisory organizations (Höckert, 2017). This is expressed through limitations in individual knowledge, individual interpretations, lobbying, culture and mindset.

We identify a need to develop strategic management both within the organizations and in the overall agricultural entrepreneurship support ecosystem. Lack of leadership and leadership initiatives cause the institutionalization and conservation of the old and individualistic culture, with the consequence of unutilized competence. The support actors clearly outline a common vision of creating sustainable rural areas in Sweden, while goal congruence, management and the fact that the actors are also competitors obstruct the collaborative effort to work towards the goals.

One challenge outlined is communication, especially communication between organizations, where no common communication platform or method of effective interaction and communication currently exists. Cooperation meetings and communication forums become individual-dependent and sensitive to changes in the people composing the group. However, there have been some initiatives for facilitating innovation within the ecosystem. Some of those mentioned are relationship-building meetings and collaborative activities and meetings. There is a willingness within the system – primarily from the governmental point of view – to simplify. There are also individual initiatives aimed at encouraging innovation:

> What happens is that you get rid of the war, I would say [when communicating]. If you can use such a hard word. Because there are many misconceptions on both sides maybe. But perhaps also some relief that 'Well, that's how it works in your region.'

> [Communication] It's necessary for understanding. It's enough to meet sometimes and tell how it is. It's not that difficult.

We outline an initial conceptualization of the challenges identified in Table 7.1, which presents representative quotes and first-order concepts.

The final step in the theoretical conceptualization is presented in Figure 7.2, which outlines a model for enabling innovation in a sustainable rural entrepreneurial support ecosystem. We identified early that the organizations have 'a common vision/mission', that is, a starting point and a common ground for collaboration within the ecosystem. While this is not enough, the three blocks from Figure 7.1 highlight the need for managing the ecosystem to achieve a sustainable and innovative support system. The three blocks are: (1) a functioning collaboration model; (2) methods for managing and developing an institutionalized system; and (3) strategic management of organizations and the system. In addition, all three blocks must work together; thus, they must be embedded in a common communication platform, as discussed earlier. Facilitating actions that are adjusted to the situation are needed for the key actors to actually communicate, bring the advisory system together and accomplish change. There is both formal and informal leadership present in the model. The communication platform involves formal leadership with administrative routines and control. There, enabling leadership brings forward informal leadership. Finally, an adaptive space is created in the ecosystem, which provides the lubricant or the space where innovation can flourish. Adaptive space is created by stimulating pressure and simultaneously helping individuals to act under this pressure. The model is based on CLT and aims to enable leaders to be skilful at formulating challenges, and challenging enough to act as pressure and then help individuals to act in a safe adaptive space while processing the pressure (Arena and Uhl-Bien, 2016).

CONCLUSION AND DISCUSSION

We contribute to the field of entrepreneurship by investigating the agricultural entrepreneurial support ecosystem, specifically the complex challenges faced and the interactions in the support system that take place when seeking to foster sustainable agricultural entrepreneurship (Fitz-Koch et al., 2018). The findings indicate that the agricultural entrepreneurial support ecosystem needs to adapt to changes in the environment to provide the support needed by agricultural entrepreneurs exposed to innovative challenges. The pressure in the environment requires changes in innovation practices and in the management and control of such changes in the support ecosystem, in Sweden and in other countries (Höckert, 2017; OECD, 2018). We highlight a number of challenges for creating a sustainable agricultural entrepreneurship ecosystem and identify a cognitive embeddedness, that is, mental processes, among individuals and groups of actors. These impacts on the interaction between actors also hinder the mutual change process and the development of a common ground of economic reasoning (cf. Zukin and DiMaggio, 1990, pp. 15–16). We identify leadership structures and everyday practices shaping and reshaping the work processes that also hinder the adoption of new innovation practices.

Complexity and institutionalization, together with the lack of collaboration, communication and strategic management, are identified as recurring obstacles. There are stabilizing mechanisms in the ecosystem that strive to maintain familiar structures even as the organizations are forced to change under pressure. There is a need for innovation within the system to face challenges, make the system work and adapt to new opportunities and conditions. We identify cultural barriers consisting of internal and external competition within and between actors and organizations in the ecosystem. The poor strategic management cannot effectively coordinate key actors' interrelations and exchanges. Individual actors and organizations primarily consider their own personal brand, identity and benefits: 'what's in it for us'. The individualistic competitive culture within and between the support organizations spills over to challenge collaboration, learning and knowledge-sharing (cf. Höckert, 2017), which in turn impact upon the support provided. We identify barriers that hinder agricultural entrepreneurial support ecosystems from thriving, affecting organizations' incentives for innovation and providing support for innovation. Like previous studies, we identify a strongly path-dependent support ecosystem, where social constructions are strongly manifested over a long period (Höckert, 2017; Nee, 1998, p. 86) based on the 200-year-old culture and traditions. The ecosystem is highly institutionalized, dominated by bureaucratic behaviour, encapsulating routinized acting and behaviour according to cognition and norms. This is also the case in other types of entrepreneurship support organizations (Johansson et al., 2019; Malmström et al., 2017). We identify a need to develop adaptive practices that nurture the informal adaptive system and bring forth creativity. There is also a need to combine these informal systems with formal administrative systems that develop goals and routines that challenge established practices. Bridging leadership can connect different perspectives to facilitate collaboration without merging or reducing the perspectives (Ospina and Foldy, 2010). The results indicate a need to create an adaptive space for reflection and learning (Höckert, 2017), a space which is a relational environment and not necessarily a physical place. In this innovative way of working, prestige and old structures may be questioned, and leadership may be developed within the ecosystem.

We can conclude that the entrepreneurial support ecosystem has not developed in parallel with the changes in the world surrounding agricultural entrepreneurship and its support system as expected after Sweden's entry into the EU in 1995, which opened up a free market. Under the right conditions and connections, the key actors may become cohesive groups that contribute to the development of the system (Arena and Uhl-Bien, 2016; Fleming et al., 2007). We agree with Arena and Uhl-Bien (2016, p. 25) that 'pressures are at the heart of adaptive space'.

This study sheds light on the importance of bringing agriculture into entrepreneurship, and enriches entrepreneurship theory by modifying the theory to fit the agricultural entrepreneurship context (Fitz-Koch et al., 2018; Welter et al., 2017). Much previous work has focused on this ecosystem. We provide knowledge on the behaviour of the key actors in the support ecosystem by offering a new theoretical model of the dynamics in the ecosystem that is based on inductive analyses and CLT (cf. Arena and Uhl-Bien, 2016). With this study as a starting point, future work can focus on creating a sustainable innovative system. We conclude in line with Burnes (2005, p. 74) that: 'If organizations are too stable, nothing changes and the system dies; if too chaotic, the system will be overwhelmed by change. In both situations, an organization can only survive and prosper if a new, more appropriate, set of order-generating rules is established'.

Like any study, ours is not without limitations. First, we limit the study to the Swedish agricultural entrepreneurial support ecosystem. The Swedish context is highly embedded in the European system, and this may provide some grounds for the generalization of the research together with findings from previous studies in other countries. We suggest that future research explores the agricultural entrepreneurship advisory system in other international contexts, and tests and develops our conceptual model in a broader contextual setting. Second, the conceptual model adopts an organizational perspective of the entrepreneurial support system, while the field would benefit from digging deeper into the cognitive foundations of social construction and action within the ecosystem. We suggest that further studies explore the cognitive level to reveal conscious and less unconscious dimensions. Finally, the study focuses on the key actors in support organizations, while there is a need to further highlight the expectations, needs and wants that the agricultural entrepreneurs have concerning the agricultural entrepreneurial support ecosystem. In line with this, we recommend that future studies consider the entrepreneurs' perspective as a complement to the current study.

NOTES

1. See http://www.lantbruketsaffarer.se/efterlyses-radgivning-vard-namnet/ accessed 13 May 2020, published 15 September 2017.
2. An actor in the agricultural support ecosystem.
3. Involving the Swedish standards for industrial classification, SNI 0111–0170.

REFERENCES

Allen, T.D. (2001), 'Family-supportive work environments: the role of organizational perceptions', *Journal of Vocational Behavior*, **58** (3), 414–435.
Arena, M.J. and M. Uhl-Bien (2016), 'Complexity leadership theory: shifting from human capital to social capital', *People and Strategy*, **39** (2), 22–29.
Berger, P.L. and T.T. Luckmann (1966), *The Social Construction of Reality: A Treatise in the Sociology of Knowledge*, New York: Double & Company.
Burnes, B. (2005), 'Complexity theories and organizational change', *International Journal of Management Reviews*, **7** (2), 73–90.
Carley, K.M. and V. Hill (2001), 'Structural change and learning within organizations', in A. Lomi and R.E. Larsen (eds), *Dynamics of Organizations: Computational Modeling and Organizational Theories*, Menlo Park, CA, USA and London, UK: AAAI Press/MIT Press, pp. 63–92.
Cederholm Björklund, J. (2018), 'Barriers to sustainable business model innovation in Swedish agriculture', *Journal of Entrepreneurship, Management and Innovation*, **14** (1), 65–90.
Cilliers, P. (1998), *Complexity and Postmodernism: Understanding Complex Systems*, New York: Routledge.
Denzau, A.T. and D.C. North (1994), 'Shared mental models: ideologies and institutions', *Kyklos*, **47** (1), 3–31.
Dias, C.S.L., R.G. Rodrigues and J.J. Ferreira (2018), 'What's new in the research on agricultural entrepreneurship?', *Journal of Rural Studies*, **65**, 99–115.
Fitz-Koch, S., M. Nordqvist, S. Carter and E. Hunter (2018), 'Entrepreneurship in the agricultural sector: a literature review and future research opportunities', *Entrepreneurship Theory and Practice*, **42** (1), 129–166.
Fleming, L., S. Mingo and D. Chen (2007), 'Collaborative brokerage, generative creativity, and creative success', *Administrative Science Quarterly*, **52** (3), 443–475.
Food and Agricultural Organization of the United Nations (FAO) (2016), *FAO Statistical Yearbook 2012, Part 1 – The Setting*. Accessed 9 July 2019 at www.fao.org/docrep/015/i2490e/i2490e00.htm.

Gartner, W.B., P. Davidsson and S.A. Zahra (2006), 'Are you talking to me? The nature of community in entrepreneurship scholarship', *Entrepreneurship Theory and Practice*, **30** (3), 321–331.

Gioia, D.A., K.G. Corley and A.L. Hamilton (2012), 'Seeking qualitative rigor in inductive research', *Organizational Research Methods*, **16** (1), 15–31.

Government Offices of Sweden (2018), *Sveriges regioner kraftsamlar inför programperioden 2020–2026*. Accessed 9 July 2019 at https://www.regeringen.se/artiklar/2016/05/sveriges-regioner-kraftsamlar-infor-programperioden-2020-2026/.

Höckert, J. (2017), 'Sharing lifeworlds and creating collaborative cultures', Doctoral thesis, Swedish University of Agricultural Sciences, Uppsala.

Hörnsten, C. (2017), 'Slututvärderingar av landsbygdsprogrammet 2007–2013 – en sammanfattning', *Jordbruksverket*, **36**. https://doi.org/10.1007/s11187-019-00273-3. https://www2.jordbruksverket.se/download/18.48a7452e15c7b4a5a65a4ec5/1496909718649/ra17_1.pdf.

Jack, S.L. and A.R. Anderson (2002), 'The effects of embeddedness on the entrepreneurial process', *Journal of Business Venturing*, **17** (5), 467–487.

Johansson, J., M. Malmström, J. Wincent and V. Parida (2019), 'How individual cognitions overshadow regulations and group norms: a study of government venture capital decisions', *Small Business Economics*, pubished online 26 October 2019 at https://link.springer.com/content/pdf/10.1007/s11187-019-00273-3.pdf.

Kontopoulos, K.M. (2006), *The Logics of Social Structure*, Cambridge: Cambridge University Press.

Korsgaard, S., R. Ferguson and J. Gaddefors (2015), 'The best of both worlds: how rural entrepreneurs use placial embeddedness and strategic networks to create opportunities', *Entrepreneurship and Regional Development*, **27** (9–10), 574–598.

Korsgaard, S., S. Müller and H.W. Tanvig (2015), 'Rural entrepreneurship or entrepreneurship in the rural – between place and space', *International Journal of Entrepreneurial Behavior and Research*, **21** (1), 5–26.

Malmström, M., J. Johansson and J. Wincent (2017), 'Gender stereotypes and venture support decisions: how governmental venture capitalists socially construct entrepreneurs' potential', *Entrepreneurship Theory and Practice*, **41** (5), 833–860.

Mumford, M.D., K.E. Bedell-Avers and S.T. Hunter (2008), 'Planning for innovation: a multi-level perspective', *Research in Multi Level Issues*, **7** (7), 107–154.

Nee, V. (1998), 'Norms and networks in economic and organizational performance', *American Economic Review*, **88** (2), 85–89.

OECD (2018), *Innovation, Agricultural Productivity and Sustainability in Sweden*, Paris: OECD Food and Agricultural Reviews, OECD Publishing.

OECD (2019), *Innovation, Productivity and Sustainability in Food and Agriculture: Main Policy Lessons from Selected OECD Country Reviews*. Accessed 9 July 2019 at https://issuu.com/oecd.publishing/docs/innovation__productivity_and_sustai.

Ospina, S. and E. Foldy (2010), 'Building bridges from the margins: the work of leadership in social change organizations', *Leadership Quarterly*, **21** (2), 292–307.

Phillipson, J., M. Gorton, M. Raley and A. Moxey (2004), 'Treating farms as firms? The evolution of farm business support from productionist to entrepreneurial models', *Environment and Planning C: Government and Policy*, **22** (1), 31–54.

Stacey, R.D., D. Griffin and P. Shaw (2000), *Complexity and Management: Fad or Radical Challenge to Systems Thinking*, London, UK and New York, USA: Routledge.

Swedish Board of Agriculture (2018a), 'Statistiken med kommentarer'. Accessed 9 July 2019 at http://www.jordbruksverket.se/webdav/files/SJV/Amnesomraden/Stat

istik,% 20fakta/Foretag%20och%20foretagare/JO34/JO34SM1801/JO34SM1801_
kommentarer.htm.

Swedish Board of Agriculture (2018b), *Sweden – Rural Development Programme
(National). 5.1.* Accessed 9 July 2019 at http://www.jordbruksverket.se/download/
18.4c6ca46b16724f1cf99de438/1542721517340/Programme_2014SE06RDNP001
_5_1_sv.pdf.

Uhl-Bien, M. and R. Marion (2009), 'Complexity leadership in bureaucratic forms of
organizing: a meso model', *Leadership Quarterly*, **20** (4), 631–650.

Uhl-Bien, M., R. Marion and B. McKelvey (2007), 'Complexity leadership theory:
shifting leadership from the industrial age to the knowledge era', *Leadership
Quarterly*, **18** (4), 298–318.

Welter, F. (2011), 'Contextualizing entrepreneurship-conceptual challenges and ways
forward', *Entrepreneurship Theory and Practice*, **35** (1), 165–184.

Welter, F., T. Baker, D.B. Audretsch and W.B. Gartner (2017), 'Everyday entrepreneurship – a call for entrepreneurship research to embrace entrepreneurial diversity',
Entrepreneurship Theory and Practice, **41** (3), 311–321.

Zahra, S.A. (2007), 'Contextualizing theory building in entrepreneurship research',
Journal of Business Venturing, **22** (3), 443–452.

Zukin, S. and P. DiMaggio (1990), 'Introduction', in S. Zukin and P. DiMaggio
(eds), *Structures of Capital: The Social Organization of the Economy*, Cambridge:
Cambridge University Press, pp. 1–6.

PART III

Entrepreneurial conditions

8. Does family business background matter? Career decisions of postgraduate students

Clara Cardone-Riportella, Isabel Feito-Ruiz and David Urbano

INTRODUCTION

Entrepreneurship has been recognized as a distinct field of study for several decades (McCaffrey, 2018). Although the field of family business and entrepreneurship has developed separately (Nordqvist and Melin, 2010), these branches of literature are related in that people could have entrepreneurial intention (EI) inside the family business as well.

A family business tradition helps an individual to acquire business knowledge and skills, which can motivate entrepreneurial activity if harnessed with the individual's personality traits. Individuals with a family business background (FBB) may plan their career thinking around their personal interests, family interests and employment opportunities within the family business (Schröder et al., 2011). Therefore, FBB may influence children's future EIs by modelling attitudes and beliefs (Krueger et al., 2000; Shapero and Sokol, 1982). Nevertheless, career decisions could be based on the long-term well-being of the family business instead of personal career interests (Murphy and Lambrechts, 2015). The entrepreneurial behaviour (EB) of these individuals may depend on the predominance of their career choice (pursuing either the continuity of their family business or their personal career interests), as well as family support. To nurture or groom a child successor may also be influenced by their different career choices (McMullen and Warnick, 2015).

As Schröder and Schmitt-Rodermund (2013) have shown, the vocational decisions of individuals with an FBB may influence the future of their family businesses. Eckrich and Loughead (1996) claim that the career interests, goals and talents of individuals with an FBB is less clear than individuals without an FBB, which suggests that they have difficulties in establishing their vocational identity. Parental behaviours (support or control), emotional support and verbal encouragement may be relevant aspects which determine whether or not they decide to continue in the family business as a successor (García et al., 2019).

Family businesses as a career choice could be explained by the commitment of family members toward their businesses (Chirico et al., 2011; Mahto et al., 2014; Dawson et al., 2015). This is understandable, since the family business represents a hybrid combination of family and business that cannot survive if the family is no longer committed to keeping the business in the family (Haynes et al., 1999). Sharma and Irving (2005) claim that there are many reasons for successors to join their family firm. They refer to four different types of commitment that define the mindset of next-generation family members: affective, based on desire; normative, based on obligation; calculative, based on opportunity costs; and imperative, based on need. Recently, García et al. (2019) have theorized the indirect effect of perceived parental support and psychological control on next-generation engagement, a key contributor to the success and continuity of the family business.

Global studies reveal low levels of interest and intention of potential successors to join their family businesses (Sieger et al., 2014, 2016; Zellweger, 2017). Based on a survey across 50 countries under the Global University Entrepreneurial Spirit Students' Survey (GUESSS) project, Sieger et al. (2016) claim that five years after graduation, a pattern of 'employee first, then founder' emerges, whereby 38.2 per cent of the graduates expected to own a business, but only 4.8 per cent saw themselves as working in their family business. Furthermore, the individual or psychological perspective has received limited attention, and is focused on understanding the influence of successor attributes on the succession process (De Massis et al., 2016), with little attention on motivation or preparation for leadership roles (Daspit et al., 2016).

We know of no extant studies that analyse years after completion of an MBA the influence of the FBB on student professional career decisions (entrepreneur, successor, or work for others), and the mediating effect of both entrepreneurial self-efficacy (ESE) and entrepreneurial intention (EI), in the case of entrepreneurial behaviour (EB), when the students are from different countries. This is the main objective of this study. To cover this gap in the family business literature, we propose the following research questions:

1. How does the family business background (FBB) of postgraduate students affect their professional career decisions?
2. Does an FBB affect postgraduate student entrepreneurial self-efficacy (ESE)?

3. Do entrepreneurial self-efficacy (ESE) and entrepreneurial intention (EI) act as mediators of the effect of the FBB on postgraduate career decisions (EI and EB)?

This chapter contributes to the family business and entrepreneurship literature in several ways. Students who belong to a family business have been involved in this situational environment since childhood, and have specific skills transmitted to them by their parents. There is also a commitment to the family which may determine their future career, and the future of the family business, if they decide to become successors. The perspective of students without this background could be different. Entrepreneurship is something new, attended by risk. The level of EB in family businesses is discussed ambiguously. Therefore, successors need to be trained to be the creators of new wealth rather than merely guardians of created wealth in the family business (Mitchell et al., 2009).

Students from an FBB may also have career intentions that differ from working in their current family business or running their own business. The skills acquired in their lives may contribute to success in other jobs or businesses, and they could help others to run businesses while remaining in the shadows. Previous experience in family firms may make these students less confident about developing other tasks outside the family firm. Considering the different types of commitment, those students without affective commitment or family support could be better off working outside the family firm, thereby serving both the interests of the individual and the success of the family firm.

This study serves to fill the research gap with respect to evaluating policies based on the FBB and its impact on career decisions, EI and real activity (EB), as well as links to succession in family firms. After this introduction, we draw on the family business and entrepreneurial literature to present a brief review with specific reference to individuals with an FBB. We then present the hypotheses we tested about the influence of the FBB on professional career decisions. Next, the sample and the methodology are described, followed by the results. Finally, we conclude with a discussion of the main findings, as well as the study's limitations and implications.

THEORETICAL BACKGROUND

Family Business Background and Professional Career Decisions

The FBB could be an example of how the social environment and belonging to a certain social group affect individual EI or EB, given that role models, skills transfer, previous learning, emotional support, verbal encouragement and other previous experiences influence career interests and choice behaviour.

In addition, financial and non-financial family support reduce the barriers to creating a new business.

Social cognitive career theory (SCCT) (Lent et al., 1994, 2000) argues that the choice of career is a function of dynamic interaction among self-efficacy, outcome expectations and personal goals. These are constructs that mediate the influence of personal or external factors. The SCCT model suggests that the development of entrepreneurial aspirations depends on interaction between self-efficacy and outcome expectations. The interaction of these key constructs leads to the formation of the EI. Individuals are expected to have higher EI and EB if they feel more capable of undertaking entrepreneurial activities (self-efficacy), hope for positive outcomes from the entrepreneurial activity (outcome expectations) and show high personal interest or aspirations toward entrepreneurship (personal goals).

The presence of intention precedes behaviour. In turn, intention is determined by attitudes that are influenced by external factors, such as training and situational variables (Krueger et al., 2000). Past experience in a family business may be one of these determinants, given that previous behaviour may affect behavioural intention.

It is well known that many individuals choose to become entrepreneurs because they are the daughters and sons of entrepreneurs. Theoretical research suggests that previous experience in a family business could be a mechanism that explains the effects of past behaviour on intentions, defined as an intergenerational (IG) influence (Mead, 1934). The literature notes that two specific factors lead to this outcome (Hamidi et al., 2008; Schröder et al., 2011): parents act as role models (Delmar and Davidsson, 2000), and parents transfer skills to their daughters and sons in the hope of carrying forward the firm they manage (Westhead, 2003). Role models are those with whom individuals make a social comparison about their own abilities, situations, experiences and possible actions to understand or evaluate their future achievements. Furthermore, role models can provide encouragement and support (Bandura, 1989), and can constitute part of the contextual background that influences career choices (Lent et al., 1994). Related to skills transfer, studies in the entrepreneurship literature have explained the formation of EIs using perceptions of the feasibility or desirability of the career choice (Fitzsimmons and Douglas, 2011; Krueger et al., 2000). Laspita et al. (2012) explain how EIs are transmitted within families across generations, and consider that three factors may determine this transmission: (1) genetic inheritance; (2) provision of resources; and (3) education and socialization. Genetic factors that children inherit from their parents may influence the tendency to develop EI. Brain mechanisms may be affected by genes that increase the perception of entrepreneurship as a potential career option (Danes et al., 2009; Davidsson and Honig, 2003). Entrepreneurial parents can trigger their offspring, as can education and socialization, the conscious or unconscious transmission of entrepreneurial values, knowledge and skills across generations. These parents may instil attitudes in their children that make entrepreneurship a desirable career option (Laspita et al., 2012).

Potential entrepreneurs may use family support to provide subjective norms that determine whether their intention to start a business is accepted and supported by others who they deem significant. Children may build self-identities through a socialization process that is both reflective and action-oriented. Ajzen (2002) suggests that the levels of EI are likely to be higher for individuals with prior exposure to family businesses if they perceive that their family supports such actions. Family business owners often involve another family member in their businesses (Aldrich and Cliff, 2003; Carr and Sequeira, 2007; Olson et al., 2003; Zahra, 2005). Family members' understanding of competitive challenges and opportunities could be improved because of this involvement (Chrisman et al., 2010; Mahto et al., 2014). Therefore, these individuals may have more EI than those without FBB.

Hypothesis 1: Postgraduate students with an FBB are more likely to recognize their EI.

Students with an FBB have the option not only to start their own businesses or find employment, but also to become successors (Zellweger et al., 2011). Belonging to certain social groups or categories may influence the complete and complex image that people have of themselves concerning the physical and social world around them. Tajfel and Turner (1985) and Sharma and Irving (2005) propose that the alignment between an individual's self-identity and the family business is a relevant antecedent of an affective commitment to pursuing a career within the family business context. Offspring who consider that the family firm is an important part of themselves have more incentive to start a career within the family firm and contribute to the firm's success. Also, normative (based on obligation), calculative (based on opportunity costs) and imperative (based on need) commitment may be reasons for succession in a family firm. García et al. (2019) also emphasize the importance of parents providing emotional support and verbal encouragement.

The choice of successor varies according to the particular family and firm. Focusing on the personal perspective,[1] children of self-employed parents may be more likely to become self-employed because they inherit the family business or the wealth to acquire a business. The children of self-employed parents build entrepreneurial cultural capital by working in their parents' firms, providing them with advantages in self-employment activities. Children may also genetically or socially inherit preferences or abilities because their parents serve as role models (Hoffman et al., 2015). However, they will not be able to create their own businesses if they consider the role of family successor as more cultural or as symbolic capital (Bourdieu, 1986; Glover, 2010). Parker (2016) points out that a fundamental challenge to the transfer is ensuring the willingness of the next-generation family members to take over and run the firm. Nurturing or grooming successors can be useful (McMullen and Warnick, 2015). Willingness could be higher if the potential successors perceive parental support. In contrast, it disappears if parental psychological, rather than behavioural, control emerges. Psychological control concerns the excessive control of a domineering parent who intrudes on a child's sense of self by manipulating and constraining interactions, and invalidating choices and feelings. Parker (2016) also argues that the altruistic and dynastic motives of founders can improve firm performance and increase firm value, while at the same time providing incentives for offspring to take over the firm. Based on the above, we hypothesize as follows:

Hypothesis 2: Postgraduate students with an FBB are more likely to run a new venture or be a successor than to work for others.

Family Business Background: The Mediating Roles of Entrepreneurial Self-Efficacy

Entrepreneurial self-efficacy (ESE) has emerged as a key psychological construct in entrepreneurship research (Miao et al., 2017) due to its influence on entrepreneurial motivation, intention, behaviour and performance (Newman et al., 2019). Furthermore, the growing influence of entrepreneurial thinking and acting on career development and vocational behaviour (Obschonka et al., 2017; Uy et al., 2015) has increased its relevance.

In the context of SCCT, ESE is influenced by personal factors, such as the initiative to create a new company, and leadership and teamwork skills. Not only does entrepreneurship involve these factors, but it also requires persistence and passion. For this reason, ESE is highly relevant (Newman et al., 2019).

Perceived behavioural control refers to the perception of resource availability, as well as the individual's perceived ease/difficulty in completing a task (Carr and Sequeira, 2007). Individuals understand they have ESE when they choose to carry out activities requiring great effort, or they overcome and show resilience in the face of obstacles (Bandura, 1997; Vanevenhoven and Liguori, 2013). Scherer et al. (1989) suggest that individuals may formulate perceptions that influence their self-efficacy beliefs through observing those who act as role models. Zellweger et al. (2011) highlight the role of observational learning as a mechanism that contributes to self-efficacy development. García et al. (2019) extend this work, indicating that parents are fundamental in assisting skill development and providing emotional support and verbal encouragement, which may actively influence the leadership and sustainability of their family business. Therefore, the family business environment may also determine the strength of an individual's belief that they could become a successful entrepreneur. In the context of SCCT, the family business environment or contextual background may influence postgraduate ESE (Carr and Sequeira, 2007; Tolentino et al., 2014; Pfeifer et al., 2016); in turn, this ESE, also influenced by personal factors, may mediate a person's EI. Having family support in creating a business may also increase student ESE. Under the role model perspective, individuals will increase their inclination toward business ownership if they perceive that others who are important to them positively evaluate the decision of becoming an entrepreneur.

Individuals may try to undertake tasks they consider to be possible to achieve (Bandura, 1997), and those with a strong perception of their abilities are more likely to pursue and persist in such tasks (Bandura, 1992). Therefore, higher levels of self-confidence in relation to the accomplishment of an entrepreneurial task can be positioned as increased volitional control (Carr and Sequeira, 2007).

The family business environment, as contextual background according to SCCT, increases the ESE of family members as well as their identity aspiration such that they see entrepreneurship as a feasible career choice (Krueger et al., 2000). Parents can increase self-efficacy through emotional support, particularly influencing children's affective reactions toward participation in the family business. In the family business context, where the family and the firm are linked, it is necessary to help potential successors manage negative emotions (Zellweger and Dehlen, 2012). Successors may suffer from fear or anxiety arising from the need to differentiate themselves from incumbents as they exert their own personal identities (Dunn, 1999). Positive reactions toward children's entrepreneurial aspirations lead to higher succession intention (Zellweger, 2017). In this sense, ESE mediates the relationship between individuals with an FBB and both EI and EB. Thus, we pose the following hypotheses:

Hypothesis 3: An FBB increases the ESE of postgraduate students.

Hypothesis 4: ESE mediates the relationship between the FBB and postgraduate students' EI and EB.

In addition to this, the presence of intention precedes behaviour. Therefore, the EI could mediate the effect of FBB on the EB. Therefore, we propose the following hypothesis:

Hypothesis 5: EI mediates the relationship between the FBB and postgraduate students' EB.

In summary, an FBB may have both a direct and an indirect effect on EI and EB, showing that past experience in a family business may influence future behavioural intentions and determine professional career choice.

METHODOLOGY

Sample Description

A questionnaire was sent to the alumni of an international MBA programme in 2010[2] offered by three public universities in Spain (Universidad de Alicante, Universitat Autònoma de Barcelona and Universidad Carlos III de Madrid). Students followed the MBA programme in the period 2002–08, so the alumni answered the survey at least two years after finishing their MBAs. October 2002 was the first year in which the MBA programme was offered. Unlike the majority of studies that analyse high school or undergraduate students (Althayde, 2009; Peterman and Kennedy, 2003; Souitaris et al., 2007), this chapter concerns former MBA students, who are more likely to consider the possibility of developing their own businesses than students at a lower level of education. The MBA programme was part-time. We used a locally developed questionnaire that consisted of 44 questions requesting information about FBB, personal perceptions with respect to the ability to carry out initiatives, leadership skills, teamwork skills, previous studies, gender, age, previous and current employment (sector and position within the firm) and country of origin.

The survey encompassed an alumni population of 930 people. The number of responses received was 190, representing 20.43 per cent of the population.[3] The programme included students of varying ages from 25 different countries.[4]

The sample and the characteristics of the dataset are briefly as follows: 33.15 per cent of the MBA students in the sample intended to set up their own businesses when they finished the MBA programme (63 students). Of this group, 53.98 per cent of the students started their own business (not including succession); 61.58 per cent of the students had a family member who was an entrepreneur; 23.93 per cent started their own business outside of the family firm; 7.69 per cent became successors; and the rest decided to work for another firm, different from the family business. In addition, 23.68 per cent of the students were female; 46.32 per cent of the students had received specific entrepreneurship training or education during their lifetime; and the age of the students averaged 38.74 years. The countries of origin for the students were as follows: 77.37 per cent of the students were from Latin America,[5] 17.90 per cent were from Europe (15.79 per cent from Spain), and 4.73 per cent were from Africa. The survey revealed that the main reason the MBA students decided to start their own businesses was entrepreneurial vocation (career flexibility); the second main reason was to discover business opportunities.

Method

To empirically analyse the hypotheses concerning the influence of FBB on EI and EB and the mediating effect of ESE and EI, we applied structural equation modelling (SEM), whose use is scarce in family business research (Sarstedt et al., 2014). Given that we have endogenous dichotomous variables, the error term is not normally distributed (for any value of x, there are only two possible values that the residuals can take). To solve this problem, we followed Bodoff and Ho (2016) and ran the first stage of partial least squares SEM (PLS-SEM), then took the binary variable and its latent variable antecedents as saved outputs and used logistic regression to estimate path coefficients. We use generalized SEM (GSEM) in Stata to estimate these coefficients when the endogenous variable is a dichotomy.

SEM has the advantage of permitting the approximation of the different explanatory variables using various attributes or determinant variables, and avoiding problems of significant correlation. It also has the advantage of considering the multiple causal relationships among endogenous and exogenous variables without fixing the causality direction. Before showing the findings of the structural model, we follow the typical stages of the modularization process with structural equations: (1) conceptualization and structural diagram of the model; (2) formal specification of the model; and (3) estimation of parameters and evaluation of measurement model.

Conceptualization and structural diagram of the model

We use the following dependent variables. Entrepreneurial intention (EI) is a dummy variable that takes the value of 1 if the student intends to engage in entrepreneurial activity after finishing the MBA, and 0 otherwise (Altinay et al., 2012; Díaz-García and Jiménez-Moreno, 2010; Laspita et al., 2012; Veciana et al., 2005).

Entrepreneurial behaviour (EB) is a dummy variable that takes the value of 1 if the student is currently developing (or developed after finishing the MBA programme) an entrepreneurial activity (new venture) or if they are a successor (Start_Succession), and 0 otherwise. It takes the value of 0 if students had worked (or currently work) for someone else since the end of the MBA. Alternatively, we define another dummy variable that takes the value of 1 if the student is currently developing (or developed after finishing the MBA programme) an entrepreneurial activity (new venture outside the family firm, Start_New), and 0 otherwise. Since all successions involve students with FBB, it is not possible to define a variable to distinguish succession from a new venture in any other way.

In terms of explanatory variables, we first use FBB, which takes the value of 1 if the MBA student comes from an entrepreneurial family, and 0 otherwise. To create this variable, we consider a similar index to that used by Carr and Sequeira (2007). We also add the response 'Yes' to the following questions: 'Does a family member own or has a family member ever owned a business?', 'Do you consider that you belong to a family business?' and 'Have you ever worked in a family member's business?'

As latent explanatory variables, we consider entrepreneurial self-efficacy (ESE). The difference between factors (or latent variables) and observable variables is that the former includes the effect of a group of variables that tries to approximate them. To measure ESE, we use reflective indicators. Entrepreneurial self-efficacy predicts initiative, leadership and teamwork. These indicators were measured following a Likert scale (1–5). A confirmative factor analysis (CFA) is followed to estimate these constructs.

We include as control the following variables. First, entrepreneurial education (a dummy variable that takes the value of 1 if the students follow entrepreneurial formation). Souitaris et al. (2007) test the effect of entrepreneurship programmes on the attitudes and intentions of students and show that some programmes increase attitudes and EI. The choice of successors may also vary according to the particular family and firm. In some cases, parents evaluate the interest shown by their descendants considering their skills, education, previous experience and leadership capacity (Martinez-Jimenez, 2009).

The second variable is female (a dummy variable that is equal to 1 if the student is a female and 0 if male). Despite some cultural nuances between countries, it can be said that entrepreneurship has traditionally been associated with men (Greene et al., 2013; Gupta et al., 2009; Gupta et al., 2014). Empirical results show that there are many similarities between female and male EI among postgraduate students. However, women and men have different motivations to engage in EB (DeMartino and Barbato, 2003). Mueller and Conway Dato-on (2013) suggest that a gender gap exists within entrepreneurial orientation, as well as in the motivation, desire and intention to become an entrepreneur. Previous studies (Maes et al., 2014) claim that women choose not to become entrepreneurs because it is an undesirable career option.

Women in family firms suffer 'women's invisibility' (Martinez-Jimenez, 2009). Although they are a highly valuable and critical resource to the family firm, a daughter's abilities and skills are underused and are prevented from developing professionally within the family firm. Females may be considered as potential successors only when all of the founders' descendants are female (Martinez-Jimenez, 2009). Schröder et al. (2011) and Zellweger et al. (2011) show that females are more likely to choose employment than to succeed in the family business. Schröder et al. (2011) also find that females in Germany are more inclined to start a new company than to be a successor in the family business.

The third variable is age (a continuous variable that is equal to the students' years). Previous studies show that being older affects EB negatively (Gielnik et al., 2012). Other studies have shown two contradictory views related to how age could increase or decrease the likelihood of entrepreneurship (Levesque and Minniti, 2011; Minola et al., 2016). On the one hand, older people have gained human, social and financial capital over the years which should be

Table 8.1   Definition of variables

Dependent variables	
Variable	**Definition**
EI	Entrepreneurial intention: a dummy variable that takes the value of 1 if the student had the intention of developing an entrepreneurial activity after finishing the MBA, and 0 otherwise.
EB	Entrepreneurship behaviour: a dummy variable that takes the value of 1 if the student is currently developing (or developed after finishing the MBA program) an entrepreneurial activity (new venture, Start_New). It takes the value of 0 if students have worked for others since the end of the MBA. Alternatively, we define another dummy variable that takes the value of 1 if the student is currently developing (or developed after finishing the MBA programme) an entrepreneurial activity (new venture) or they are a successor (Start_Succesion).
Explanatory variables	
FAM_ENT	Family entrepreneur: a dummy that takes the value of 1 when the MBA student comes from an entrepreneurial family and 0 otherwise. To create this variable, we consider a similar index to that in Carr and Sequeira (2007). We add the response 'Yes' to the following questions: 'Does a family member own or has a family member ever owned a business?', 'Do you consider that you belong to a family business?' and 'Have you ever worked in a family member's business?'
Entrepreneurial self-efficacy	Core construct: a latent variable with indicators of being initiative, leadership and teamwork.
Control variables	
Entrepreneurial education	Entrepreneurial education (EE): a dummy variable that takes the value of 1 if the MBA student has received any specific training/education on entrepreneurship in their lifetime and 0 otherwise.
Gender	Female: a dummy variable that takes the value of 1 when the student is female and the value 0 when male.
Age	Age: a continuous variable that represents the students' age.

Note: Standard errors in parentheses; *** $p<0.01$, ** $p<0.05$, * $p<0.1$.

Table 8.2   *Mean, standard deviation and correlation matrix*

Variable	#Obs.	Mean	SD	1	2	3	4	5	6	7	8
1. FBB	190	0.615	0.487	1.000	0.153*	0.120	0.137*	0.056	-0.069	0.033	0.101
2. Self-efficacy	190	-3.71E16.	1.003		1.000	-0.030	-0.034	0.007	-0.096	-0.065	-0.155*
3. EI	190	0.332	0.472			1.000	0.507***	0.541	-0.004	0.055	-0.044
4. EB (Start_Succession)	190	0.268	0.444				1.000	0.880***	0.090	0.026	0.141
5. EB (Start_New)	190	0.221	0.416					1.000	0.039	-0.028	0.152**
6. Entrepreneurial education	190	0.463	0.499						1.000	0.039	-0.060
7. Female	190	0.237	0.426							1.000	-0.067
8. Age	190	38.74	8.04								1.000

beneficial for starting a business. On the other hand, older people may lose interest in entrepreneurship.

As mentioned before, the variables for this chapter are drawn from the original data obtained from the survey that is produced ad hoc for this research. These are reported in Table 8.1 and their correlations are presented in Table 8.2.

The relations proposed between all of the variables – endogenous and exogenous, observable and latent – are reflected in Figure 8.1, indicating both the correlations subjected to evaluation and the possible correlations between variables and factors.

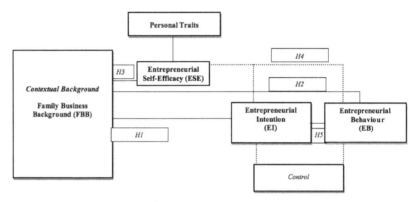

Source: Based on Vanevenhoven and Liguori (2013).

Figure 8.1   *Social Cognitive Career Theory: influence of postgraduate studies of individuals with FBB on EI and EB*

Formal specification of the model

The relationships of the structural diagram lead to the following specification of the model, where η refers to the endogenous latent variables and ξ, to the latent exogenous variables (factors). The observable exogenous variables and the observable endogenous variables are substituted by their nomenclatures. The error of the latent endogenous variable is indicated by ζ, the error of the observable endogenous variable by ε and the error of the observable exogenous variable by δ. Regarding the coefficients, γ indicates the relation between the exogenous variable and another endogenous variable and λ indicates the relation of the latent variable with its indicators. Thus, the structural model:

$$\eta_1\ (EI) = \gamma_{11}FBB + \gamma_{12}ESE + \gamma_{13}CONTROLS + \zeta_1$$
$$\eta_2\ (EB) = \gamma_{21}EI + \gamma_{22}FBB + \gamma_{23}ESE + \gamma_{24}CONTROLS + \zeta_2$$

We propose two models. The first model considers EI as a dependent variable and the following as explanatory variables: family background (FBB), entrepreneurial self-efficacy (ESE) and controls. The second model includes EB (Start_Succession and Start_New) as an entrepreneurial goal, which is predicted by EI and the other previously mentioned variables.

The measurement model: core construct, entrepreneurial self-efficacy (ESE); we include the following indicators for the core construct:

$$\text{Initiative} = \lambda_{11}\,\xi_1 + \delta_1$$
$$\text{Leadership} = \lambda_{21}\,\xi_1 + \delta_2$$
$$\text{Teamwork} = \lambda_{31}\,\xi_1 + \delta_3$$

Estimation of parameters and evaluation of measurement model

At the item level, the correlation between items and constructs (λ) being $\lambda > 0.50$, so that all items load significantly on their respective constructs, demonstrating convergent validity. Loadings above 0.70 indicate that the construct explains over 50 per cent of the indicator's variance. At the construct level, the assessment of construct internal consistency reliability is evaluated using Cronbach's alpha and composite reliability (ρ_c). Values between 0.60 and 0.70 are considered 'acceptable', whereas 0.70 and 0.95 are 'satisfactory to good' (Hair et al., 2014a, 2014b). Convergent validity of the reflectively measured constructs is assessed by the average variance extracted (AVE) for all items associated with the construct. The AVE value is calculated as the mean of the squared loadings for all indicators associated with a construct. An acceptable AVE is 0.50 or higher, which means the construct explains on average over 50 per cent of the variance of its items (see Table 8.3). To test for multicollinearity, we use the variance inflation factor analysis (VIF), which is lower than five for the whole study.

Table 8.3   Feasibility and validity of measurement

Entrepreneurial self-efficacy (ESE)					
Item/Construct	λ	α (alpha Cronbach)	Rho A	Composite Reliability (ρ_c)	AVE
Initiative	0.888				
Leadership	0.808	0.776	0.799	0.869	0.689
Teamwork	0.792				

FINDINGS AND DISCUSSION

Tables 8.4 and 8.5 present the results of the logit model through GSEM in Stata. Table 8.4 shows the results for EI (panel A) and the estimation for the mediating variable ESE (panel B) and Table 8.5 shows the results for both EB as Start_Succession or Start_New (panel A), as well as the estimations for the mediating variables EI (panel B) and ESE (panel C).

In Table 8.4, the results show that FBB is positively associated with EI, which supports our Hypothesis 1. This result is in line with the argument that FBB influences career interests (Laspita et al., 2012), given that parents act as role models (Delmar and Davidsson, 2000), transfer skills to their children (Westhead, 2003) and provide support reducing the perception of barriers that limit this intention (Carr and Sequeira, 2007).

However, the FBB effect is not significant on EB (Start_Succession and Start_New), indicating that offspring in a family business who feel that the family business is a relevant part of themselves have more incentives to start a career within the family firm rather than starting their own business (affective commitment). In addition to this commitment, Sharma and Irving (2005) consider a mindset of 'having to' remain within the family firm due to a sense of obligation (normative commitment), the prohibited costs of leaving (calculative commitment), as well as having a mindset of 'needing to' keep a career in the family business associated with a perceived lack of alternative employment opportunities (imperative commitment). Family successors may identify themselves with the family business, feel pressure from family expectations and the need to support familial goals and values, or perceive that they have few career alternatives outside the family firm (Dawson et al., 2015). Therefore, family members could become successors (Zellweger et al., 2011), which reduces student incentives to run their own businesses. This result supports our Hypothesis 2. The previous estimated EI has a positive and significant effect on the EB, which is consistent with the argument that intention precedes behaviour. We also found that age has a positive and significant effect on the EB, which is in line with the argument that older people have gained human, social and financial capital over the years and are thus more likely to run a new venture.

To test the mediating effect of ESE and EI, our analysis draws on Hair et al. (2014a) by answering the following three questions:

1. Is the direct effect between FBB and EI significant when the mediator variable is excluded from the model?
2. Is the indirect effect via the mediator variable significant after this variable has been included?
3. How much of the direct effect does the indirect effect via the mediator absorb?

For the first model, the direct effect between FBB and EI when the mediating effect (ESE) is not included is 0.2715 and significant (p = 0.092). After ESE inclusion, as we can see in Table 8.4 that the FBB effect is 0.2956 and significant. The indirect effect (_b[EI:ESE]*_b[ESE:FBB]) is not significant. The variance accounted for (VAF), defined as VAF = indirect effect/total effect, is lower than 0.2.

Regarding the mediating effect of EI, the results show that the direct effect between FBB and EB (Start_Succession) before including the mediating var-

Table 8.4   Family business background (FBB) on entrepreneurial intention (EI), mediating effect of entrepreneurial self-efficacy (ESE)

Variables	Model 1
Panel A: Dependent variable, entrepreneurial intention (EI)	
Main variable	
Family business background (FBB)	0.2956*
	(1.79)
Mediating variable	
Entrepreneurial self-efficacy (ESE)	-0.1287
	(-0.80)
Controls	
Entrepreneurial education (EE)	-0.008
	(-0.05)
Female	0.0879
	(0.57)
Age	-0.1412
	(-0.86)
Constant	-0.7200***
	(-4.59)
VAF test (FBB and ESE)	-0.07
Observations	190
Panel B: Dependent variable, entrepreneurial self-efficacy (ESE)	
Family business background (FBB)	0.1531**
	(2.14)
Constant	0.000
	(-0.00)
Observations	190

Note: Standard errors in parentheses; *** $p < 0.01$, ** $p < 0.05$, * $p < 0.1$.

Table 8.5   *Family business background (FBB) on entrepreneurial behaviour*
(EB), mediating effect of entrepreneurial intention (EI) and
entrepreneurial self-efficacy (ESE)

Variables	Model 1 (Start_Succession)	Model 1 (Start_New)
Panel A: Dependent variable, entrepreneurial behaviour (EB)		
Main variables		
Family business background (FBB)	0.1827	-0.1028
	(0.88)	(-0.45)
Mediating variables		
Entrepreneurial intention (EI)	2.6558***	3.3266***
	(6.31)	(6.35)
Entrepreneurial self-efficacy (ESE)	0.2177	0.2464
	(1.19)	(1.21)
Controls		
Entrepreneurial education (EE)	0.1312	0.2441
	(0.66)	(1.09)
Female	0.0138	-0.1789
	(0.07)	(-0.82)
Age	0.5637***	0.7500***
	(2.70)	(3.05)
Constant	2.2575***	3.0393***
	(7.26)	(7.19)
VAF test (FBB and EI)	**0.7851**	-2.2102
VAF test (FBB and ESE)	0.1543	**-0.5795**
Observations	190	190
Panel B: Dependent variable, entrepreneurial intention (EI)		
Family business background (FBB)	0.2956*	0.2956*
	(1.79)	(1.79)
Constant	-0.7201***	-0.7201***
	(-5.59)	(-5.59)
Observations	190	190
Panel C: Dependent variable, entrepreneurial self-efficacy (ESE)		
Family business background (FBB)	0.1531**	0.1531**
	(2.14)	(2.14)
Constant	0.000	0.000
	(-0.00)	(-0.00)
Observations	190	190

Note: Standard errors in parentheses; *** $p < 0.01$, ** $p < 0.05$, * $p < 0.1$.

iable EI is 0.2864 and almost significant (p = 0.108). After EI inclusion (see Table 8.5), the direct of FBB is 0.1827 and insignificant. The indirect effect (_b[START_SUCCESSION:EI]*_b[EI:FBB]) is 0.7851 and significant (p = 0.085). The VAF is 0.811, which is higher than 0.2. Therefore, the EI has a mediating effect between FBB and EB.

For robustness, in a non-reported analysis, we test the influence of FBB on EB (Start_Succession and Start_New) without including EI and ESE. The results show that FBB has a positive and significant effect on Start_Succession but turns insignificant in the case of Start_New. These results seem to indicate that students with FBB are more likely to continue in the family business rather than start a new venture.

CONCLUSIONS AND IMPLICATIONS

This chapter has aimed to analyse the influence of the family business background (FBB) of postgraduate students on entrepreneurial intention (EI) and entrepreneurial behaviour (EB) from the social cognitive career theory (SCCT). Students with an FBB may start their own business, or continue as a successor in the next generation of the family business, or work for others outside of the family business. Student ESE may be a construct that explains their EI and EB, and both ESE and EI could mediate the effect of FBB.

In terms of the research questions, with a sample of 190 responses from national and international students previously enrolled in an MBA programme, the main results show that an FBB is positively associated with EI and ESE. However, the direct effect of the FBB on EB is not significant, being the indirect and total effect through EI is positive and significant. These results may indicate that students with an FBB have EI, and intention precedes behaviour. Previous experience in a family business and interaction with this environment enhance the entrepreneurial skills of these students. However, the different types of commitment (affective, normative, calculative and imperative) and the risk associated with undertaking their own business (outside the comfort zone) reduce the probability that these students will start a business outside their family firm.

This study serves to fill the research gap with respect to evaluating policies based on the FBB and its impact on EI and real activity, as well as links to succession in family firms. The level of EB in a family business is discussed ambiguously. On the one hand, family firms are often referred to as being conservative, risk-averse and cautious about innovation if they perceive a potential loss of their socio-emotional wealth (SEW) (Sciascia et al., 2010). On the other hand, the EB of established businesses is seen as an important prerequisite for family business survival. Successors need to be trained to be the creators of new wealth rather than merely guardians of created wealth in family businesses (Mitchell et al., 2009).

The results reflect that family businesses may provide an environment for training their members. Depending on better relationships with their parents, descendants would prefer to work for the family firm rather than work elsewhere (Houshmand et al., 2017). Moreover, family businesses may create jobs, foster economic development and provide revenues to support local governments. Family members tend to follow careers in the family business, thus making it necessary that the content and the form of academic entrepreneurial programmes try to differentiate between founder and successor entrepreneurs to motivate (or not) students to choose careers in the family business. Specific postgraduate programmes that include a perspective differentiating between next-generation and family firms are quite limited.

Among the main conclusions from the GUESSS REPORT-2016,[6] our results are quite similar to those that find: (1) 80.3 per cent of all students want to become employees after finishing their studies; (2) only 8.8 per cent of this group intend to work in their own business after finishing their studies; (3) 38.2 per cent show interest in working in their own business five years after completion of their studies; (4) the share of international founders in developing countries is significantly higher than in developing countries; and (5) there is a gender gap, with females having weaker EI than males (Sieger et al., 2016).

This study presents some limitations, but these provide a window in terms of research opportunities in this field. First, from the point of view of family business research, future studies could provide additional insight by focusing on the quality of the family business experience and information concerning financial support and commitment. In addition, it could be relevant to compare EI and EB when family members come from a firm with a well-developed succession plan. Second, the model could be used in a transversal way to understand factors (for example, personal factors and contextual background) that influence the EI and EB of future MBA postgraduate students. Longitudinal studies would make it possible to understand the complete evolution of the initial choice of processes that culminate in the development of stable enterprises. A third limitation of this study is the information available. More information about family firms in terms of financial performance and wealth could allow us to understand their heterogeneity and succession process. More information about the relationship between the students and their parents and the birth order of the student as potential successor could also be useful.

We believe that we have provided both theoretical and empirical insights that may be used in designing future research that allows a further conceptualization of management practice. The results associated with social characteristics may provide academics, advisors and politicians with valuable knowledge concerning the development and implementation of formative programmes to motivate entrepreneurial activity, distinguishing between potential founders and successors. Accordingly, the cognitive social model offers a theoretical framework that allows academic interventions. Expectations of self-sufficiency are understood as dimensions that are susceptible to improvement through education, which is an important aspect to be considered when designing postgraduate programmes (Blanco-Blanco, 2009). In addition, policy-makers and universities may provide students with financial support and networking to start their own businesses. From a human capital perspective, family businesses may add another benefit, given that such enterprises could be 'business incubators' for future business start-ups by serving as a training camp for those students with an FBB (Carr and Sequeira, 2007). Given that governments have implemented different laws to support entrepreneurial activity around the world, this study could influence policy measures (OECD, 2009). Governments are seeking to promote policies to generate self-employment and promote EI among young people (Fretschner and Weber, 2013; Katz, 2003); they should also focus on young family members to guarantee the success of current family firms.

ACKNOWLEDGEMENTS

Isabel Feito-Ruiz acknowledges the financial support of the Spanish Ministry of Economy and Competitiveness and European Regional Development Fund (ERDF) (Project MINECO-16-ECO2015-66184-R) and Regional Government of Castilla y Leon (Spain) under Grant (Project LE103G18). David Urbano acknowledges the financial support from the Spanish Ministry of Economy and Competitiveness (project ECO2017-87885-P), the Economy and Knowledge Department – Catalan Government (project 2017-SGR-1056), and ICREA under the ICREA Academia Programme. The authors also acknowledge the useful comments on the survey made by Alicia Coduras (IE Business School, Spain), the useful comments received from Hermann Frank, two anonymous referees and of the participants at XXXII RENT, Toledo, Spain, November 2018. The usual disclaimer applies.

NOTES

1. The lack of information about firm characteristics does not allow us to deepen the analysis of succession from the point of view of the firm.
2. Although the programme analysed is an international MBA, and the students are from different countries, it is important to note at this point that the initiative for the launch of this programme came from three innovative universities, two located in the most heavily populated Spanish cities (Madrid and Barcelona) and the other in a small city. The programme was taught through Madrid University.

3. Previous studies have presented a sample size of approximately this number of students (see Althayde, 2009; Peterman and Kennedy, 2003; Souitaris et al., 2007).
4. Angola, Argentina, Cabo Verde, Chile, Colombia, Cuba, Dominican Republic, Ecuador, El Salvador, Estonia, France, Guatemala, Guyana, Honduras, Mexico, Moldova, Mozambique, the Netherlands, Panama, Paraguay, Peru, Portugal, Spain, the United States, Venezuela.
5. The programme was taught in Spanish, reflecting that nearly two-thirds of the students were from Latin America. The programme gave them the opportunity to study European strategies in their mother tongue to be applied in their own countries. In addition to the fact that smaller cultural differences may motivate Latin American students to undertake this programme, an advertising campaign was developed for the MBA programme, but this campaign was not used in other countries.
6. Global University Entrepreneurial Spirit Students' Survey (GUESSS REPORT-2016) is 'one of the largest entrepreneurship research projects in the world. The main research focuses on students' entrepreneurial intentions and activities, including the topic of family firm succession'. The 7th edition in 2016 provides answers to these questions based on more than 122 000 completed responses from students who were from 50 countries and more than 1000 universities.

REFERENCES

Ajzen, I. (2002), 'Perceived behavioral control, self-efficacy, locus of control, and the theory of planned behavior', *Journal of Applied Social Psychology*, **32**, 665–683.

Aldrich, H.E. and J.E. Cliff (2003), 'The pervasive effects of family on entrepreneurship: toward a family embeddedness perspective', *Journal of Business Venturing*, **18** (5), 573–596.

Althayde, R. (2009), 'Measuring enterprise potential in young people', *Entrepreneurship Theory and Practice*, **33** (2), 481–500.

Altinay, L., M. Madanoglu, R. Daniele and C. Lashley (2012), 'The influence of family tradition and psychological traits on entrepreneurial intention', *International Journal of Hospitality Management*, **31**, 489–499.

Bandura, A. (1989), 'Regulation of cognitive processes through perceived self-efficacy', *Developmental Psychology*, **25** (5), 729–735.

Bandura, A. (1992), 'Self-efficacy mechanism in psychobiologic functioning', in R. Schwarzer (ed.), *Self-efficacy: Thought Control of Action*, Washington, DC: Hemisphere, pp. 355–394.

Bandura, A. (1997), *Self-efficacy: The Exercise of Control*, New York: Freedman.

Blanco-Blanco, A. (2009), 'Social cognitive career model: a review of more than a decade of empirical research', *Revista de Educación*, **350**, 423–445.

Bodoff, D. and S.Y. Ho (2016), 'Partial least squares structural equation modeling approach for analyzing a model with a binary indicator as an endogenous variable', *CAIS*, **38** (23), 400–419.

Bourdieu, P. (1986), 'The forms of capital', in J. Richardson (ed.), *Handbook of Theory and Research for the Sociology of Education*, New York: Greenwood, pp. 241–258.

Carr, J.C. and J.M. Sequeira (2007), 'Prior family business exposure as intergenerational influence of entrepreneurial intent: a theory of planned behavior approach', *Journal of Business Research*, **60** (10), 1090–1098.

Chirico, F., D. Ireland and D. Simon (2011), 'Franchising and the family firm: creating unique resources of advantage through familiness', *Entrepreneurship Theory and Practice*, **35** (3), 483–501.

Chrisman, J.J., F.W. Kellermanns, K.C. Chan and K. Liano (2010), 'Intellectual foundations of current research in family business: an identification and review of 25 influential articles', *Family Business Review*, **23** (1), 9–26.

Danes, S.M., K. Stafford, G. Hayes and S.S. Amarapurkar (2009), 'Family capital of family firms: bridging human, social, and financial capital', *Family Business Review*, **22** (3), 199–216.

Daspit, J.J., D.T. Holt, J.J. Chrisman and R.G. Long (2016), 'Examining family firm succession from a social exchange perspective: a multiphase, multistakeholder review', *Family Business Review*, **29** (1), 44–64.

Davidsson, P. and B. Honig (2003), 'The role of social and human capital among nascent entrepreneurs', *Journal of Business Venturing*, **18**, 301–331.

Dawson, A., P. Sharma, P.G. Irving, J. Marcus and F. Chirico (2015), 'Predictors of later-generation family members' commitment to family enterprises', *Entrepreneurship Theory and Practice*, **39** (3), 545–569.

Delmar, F. and P. Davidsson (2000), 'Where do they come from? Prevalence and characteristics of nascent entrepreneurs', *Entrepreneurship and Regional Development*, **12**, 1–23.

DeMartino, R. and R. Barbato (2003), 'Differences between women and men MBA entrepreneurs: exploring family flexibility and wealth creation as career motivators', *Journal of Business Venturing*, **18**, 815–832.

De Massis, A., P. Sieger, J.H. Chua and S. Vismara (2016), 'Incumbents' attitude toward intrafamily succession: an investigation of its antecedents', *Family Business Review*, **29** (3), 278–300.

Díaz-García, M. and J. Jiménez-Moreno (2010), 'Entrepreneurial intention: the role of gender', *International Entrepreneurship Management Journal*, **6**, 261–283.

Dunn, B. (1999), 'The family factor: the impact of family relationship dynamics on business-owning families during transitions', *Family Business Review*, **12**, 41–57.

Eckrich, C.J. and T.A. Loughead (1996), 'Effects of family business membership and psychological separation on the career development of late adolescents', *Family Business Review*, **9**, 369–386.

Fitzsimmons, J.R. and E.J. Douglas (2011), 'Interaction between feasibility and desirability in the formation of entrepreneurial intentions', *Journal of Business Venturing*, **26** (4), 431–440.

Fretschner, M. and S. Weber (2013), 'Measuring and understanding the effects of entrepreneurial awareness education', *Journal of Small Business Management*, **5** (3), 410–428.

García, P.R.J.M., P. Sharma, A. De Massis, M. Wright and L. Sholes (2019), 'Perceived parental behaviors and next-generation engagement in family firms: a social cognitive perspective', *Entrepreneurship Theory and Practice*, **43** (2), 224–243.

Gielnik, M.M., H. Zacher and M. Frese (2012), 'Focus on opportunities as a mediator of the relationships between business owners' age and venture growth', *Journal of Business Venturing*, **27**, 127–142.

Glover, J. (2010), 'Capital usage in adverse situations: applying Bourdieu's theory of capital to family farm businesses', *Journal of Family and Economic Issues*, **31**, 485–497.

Greene, F.G., L. Han and S. Marlow (2013), 'Like mother, like daughter? Analyzing maternal influences upon women's entrepreneurial propensity', *Entrepreneurship Theory and Practice*, **37** (4), 687–711.

Gupta, V.K., A.B. Goktan and G. Gunay (2014), 'Gender differences in evaluation of new business opportunity: a stereotype threat perspective', *Journal of Business Venturing*, **29**, 273–288.

Gupta, V.K., D.B. Turban and S.A. Wasti and A. Sikdar (2009), 'The role of gender stereotypes in perceptions of entrepreneurs and intentions to become an entrepreneur', *Entrepreneurship Theory and Practice*, **33** (2), 397–417.

Hair, J.F., G.T.M. Hult, C.M. Ringle and M. Sarstedt (2014a), *A Primer on Partial Least Squares Structural Equation Modeling*, Thousand Oaks, CA: SAGE.

Hair, J.F., M. Sarstedt, L. Hopkins and V. Kuppelwieser (2014b), 'Partial least squares structural equation modeling (PLS_SEM): an emerging tool in business research', *European Business Review*, **26** (2), 106–121.

Hamidi, D., K. Wennberg and H. Berglund (2008), 'Creativity in entrepreneurship education', *Journal of Small Business and Enterprise Development*, **15** (2), 304–320.

Haynes, G.W., R. Walker, B.R. Rowe and G.S. Hong (1999), 'The intermingling of business and family finances in family-owned businesses', *Family Business Review*, **12**, 225–239.

Hoffmann, A., M. Junge and N. Malchow-Moller (2015), 'Running in the family: parental role models in entrepreneurship', *Small Business Economics*, **44**, 79–104.

Houshmand, M., M. Seidel and D.G. Ma (2017). 'The impact of adolescent work in family business on child–parent relationships and psychological well-being', *Family Business Review*, **30**, 242–261.

Katz, J. (2003), 'The chronology and intellectual trajectory of American entrepreneurship education 1876–1999', *Journal of Business Venturing*, **18** (2), 283–300.

Krueger, N., M.D. Reilly and A.L. Carsrud (2000), 'Competing models of entrepreneurial intentions', *Journal of Business Venturing*, **15** (5–6), 411–432.

Laspita, S., N. Breugdt, S. Heblich and H. Patzelt (2012), 'Intergenerational transmission of entrepreneurship intentions', *Journal of Business Venturing*, **27** (4), 414–435.

Lent, R.W., S.D. Brown and G. Hackett (1994), 'Toward a unifying social cognitive theory of career and academic interest, choice, and performance [monograph]', *Journal of Vocational Behavior*, **45**, 79–122.

Lent, R.W., S.D. Brown and G. Hackett (2000), 'Contextual supports and barriers to career choice: a social cognitive analysis', *Journal of Counseling Psychology*, **47**, 36–49.

Levesque, M. and M. Minniti (2011), 'Age matters: how demographics influence aggregate entrepreneurship', *Strategic Entrepreneurship Journal*, **5**, 269–284.

Maes, J., H. Leroy and L. Sels (2014), 'Gender differences in entrepreneurial intentions: a TPB multi-group analysis at factor and indicator level', *European Management Journal*, **32** (5), 784–794.

Mahto, R.V., P.S. Davis and D. Khanin (2014), 'Continuation commitment: family's commitment to continue the family business', *Journal of Family Economic Issues*, **35**, 278–289.

Martinez-Jimenez, R. (2009), 'Research on women in family firms: current status and future directions', *Family Business Review*, **22** (1), 53–64.

McCaffrey, M. (2018), 'Extending the economic foundation of entrepreneurship research', *European Management Review*, **15**, 191–199.

McMullen, J.S. and B.J. Warnick (2015), 'To nurture or groom? The parent-founder succession dilemma', *Entrepreneurship Theory and Practice*, **39** (6), 1379–1412.

Mead, G.H. (1934), *Mind, Self, and Society*, Chicago, IL: University of Chicago Press.

Miao, C., S. Qian and D. Ma (2017), 'The relationship between entrepreneurial self-efficacy and firm performance: a meta-analysis of main and moderator effects', *Journal of Small Business Management*, **55** (1), 87–107.

Minola, T., G. Criaco and M. Obschonka (2016), 'Age, culture, and self-employment motivation', *Small Business Economics*, **46**, 187–213.

Mitchell, J.R., T.A. Hart, S. Valcea and M.D. Townsend (2009), 'Becoming the boss: discretion and postsucession success in family firms', *Entrepreneurship Theory and Practice*, **33** (6), 1201–1218.

Mueller, S.L. and M. Conway Dato-on (2013), 'A cross-cultural study of gender-role orientation and entrepreneurial self-efficacy', *International Entrepreneurship and Management Journal*, **9** (1), 1–20.

Murphy, L. and F. Lambrechts (2015), 'Investigating the actual career decisions of the next generation: the impact of family business involvement', *Journal of Family Business Strategy*, **6**, 33–44.

Newman, A., M. Obschonka, S. Schwarz, M. Cohen and I. Nielsen (2019), 'Entrepreneurial self-efficacy: a systematic review of the literature on its theoretical foundations, measurement, antecedents, and outcomes, and an agenda for future research', *Journal of Vocational Behavior*, **110** (Part B), 403–419.

Nordqvist, M. and L. Melin (2010), 'Entrepreneurial families and family firms', *Entrepreneurship and Regional Development*, **22** (3–4), 211–239. https://doi.org/10.1080/08985621003726119.

Obschonka, M., K. Hakkarainen, K. Lonka and K. Salmela-Aro (2017), 'Entrepreneurship as a twenty-first century skill: entrepreneurial alertness and intention in the transition to adulthood', *Small Business Economics*, **48** (3), 487–501.

Olson, P.D., V.S. Zuiker, S.M. Danes, J. Stafford, R.K.Z. Heck and K.A. Duncan (2003), 'The impact of the family business sustainability', *Journal of Business Venturing*, **18** (5), 639–666.

Organisation for Economic Co-operation and Development (OECD) (2009), *Education at a Glance*, Paris: OECD.

Parker, S.C. (2016), 'Family firms and the "willing successor" problem'. *Entrepreneurship Theory and Practice*, **40**, 1241–1259.

Peterman, N. and J. Kennedy (2003), 'Enterprise education: influencing students' perceptions of entrepreneurship', *Entrepreneurship Theory and Practice*, **28** (20), 129–144.

Pfeifer, S., N. Šarlija and M. Zekic Sušac (2016), 'Shaping the entrepreneurial mindset: entrepreneurial intentions of business students in Croatia', *Journal of Small Business Management*, **54**, 102–117.

Sarstedt, M., C.R.D. Ringle, R. Reams and J.F. Hair (2014), 'Partial least squares structural equation modeling (PLS-SEM): a useful tool for family business researchers', *Journal of Family Business Strategy*, **5** (1), 105–115.

Scherer, R.F., J.S. Adams, S.S. Carley and F.A. Wiebe (1989), 'Role model performance effects on development of entrepreneurial career preference', *Entrepreneurship Theory and Practice*, **13** (3), 53–71.

Schröder, E. and E. Schmitt-Rodermund (2013), 'Antecedents and consequences of adolescents' motivations to join the family business', *Journal of Vocational Behavior*, **83** (3), 476–485.

Schröder, E., E. Schmitt-Rodermund and N. Arnaud (2011), 'Career choice intentions of adolescents with a family business background', *Family Business Review*, **24** (4), 305–321.

Sciascia, S., F. Chirico and P. Mazzola (2010), 'Entrepreneurial orientation and performance in family-owned firms: the role of family management' (Interactive Paper), *Frontiers of Entrepreneurship Research*, **30** (13). http://www.diva-portal .org/smash/record.jsf?pid=diva2%3A484235&dswid=-7906.

Shapero, A. and L. Sokol (1982), 'Social dimensions of entrepreneurship', in C.A. Kent, D.L. Sexton and K.H. Vesper (eds), *Encyclopedia of Entrepreneurship*, Englewood Cliffs, NJ: Prentice Hall, pp. 72–79.

Sharma, P. and P.G. Irving (2005), 'Four bases of family business successor commitment: antecedents and consequences', *Entrepreneurship Theory and Practice*, **29**, 13–33.

Sieger, P., U. Fueglistaller and T. Zellweger (2014), 'Student entrepreneurship across the globe: a look at intentions and activities', International Report of the GUESSS Project 2013/2014. http://www.alexandria@unisg.ch.

Sieger, P., U. Fueglistaller and T. Zellweger (2016), *Student Entrepreneurship 2016: Insights From 50 Countries*, St Gallen/Bern: KMU-HSG/IMU.

Souitaris, V., S. Zerbinati and A. Al-Laham (2007), 'Do entrepreneurship programmes raise entrepreneurial intention of science and engineering students? The effect of learning, inspiration and resources', *Journal of Business Venturing*, **22**, 566–591.

Tajfel, H. and J.C. Turner (1985), 'The social identity theory of intergroup behavior', in S. Worchel and W.G. Austin (eds), *Psychology and Intergroup Relations*, Chicago, IL: Nelson-Hall, pp. 7–24.

Tolentino, L., V. Sedoglavich, V. Lu, P. Garcia and S. Restubog (2014), 'The role of career adaptability in predicting entrepreneurial intentions: a moderated mediation model', *Journal of Vocational Behavior*, **85**, 403–412.

Uy, M., K. Chan, Y. Sam, M. Ho and O. Chernyshenko (2015), 'Proactivity, adaptability and boundaryless career attitudes: the mediating role of entrepreneurial alertness', *Journal of Vocational Behavior*, **86**, 115–123.

Vanevenhoven, J. and E. Liguori (2013), 'The impact of entrepreneurship education: introducing the entrepreneurship education project', *Journal of Small Business Management*, **51** (3), 315–328.

Veciana, J.M., M. Aponte and D. Urbano (2005), 'University students attitudes towards entrepreneurship: a two countries comparation', *International Entrepreneurship and Management Journal*, **1** (2), 165–182.

Westhead, P. (2003), 'Company performance and objectives reported by first and multi-generation family companies', *Journal of Small Business and Enterprise Development*, **10** (1), 93–105.

Zahra, S.A. (2005), 'Entrepreneurial risk taking in family firms', *Family Business Review*, **18** (1), 23–40.

Zellweger, T.M. (2017), *Managing the Family Business: Theory and Practice*, Cheltenham, UK and Northampton, MA, USA: Edward Elgar Publishing.

Zellweger, T.M. and T. Dehlen (2012), 'Value is in the eye of the owner: affect infusion and socioemotional wealth among family firm owners', *Family Business Review*, **25**, 280–297.

Zellweger, T., P. Siege and F. Halter (2011), 'Should I stay or should I go? Career choice intentions of students with family business background', *Journal of Business Venturing*, **26** (5), 521–536.

9. Organizational conditions stimulating the entrepreneurial mindset

Dagmar Ylva Hattenberg, Olga Belousova and Aard J. Groen

INTRODUCTION

In the past two decades, the term 'entrepreneurial mindset' (EMS) has been embraced as capturing the entrepreneurialness of individuals (Haynie et al., 2010; Shepherd et al., 2010), concerning 'the ability and willingness of individuals to rapidly sense, act and mobilize, in response to a judgmental decision under uncertainty about a possible opportunity for gain' (Shepherd et al., 2010, p. 62). Employees are at the heart of an organization (McGrath and MacMillan, 2000); without employees, an organization would not be able to create an entrepreneurial environment. Indeed, 'behaviour is the central and essential element in the entrepreneurial process' (Covin and Slevin, 1991, p. 8). Capturing individual entrepreneurialness has the potential to aid research and practice in understanding why certain individuals behave entrepreneurially within organizations (Shepherd et al., 2010; Ireland et al., 2003) whereas others do not (Shepherd and Patzelt, 2018). This, in turn, can help research understand how individual entrepreneurialness aids organizations in sustaining their competitive advantage in an increasingly competitive environment (Shetty, 2004).

Furthermore, research indicates that the organizational culture may influence employees' EMS (Shepherd et al., 2010). Nevertheless, the nature of this relationship has only been scarcely investigated. Research demonstrates the need for further consideration of how EMS works, and what one (or an organization) can do to activate or stimulate EMS (Shepherd and Patzelt, 2018; Robinson et al., 2016; Ireland et al., 2003). In this light, we discuss how organizations can stimulate the individual EMS; specifically, to what extent organizational conditions play a role.

Shepherd et al. (2010) argue that there is a learning spiral between an individual's entrepreneurialness, as captured in EMS, and the entrepreneurial culture at the organizational level. Our research extends this work, building on

Hornsby et al. (2013), who discuss the importance of a heterogeneous approach of employee level characteristics with regard to the interaction with corporate entrepreneurship (CE). A detailed understanding of the ways in which varying organizational conditions can impact employees' EMS may aid in uncovering intricacies related to research and management of CE. Our exploration of how organizations, building on the conditions as perceived by employees, can stimulate EMS within an entrepreneurial, organizational environment extends and deepens current discussions, to understand the relationship between organizational conditions and EMS.

We explore the relationship between specific organizational conditions (Hornsby et al., 2013) and EMS in an organizational context, by surveying and interviewing employees of all levels throughout an organization. Our findings emphasize the importance of organizational stimulation with regard to EMS, thus acknowledging and strengthening the work of Shepherd et al. (2010) and Hornsby et al. (2013).

The structure of this chapter is as follows: we discuss a theoretical background on CE and EMS, explaining our assumption that every employee in an organization is able to manage their own job tasks simultaneously with initiating entrepreneurial initiatives, and we argue that the mechanism explaining our assumption is EMS. Next, we perform an explorative analysis according to well-established procedures. Finally, we discuss our exploratory findings and we develop propositions and avenues for future research.

THEORETICAL DEVELOPMENT

Corporate Entrepreneurship

Frequently, researchers and practitioners see CE as a solution to survive in a volatile environment and to maintain a sustained competitive advantage as an organization (Kuratko et al., 2017; Birkinshaw, 1997). Sharma and Chrisman (1999, p. 18) define it as: 'the process whereby an individual or a group of individuals, in association with an existing organization, create a new organization or instigate renewal or innovation within that organization'. A typical example of CE is Hewlett Packard in the 1990s, where a group of employees obtained $8 million to create a new entrepreneurial initiative regarding e-commerce development (Hisrich and Ramadani, 2017). These employees worked on an entrepreneurial initiative alongside their daily job tasks.

To promote such entrepreneurial initiatives, research has identified several factors of the organizational environment that may be fruitful and stimulating for employee entrepreneurial behaviour (Hornsby et al., 2013). At the same time, a central mechanism explaining the interaction of the context with the entrepreneurial initiatives within an organization is yet to be developed

(Belousova and Gailly, 2013; Shetty, 2004), and we believe it can be captured by EMS. Specifically, we believe that the CE process is important to investigate, because of the likelihood that this environment provides room for employees to act on entrepreneurial opportunities.

Belousova and Gailly (2013) discuss and emphasize a distinction between two types of CE: dispersed CE (DCE) and focused CE (FCE). FCE and DCE differ in nuances, and the interaction with employees can result in different consequences for both employees and the organization. With an FCE perspective, one perceives the entrepreneurial effort as concentrated and structurally separated; whereas with a DCE perspective, every employee is considered capable of coming up with entrepreneurial initiatives (Belousova and Gailly, 2013; Birkinshaw, 1997). Viewed from the DCE perspective, every employee has a latent dual role within the organization.

Extending the work of Belousova and Gailly (2013), we believe that the individual commencement of initiatives should be emphasized: DCE has an effect on entrepreneurial initiatives through an individual process, underlining the idea that organizational conditions relate to EMS (Shepherd et al., 2010). Specifically, one may argue that these individual employees are able to utilize resources and transform them into knowledge, skills, networking opportunities and communication abilities (Culkin and Mallick, 2011), which leads the discussion away from who is an entrepreneur (Gartner, 1988), towards what a (potential) entrepreneur is willing and able to do, as captured in EMS (Haynie et al., 2010).

Entrepreneurial Mindset

EMS captures whether one perceives oneself to have the skillset and abilities to act entrepreneurially, whether one would actually like to be entrepreneurial, and whether one makes a judgement call about the consequences of one's actions (Culkin and Mallick, 2011). EMS specifically concerns a distinction between willingness and ability aspects (Shepherd et al., 2010). Willingness and ability both consist of the aspects of affect (Campos et al., 2017; Makimurto-Koivumaa and Belt, 2016; Shepherd et al., 2010), skills (Laalo and Heinonen, 2016; Culkin and Mallick, 2011) and cognition (Campos et al., 2017; Robinson et al., 2016; Haynie et al., 2010).

Affect refers to whether one likes to be entrepreneurial: a positive attitude (Makimurto-Koivumaa and Belt, 2016), emotions (Noble, 2015) and identity (Shepherd et al., 2010). Skills refer to the skillset and abilities of individuals, such as growth and exploitation skills, and abilities (Haynie et al., 2010). Cognition refers to the judgement call and cognition needed to make such a decision, for instance metacognition (Patel and Mehta, 2016) and knowledge (Shams and Kaufmann, 2016).

EMS can arguably be developed over time (Shepherd et al., 2010); specifically viewed from a DCE perspective where every employee has the ability to act and behave entrepreneurially (Belousova and Gailly, 2013), we argue that every employee can utilize EMS to initiate an entrepreneurial initiative. To date, there has been little empirical consideration of EMS in an organizational context, with the few exceptions targeting mid- to high-level management (Shepherd et al., 2010; Wright, 2001), though not employees specifically. The entire range of employees has not been investigated before. Based on the DCE perspective, we argue that any employee within an organization is capable of seeing and sensing entrepreneurial opportunities. We believe that EMS better captures the individual characteristics of employees regarding their entrepreneurialness than previous work on concepts such as 'individual entrepreneurial orientation' (IEO); and building on the theoretical work of Shepherd et al. (2010), we argue that EMS is an appropriate concept to capture individual entrepreneurialness in an organizational context.

Within an organizational context, employees with EMS need to be able to spot market opportunities both within and outside the business (Kyrgidou and Petridou, 2011), and mobilize resources within an existing organization by strategically reallocating them (Shams and Kaufmann, 2016). Resources can refer to internal individual resources, such as knowledge and skills (Shepherd et al., 2010), or external resources such as co-workers (that is, social resources and human resources) (Robinson et al., 2016; Shams and Kaufmann, 2016), investments or funding (that is, financial resources) (Mitchell, 2007; McGrath and MacMillan, 2000), or tools (that is, technical resources) (Mitchell, 2007). Thus, varying resources within an organization will act as stimulants or inhibitors of employees' willingness and ability to see and act on an opportunity.

An increasing amount of research focuses on organizational antecedents with regard to EMS, such as an entrepreneurial culture (Shepherd et al., 2010; Ireland et al., 2003), management (Culkin and Mallick, 2011; Mitchell, 2007), strategy (Kyrgidou and Petridou, 2011) and the social environment (Smith et al., 2009). Whilst these studies have contributed to our understanding of the contextualization of EMS, they have only just begun to understand how to stimulate EMS within an organizational environment.

Organizational Conditions

According to Hornsby et al. (2013), several organizational conditions can influence the engagement of employees in CE. Organizational conditions concern conditional variables influencing individual employees through job tasks, culture, perceived leadership and the perceived environment (Hornsby et al., 2013; Shepherd et al., 2010). Hornsby et al. (2013) measured a specific set of organizational conditions, building on the work of Hornsby et al. (2009),

Ireland et al. (2009) and Kuratko et al. (1990). The organizational conditions concern the perception of work discretion, rewards and reinforcements, time availability and management support within the organization (Kuratko et al., 2014).

Work discretion captures job autonomy, perceived freedom and individual decision-making (Hornsby et al., 2013), making up a large proportion of an organizational culture (Shepherd et al., 2010). Whether an employee experiences a high amount of work discretion appears to relate positively to entrepreneurial initiatives (Kuratko et al., 2005). Time availability captures the experiences of employees regarding their workload, yet another aspect of an organizational culture (Shepherd et al., 2010). Time availability is considered an 'important resource for generating entrepreneurial initiatives' (Kuratko et al., 2014, p. 39), though research is enigmatic about the nuances of this relationship. If an employee perceives time as available and unstructured, with the opportunity to fill in this time with their own ideas, though related to work activities, it appears that they tend to initiate entrepreneurial initiatives (Kuratko et al., 2014). Rewards and reinforcements, capturing how employees perceive tangible and intangible rewards, and captured within an organizational culture as stimulating employee behaviour (Shepherd et al., 2010), likewise positively correlate with entrepreneurial initiatives (Ireland et al., 2009). Rewards and reinforcement can have a direct effect on entrepreneurial initiatives; nevertheless, this relationship appears likely, yet not solid (Ireland et al., 2009): employees can still defy the tendency to behave entrepreneurially, and the reason why remains unknown. Management support, lastly, captures 'the willingness of top-level managers to facilitate and promote entrepreneurial behaviour' (Hornsby et al., 2013, p. 939). Management support aids in starting an interaction spiral between an entrepreneurial culture and EMS (Shepherd et al., 2010). Specifically, Shepherd et al. (2010) argue that employees should be championed to commence entrepreneurial initiatives, and management plays an important, if not critical role.

Regarding the named organizational conditions, we believe that Hornsby et al. (2013) have developed a strong approach to measure them. Therefore, we build on the work of Hornsby et al. (2013), by utilizing their conceptualization and operationalization of organizational conditions. Specifically, based on the spiral theory (that is, the deviation-amplifying loop) by Shepherd et al. (2010), we argue that organizational conditions can shape employees' EMS and consequently entrepreneurial initiatives by inhibiting or fuelling EMS.

METHODOLOGY

Research Approach

We employ a single in-depth case study, using a survey method to investigate the potential relations between the organizational conditions and EMS, followed up by semi-structured interviews with 12 employees. Surveys are arguably useful in situations where a social phenomenon needs to be studied within a specific context and in relationship with other variables (Davidsson, 2009) in a variety of natural settings (Pinsonneault and Kraemer, 1993). A survey is useful as an objective measurement, capturing multiple variables and relationships, which can be pre-tested and controlled. Our survey contains well-developed and often-utilized scales, which provides our research with the possibility to compare results to earlier findings in the literature. Finally, a survey is appropriate if it aids in identifying an answer to how and why a certain phenomenon is happening (Pinsonneault and Kraemer, 1993). Next, the interviews are used to strengthen and validate the exploratory findings from the survey, highlighting and deepening these initial results.

Research Setting

The study setting is a Dutch pharmaceutical family firm ('PharmaCo'), with headquarters based in the Northern Netherlands and offices spread over five countries on three continents, founded over 40 years ago. The company employs approximately 65 employees in the Netherlands and holds world-leading positions in the distribution and trading of raw and processed pharmaceutical materials. The industrial pharmaceutical environment is characterized as rather traditional, and a dispersed approach can bring multiple benefits to the organization. We followed a complete sampling approach. The survey was introduced via intranet, by presenting at several internal meetings and via e-mail. For the interviews, the first author invited people on a one-on-one basis.

Data Collection

The concern of this research is to identify the relationship between EMS phenomenon and its environment. We derived our concepts from the literature (McMullen and Kier, 2016; Shepherd et al., 2010; McMullen and Shepherd, 2006; McGrath and MacMillan, 2000).

Interviews

Twelve employees from different departments and holding different hierarchical positions were asked to participate in a semi-structured interview, before the start of the survey. Each interview lasted 45–75 minutes, and the interviews were transcribed in verbatim.

Survey

We used an online anonymous survey, distributed in English and Dutch at a single point in time; a weekly reminder was sent twice. For Dutch participants, the English scales were translated utilizing a back-and-forth translation method, executed by a professional translation agency. The software 'Typeform' was used to collect the data. A preliminary notice emphasized the anonymity, confidentiality and voluntariness of participation. Demographic variables concerned gender, business unit, job position and education. The survey consisted mainly of closed-ended items, indicated in the description of the different scales. At the end of the survey, participants were debriefed.

Entrepreneurial Mindset

To measure EMS, we used the Intrapreneurial Attitude Orientation (IAO) scale developed by Shetty (2004). The IAO scale appears to be one of the first scales that measure the proclivity to entrepreneurial behaviour within an organizational context. The IAO scale is an adapted version of the well-established Entrepreneurial Attitude Orientation (EAO) scale, developed by Robinson et al. (1991). Shetty's (2004) adaptation made it possible to utilize the scale in an organizational context. The aim of the IAO scale is to measure attitudes and skills of individuals related to entrepreneurship in an organization. The IAO scale is a content-wise valid instrument to capture EMS, as it comprises ability, willingness and attitudes of individuals. We thus believe that the IAO scale is currently the most appropriate scale to measure EMS; an example item is: 'I believe that to become successful in business you must spend time every day developing opportunities'. All items could be answered by means of a five-point Likert formatted scale, ranging from 'completely disagree' to 'completely agree'. Although EMS is a multidimensional construct, we consider the composite, as we believe that in order to engage in entrepreneurial initiatives an employee would need to possess both willingness and perceived ability to do so.

Organizational Conditions

We measured organizational conditions using the measurement for organizational preparedness for corporate entrepreneurship, called the Corporate Entrepreneurship Assessment Instrument (CEAI), developed by Hornsby et al. (2013). An example item of the CEAI is: 'Money is often available to get new ideas of the ground'. Hornsby et al. (2013) built the CEAI on established work dating back to the 1990s. Hornsby et al. (2013) performed several validation studies, concluding on its usefulness and comprehensiveness with regard to measuring organizational conditions. The four dimensions of the CEAI are work discretion (WD), time availability (TA), management support (MS), and rewards and reinforcements (RR).

Control variables
Though not part of our main model, we measured control variables, to take into account for our regression analysis. We concerned ourselves with gender, education, business unit and department.

Sample
In total, 65 respondents were approached and 48 respondents participated in the survey. We excluded 16 respondents from the final analysis. The final analysis was thus run with 32 respondents: 21 men (65.6 per cent) and 11 women (34.4 per cent). The tenure of respondents ranged from 1 to 12 years, with 46.9 per cent working a year or less for the organization. The majority of the sample was bachelor degree educated: 14 out of 32 respondents (43.8 per cent). Most respondents work in the lab department (21.9 per cent), production (18.8 per cent) or research and development (15.6 per cent).

Data Analysis

Based on Podsakoff et al. (2003), we compared our correlations between the constructs to the true variance as indicated by Cote and Buckley's (1988) formula. Since we measured attitude-related concepts, common method variance may bias the results, by either inflating or deflating the correlations due to systematic measurement variance and random measurement variance (Podsakoff et al., 2003). To prevent respondents' tendency to avoid cognitive dissonance and employ a consistency motif (Podsakoff et al., 2003), we combined retrospective and prospective items. We work with established, well-developed and often used scales, lowering the possible influence of the consistency motif and acquiescence (see also Winkler et al., 1982).

Before conducting regression analyses, we investigated the necessary assumptions, as indicated by Field (2013), which were met. Our data (including error terms) appeared normally distributed, with no influential cases or outliers. There is thus no cause for deleting cases. For instance, the Mahalanobis score, leverage and Cook's distance indicate that there are no specific influential cases that may cause concern. Furthermore, the P-Plots indicated a linear distribution. We analyzed the data using the forced entry approach (Field, 2013). If there is no strong theoretical reasoning for adding the predictors in another fashion (that is, stepwise or hierarchical), Studenmund and Cassidy (1987) argue that the forced entry method is the most appropriate and robust.

RESULTS

Table 9.1 shows the means, standard deviations and intercorrelations. Organizational conditions are abbreviated to 'Org. Cond.'. The correlation matrix shows no signs for multicollinearity. It shows a high intercorrelation between the sub-dimensions and the composite of organizational conditions. This is expected, as the sub-dimensions combined form the composite of organizational conditions.

To explore the DCE assumption, we compared the means of the different business units and departments in terms of the dependent variable EMS, using a one-way ANOVA (Field, 2013). The ANOVA indicates no significant differences between groups ($F = 1.895$, $p = 0.104$), supporting the dispersed perspective that EMS is pervasive throughout an organization with no differences between groups of people. Furthermore, we found no differences between men and women in terms of EMS ($t = 0.795$, $p = 0.436$, df $= 18.644$).

However, we found qualitative differences in the interviews of employees and managers: while one employee answered that 'every employee needs to be entrepreneurial, otherwise the company would not be entrepreneurial', a manager indicated that 'everyone is entrepreneurial to a certain extent, but this does depend on the department and the necessity: not everyone shows to be entrepreneurial'. Based on these explorative findings, we propose that EMS is pervasive throughout an organization, although manifestations of EMS may differ depending on the person or the department.

To further investigate the relationship between the organizational conditions and EMS, we created forced entry models, controlling for education, department and gender. As the sample is relatively small, and to enable ourselves to analyze the data in a comparable manner, we standardized all the variables into z-scores (Field, 2013). Table 9.2 shows the associated statistics. The control variables (Model 1) explain 8.1 per cent of the variance of EMS and the model is non-significant.

Whilst exploring the relationship between work discretion and EMS, we found a positive effect ($\beta = 0.583$, $p = 0.001$); adding work discretion to the original model (2a) explains 32.6 per cent of the variance of EMS ($R^2 = 0.407$). One manager confirms the importance of autonomy in one's job, captured in work discretion: 'it is my job to plant a seed, but from that point on, initiative needs to come from employees, and this usually works out well'. An employee also indicates that it is necessary that an organization facilitates job autonomy: 'our organization needs to and does everything within its power to stimulate and facilitate entrepreneurship, though time can be a limiting factor'.

Table 9.1   *Means (M), standard deviations (SD) and correlations*

	M	SD	Org Cond TA	Org Cond MS	Org Cond RR	Org Cond WD	Composite Org Cond	Composite EMS	Education Level	Business Unit
Org Cond TA	4.01	1.05								
Org Cond MS	3.93	1.09	0.085							
Org Cond RR	4.49	1.04	0.206	0.434*						
Org Cond WD	5.04	0.97	0.011	0.587**	0.421*					
Composite Org Cond	4.37	0.71	0.482+	0.775**	0.753**	0.726**				
Composite EMS	4.98	0.47	0.176	0.570**	0.387*	0.564**	0.619**			
Education Level	2.00	0.88	0.293	0.262	0.106	0.060	0.269	0.270		
Business Unit	5.44	3.61	-0.036	-0.143	0.412*	0.107	0.119	0.024	-0.030	
Gender	1.34	0.48	-0.183	-0.076	0.276	0.164	0.060	-0.148	-0.304	0.318

Note: $n = 32$; * $p < 0.05$; ** $p \leq 0.001$; + $p = 0.005$.

Table 9.2   Regression and ANOVA coefficients of the hypothesized relationships[a, d, f]

	B [SE]	*t*	CI [b]	*F*	df [c]	*R²* [e]
Model 1:				0.825	3, 28	0.081
Gender	-0.094 [0.417]	-0.467	[-1.048 -0.659]			
Business Unit	0.061 [0.053]	0.319	[-0.092 -0.126]			
Education Level	0.244 [0.217]	1.278	[-0.167 -0.721]			
Model 2a:				4.628⁺	4, 27	0.407
Gender	-0.201 [0.346]	-1.204	[-1.126 -0.293]			
Business Unit	0.030 [0.043]	0.194	[-0.081 -0.098]			
Education Level	0.175 [0.178]	1.114	[-0.167 -0.565]			
WD	0.583** [0.152]	3.849	[0.272 -0.894]			
Model 2b:				0.669	4, 27	0.090
Gender	-0.084 [0.424]	-0.408	[-1.044 -0.697]			
Business Unit	0.061 [0.054]	0.312	[-0.094 -0.127]			
Education Level	0.218 [0.227]	1.090	[-0.218 -0.713]			
TA	0.099 [0.193]	0.514	[-0.297 -0.495]			
Model 2c:				3.875*	4, 27	0.365
Gender	-0.125 [0.353]	-0.733	[-0.984 -0.466]			
Business Unit	0.146 [0.045]	0.890	[-0.053 -0.134]			
Education Level	0.090 [0.190]	0.540	[-0.288 -0.493]			
MS	0.558** [0.161]	3.471	[0.228 -0.888]			

	B [SE]	t	CI [b]	F	df [c]	R^2 [e]
Model 2d: Gender Business Unit Education Level RR	-0.197 [-0.197] -0.101 [0.052] 0.158 [0.203] 0.466* [0.189]	-1.040 -0.536 0.883 2.465	[-1.215 -0.398] [-0.135 -0.079] [-0.238 -0.596] [0.078 -0.854]	2.251	4, 27	0.250
Model 3: Gender Business Unit Education Level Composite Org Cond	-0.171 [0.339] 0.007 [0.043] 0.053 [0.184] 0.614** [0.155]	-1.047 0.045 0.330 3.971	[-1.052 -0.341] [-0.087 -0.090] [-0.316 -0.437] [0.297 -0.931]	4.888**	4, 27	0.420

Notes:
[a] $N = 32$.
[b] CI = confidence interval.
[c] df = degrees of freedom.
[d] Dependent variable is composite EMS.
[e] Explained variance as compared to Model 1.
[f] All the variables have been standardized to z-scores (Field, 2013).
* $p < 0.02$.
+ $p < 0.01$.
** $p < 0.005$.

Management support was also found to positively correlate with EMS ($\beta = 0.558$, $p = 0.002$); adding management support to Model 1 explains 28.3 per cent more variance of EMS (Model 2c, $R^2 = 0.365$). Exploring the relationship between rewards and reinforcements and EMS, the relationship is found to be positive and significant as well ($\beta = 0.466$, $p = 0.02$). One employee verifies this relationship by indicating, 'I am mostly driven by monetary rewards, above and beyond my salary'. Interesting here is that the complete model, including the control variables, is not significant ($F = 2.251$, $p = 0.09$), whilst adding rewards and reinforcements to Model 1 increases the explanatory power of the variance by 16.9 per cent ($R^2 = 0.250$).

Despite the evidence from the interviews regarding the impact of time availability, and previous literature highlighting importance of time for innovation and creativity, time availability is not significantly related to EMS in our study, nor did this model explain more variance than the control variables.

To explore the overall effect of organizational conditions, we computed a composite variable of the sub-dimensions of organizational conditions. The analysis provides support for a positive relationship between organizational conditions and EMS (β = 0.614, p < 0.001). When investigating semi-partial correlations, we can understand how strong the relationship between a predictor and the composite of EMS is. Specifically, semi-partial correlations indicate how much a predictor explains the variance of an outcome variable, which is not explained by any other variables in the model. In Model 2a, the semi-partial correlation concerns 0.571; in Model 2b, 0.094; in Model 2c, 0.532; in Model 2d, 0.411; and in Model 3, 0.582. This underlines the marginal relationship between time availability and EMS, explaining why we could not find an effect.

Post Hoc Exploration

To investigate the models and relationships further to better understand the findings, we ran a multiple regression analysis. We included all the variables as separate model steps via a forced entry procedure, starting with Model 1 only including the control variables (Field, 2013); see also Table 9.2 for the specifics of Model 1. The results indicate that our model is a strong predictor of EMS, as compared to mean scores (F = 3.12, p = 0.017). The main contributor to EMS is work discretion: the more organizational conditions we add to the model simultaneously, the more it diminishes the effect of work discretion (that is, in our final model we included all the organizational conditions, resulting in work discretion results of β = 0.397, p = 0.057).

Furthermore, we explored whether the relationship between time availability and organizational conditions is curvilinear, rather than linear. Specifically, we explored whether there is a limit to the time availability condition, and whether an exponential growth of time relates to EMS. We computed a standardized squared variable of the time availability variable and though the curvilinear model explained more variability than the linear model (R = 0.159), the model was non-significant (F = 0.669, p = 0.619). Interestingly, the beta coefficient shows a negative relationship with EMS (β = -0.214), which indicates that more time in an exponential manner, may result in less EMS.

When investigating an inverted U-shape relationship, the results remain non-significant (F = 0.986, p = 0.445) and the beta coefficient remains negative. The combined model of the linear relationship and the curvilinear relationship is tested with an ANOVA and though the model remains non-significant, the F-change increases in significance. The model including the inverted U-shape relationship appears to explain more variability than the linear relationship (R^2 *change* = 0.069). However, when exploring a curve estimation in SPSS, the graphs do not indicate a linear nor a curvilinear regression line.

DISCUSSION

Interpretations and Future Research

In this explorative study, we provide a first indication that organizational conditions can be regarded as important influencers stimulating EMS. EMS seems pervasive throughout an organization, no matter the department, corroborated by employees in the interviews, though nuanced by managers. The nuance is especially interesting to investigate further, as perception seems to play a significant role. With these findings, we believe we extend the work of Shepherd et al. (2010) by investigating employees and managers, as EMS could be useful in multiple departments, basing ourselves on the DCE perspective (Belousova and Gailly, 2013). Our first exploration thus indicates that managers do not differ in EMS from other employees, and future research is advised to take the entire scope of employees into account: just focusing on managers seems not enough. Whilst our study is merely a first exploration with a small sample size, the sample does include multiple employees in a variety of roles from different departments, and we can say for certain that the inclination to focus solely on managers is not comprehensive. We thus propose:

Proposition 1: EMS is pervasive throughout all levels of an organization.

Furthermore, certain elements of organizational conditions, namely work discretion, management support, and rewards and reinforcements, strongly positively relate to EMS in our exploration. Our results thus indicate preliminary evidence that organizational conditions, as indicated by Hornsby et al. (2013), are relevant influencers of EMS; tools to stimulate EMS amongst employees. Whilst earlier research has established the relationship between organizational conditions and entrepreneurial behaviour, we can now further investigate the nuance that there might be more to this relationship, beyond what is known from the literature. We suggest future research to delve deeper into this relationship, across multiple firms, to establish more certainty with regard to the nuanced explanation. We propose the following:

Proposition 2: (a) Work discretion; (b) management support; and (c) rewards and reinforcements positively relate to EMS.

An unexpected yet interesting finding is that time availability does not significantly relate to EMS. The perception of the availability of time is what is essential, according to Hornsby et al. (2013): they describe how employees evaluate and judge their available time regarding room for entrepreneurial initiatives. We see, however, that time availability also does not correlate to other organizational conditions. One explanation could be that the actual experience of time does not outweigh the effect of feeling autonomous, as captured within work discretion. It could be that the feeling of freedom, given either in time or in another way, is far more fundamental than the factual time aspect, as is captured in time availability; whereas the feeling of autonomy and responsibility indicates that one needs to make time for it. Possibly, by structurally separating these dimensions in different types of questions, the effect of time availability is diminished.

We theorize that time availability might not serve as a single predicting variable, but rather interacts with other variables when influencing EMS, thus serving as a boundary condition. Goodale et al. (2011) have indicated that it is sensible to investigate interactions and moderating relationships when it comes to the organizational conditions, as they do not always necessarily serve as antecedents of innovation and entrepreneurship. Moreover, Hornsby et al. (2009) argue that time availability might be role-dependent. They investigated whether the number of entrepreneurial ideas increases with more time availability. They found that the number of ideas implemented decreased at a faster rate for line managers as compared to senior managers. The organization that participated in the current research has a flat structure, with only one layer of management. Therefore, we recommend that the interaction with organizational roles should be investigated in a larger, more hierarchical organization and compared to the current findings. We propose the following:

Proposition 2d: Time availability relates positively to EMS, under the boundary condition of work discretion.

Proposition 3: Time availability interacts with hierarchical roles in relationship to EMS.

Lastly, Ireland et al. (2009) argue that there is a reciprocal relationship between the entrepreneurial architecture composed of organizational conditions, and the commencement of entrepreneurial initiatives. Moreover, Hornsby et al. (2013) have calculated that organizational conditions significantly correlate with the aggregated entrepreneurial behaviours within an organization (see also Ireland et al., 2009). We believe that if organizational conditions significantly relate to the aggregated entrepreneurial behaviour of employees, it is sensible to believe that organizational conditions relate similarly significantly to individual entrepreneurial behaviours.

Moreover, Kuratko et al. (2014) investigate the same organizational conditions and conclude that the perception of the conditions is what relates to entrepreneurial initiatives. Specifically, Kuratko et al. (2014) describe the perception of managers as willingness and ability, similar to the definition of EMS (Shepherd et al., 2010), relating to entrepreneurial initiatives. Building on the work of Kuratko et al. (2014) and Hornsby et al. (2013), and our case findings, we propose that:

Proposition 4: The composite of organizational conditions relates positively to EMS.

PRACTICAL IMPLICATIONS

Our results provide insight in useful tools that an organization can utilize to stimulate employees' EMS. As work discretion is the most influential condition stimulating EMS, organizations can provide employees with more space for responsibility and freedom to make their own choices. Thinking back to the Hewlett Packard example, employees were given the freedom to work on an entrepreneurial initiative next to their daily jobs, and this turned out to be successful.

On the other hand, our results indicate that focusing on time availability might not be useful. Whereas many organizations, such as Google, attempt to stimulate entrepreneurial initiatives by allocating specific hours to 'developing entrepreneurial ideas', this may not be as fruitful for the employees' EMS, and could potentially explain why Holt et al. (2007) found no relationship between time availability and CE.

LIMITATIONS

Though we recognize the contributions and benefits of this chapter, we acknowledge that it has limitations. We draw cross-sectional, relational conclusions of the results and therefore interpret causality with caution, resulting in propositions. Our aim was to describe and analyze a population, as well as investigate differences between a subset of the population, and for this aim, a cross-sectional approach is appropriate (Pinsonneault and Kraemer, 1993). Nevertheless, the fact that the survey has been distributed at only one point in time limits the generalizability of the findings of the chapter, and future research should build on our findings to investigate the directionality and causality of the relationships.

Furthermore, although our findings are supported and extended by interviews, the combination of the survey and interviews only gives a static first indication of the relationship between organizational conditions and EMS. Whilst this first exploration is necessary, for reasons explicated, it is advisable for future research to investigate the dynamic relationship and development of EMS. After all, as some interviewees indicated, entrepreneurship is not always necessary in every job every day, and it might thus be susceptible to changes over time and context. As the aim for the current research was to deepen the understanding of the relationship between organizational conditions and EMS, such a contribution is incredibly interesting but beyond the scope of the present research, and thus a topic for future research to address.

Lastly, this study works with a representative but small sample, which is why we have chosen not to dissect EMS into the multiple facets that it consists of. We strongly suggest future research to investigate larger samples and multiple organizations, not only to verify our results but also to delve deeper into dissecting EMS in its proposed segments. To contribute to existing research, future research could in fact extend the current usage of the IAO scale, which currently seems the most appropriate measure for EMS, by investigating the multiple aspects of EMS. Whilst our research strongly argues for a relationship, a better understanding of this relationship could provide research and organizations with more hands-on tools to establish CE.

REFERENCES

Belousova, O. and B. Gailly (2013), 'Corporate entrepreneurship in a dispersed setting: Actors, behaviors, and process', *International Entrepreneurship and Management Journal*, **9**(3), 361–377.

Birkinshaw, J. (1997), 'Entrepreneurship in multinational corporations: The characteristics of subsidiary initiatives', *Strategic Management Journal*, **1**, 207–229.

Campos, F., M. Frese, M. Goldstein, L. Iacovone, H. Johnson, et al. (2017), 'Teaching personal initiative beats traditional training in boosting small business in West Africa', *Science*, **357**(6357), 1287–1290.

Cote, J. and M. Buckley (1988), 'Measurement error and theory testing in consumer research: An illustration of the importance of construct validation', *Journal of Consumer Research*, **14**(4), 579–582.

Covin, J. and D. Slevin (1991), 'A conceptual model of entrepreneurship as firm behavior', *Entrepreneurship Theory and Practice*, **16**(1), 7–26.

Culkin, N. and S. Mallick (2011), 'Producing work-ready graduates: The role of the entrepreneurial university', *International Journal of Market Research*, **53**(3), 347–368.

Davidsson, P. (2009), *The Entrepreneurship Research Challenge*, 1st edn, Cheltenham, UK and Northampton, MA, USA: Edward Elgar Publishing.

Field, A. (2013), *Discovering Statistics Using IBM SPSS Statistics*, 5th edn, London: SAGE Publications.

Gartner, W. (1988), '"Who is an entrepreneur?" is the wrong question', *American Journal of Small Business*, **12**(4), 11–32.

Goodale, J., D. Kuratko, J. Hornsby and J. Covin (2011), 'Operations management and corporate entrepreneurship: The moderating effect of operations control on the antecedents of corporate entrepreneurial activity in relation to innovation performance', *Journal of Operations Management*, **29**(1–2), 116–127.

Haynie, J., D. Shepherd, E. Mosakowski and P. Earley (2010), 'A situated metacog-nitive model of the entrepreneurial mindset', *Journal of Business Venturing*, **25**(2), 217–229.
Hisrich, R. and V. Ramadani (eds) (2017), *Effective Entrepreneurial Management*, 1st edn, Cham: Springer.
Holt, D.T., M.W. Rutherford and G.R. Clohessy (2007), 'Corporate entrepreneurship: An empirical look at individual characteristics, context, and process', *Journal of Leadership and Organizational Studies*, **13**(4), 40–54.
Hornsby, J., D. Kuratko, D. Holt and W. Wales (2013), 'Assessing a measurement of organizational preparedness for corporate entrepreneurship', *Journal of Product Innovation Management*, **30**(5), 937–955.
Hornsby, J., D. Kuratko, D. Shepherd and J. Bott (2009), 'Managers' corporate entrepreneurial actions: Examining perception and position', *Journal of Business Venturing*, **24**(3), 236–247.
Ireland, R., J. Covin and D. Kuratko (2009), 'Conceptualizing corporate entrepreneur-ship strategy', *Entrepreneurship Theory and Practice*, **33**(1), 19–46.
Ireland, R., M. Hitt and D. Sirmon (2003), 'A model of strategic entrepreneurship: The construct and its dimensions', *Journal of Management*, **29**(6), 963–989.
Kuratko, D., J. Hornsby and J. Covin (2014), 'Diagnosing a firm's internal environment for corporate entrepreneurship', *Business Horizons*, **57**(1), 37–47.
Kuratko, D., R. Ireland, J. Covin and J. Hornsby (2005), 'A model of middle-level managers' entrepreneurial behavior', *Entrepreneurship Theory and Practice*, **29**(6), 699–716.
Kuratko, D., J. McMullen, J. Hornsby and C. Jackson (2017), 'Is your organization conducive to the continuous creation of social value? Toward a social corporate entrepreneurship scale', *Business Horizons*, **60**(3), 271–283.
Kuratko, D., R. Montagno and J. Hornsby (1990), 'Developing an intrapreneurial assessment instrument for an effective corporate entrepreneurial environment', *Strategic Management Journal*, **11**, 49–58.
Kyrgidou, L. and E. Petridou (2011), 'The effect of competence exploration and competence exploitation on strategic entrepreneurship', *Technology Analysis and Strategic Management*, **23**(6), 697–713.
Laalo, H. and J. Heinonen (2016), 'Governing the entrepreneurial mindset: Business students' constructions of entrepreneurial subjectivity', *European Educational Research Journal*, **15**(6), 696–713.
Makimurto-Koivumaa, S. and P. Belt (2016), 'About, for, in or through entrepreneur-ship in engineering education', *European Journal of Engineering Education*, **41**(5), 512–529.
McGrath, R. and I.C. MacMillan (2000), *The Entrepreneurial Mindset: Strategies for Continuously Creating Opportunity in an Age of Uncertainty*, Cambridge, MA: Harvard Business Press.
McMullen, J. and A. Kier (2016), 'Trapped by the entrepreneurial mindset: Opportunity seeking and escalation of commitment in the mount everest disaster', *Journal of Business Venturing*, **31**(6), 663–686.
McMullen, J. and D. Shepherd (2006), 'Entrepreneurial action and the role of uncer-tainty in the theory of the entrepreneur', *Academy of Management Review*, **31**(1), 132–152.
Mitchell, G. (2007), 'Instill the entrepreneurial mindset', *Research-Technology Management*, **50**(6), 11–13.
Noble, C. (2015), 'Mindsets, mind sets and mind sense', *Prometheus*, **33**(4), 411–420.

Patel, S. and K. Mehta (2016), 'Systems, design, and entrepreneurial thinking: Comparative frameworks', *Systemic Practice and Action Research*, **30**(5), 515–533.

Pinsonneault, A. and K. Kraemer (1993), 'Survey research methodology in management information systems: An assessment', *Journal of Management Information Systems*, **10**(2), 75–105.

Podsakoff, P., S. MacKenzie, J. Lee and N. Podsakoff (2003), 'Common method biases in behavioral research: A critical review of the literature and recommended remedies', *Journal of Applied Psychology*, **88**(5), 879–903.

Robinson, P., D. Stimpson, J. Huefner and H. Hunt (1991), 'An attitude approach to the prediction of entrepreneurship', *Entrepreneurship Theory and Practice*, **15**(4), 13–31.

Robinson, S., H. Neergaard, L. Tanggaard and N. Krueger (2016), 'New horizons in entrepreneurship: From teacher-led to student-centered learning', *Education and Training*, **58**(7–8), 661–683.

Shams, S. and H. Kaufmann (2016), 'Entrepreneurial co-creation: A research vision to be materialised', *Management Decision*, **54**(6), 1250–1268.

Sharma, P. and S.J.J. Chrisman (1999), 'Toward a reconciliation of the definitional issues in the field of corporate entrepreneurship', *Entrepreneurship: Theory and Practice*, **23**(3), 11–27.

Shepherd, D. and H. Patzelt (2018), *Entrepreneurial Cognition: Exploring the Mindset of Entrepreneurs*, 1st edn, Cham: Palgrave Macmillan.

Shepherd, D., H. Patzelt and J. Haynie (2010), 'Entrepreneurial spirals: Deviation-amplifying loops of an entrepreneurial mindset and organizational culture', *Entrepreneurship Theory and Practice*, **34**(1), 59–82.

Shetty, P. (2004), 'Attitude towards entrepreneurship in organisations', *Journal of Entrepreneurship*, **13**(1), 53–68.

Smith, J., J. Mitchell and R. Mitchell (2009), 'Entrepreneurial scripts and the new transaction commitment mindset: Extending the expert information processing theory approach to entrepreneurial cognition research', *Entrepreneurship Theory and Practice*, **33**(4), 815–844.

Studenmund, A. and J. Cassidy (1987), *Using Econometrics: A Practical Guide*, Boston, MA: Little Brown & Company.

Winkler, J., D.E. Kanouse and J. Ware (1982), 'Controlling for acquiescence response set in scale development', *Journal of Applied Psychology*, **67**(5), 555–561.

Wright, M. (2001), 'Creating and growing wealth: Sue Birley on entrepreneurship and wealth creation', *Academy of Management Executive*, **15**(1), 37–39.

10. Growth of social and commercial SMEs: a comparative study

Annu Kotiranta, Saila Tykkyläinen and Kaisu Puumalainen

INTRODUCTION

The global economic crisis of 2008 accelerated discussion within the European political front on social enterprises' potential to contribute to solving prevalent societal and environmental challenges, such as social exclusion and climate change (Bacq and Janssen, 2011; Doherty et al., 2014; European Commission, 2011). Social enterprises are seen by politicians and academics to play a part in developing more resilient economies and creating inclusive growth (European Commission, 2015; European Commission and OECD, 2016). However, social enterprises must continue to grow in order to match the scope of these problems (Martin and Osberg, 2007).

In spite of the hype, there are few empirical studies that have assessed whether social enterprises are able to live up to these expectations. Case studies and conceptual papers have dominated the research on social enterprise growth, whereas work to test the hypotheses and propositions derived from theories is largely missing (Bacq and Janssen, 2011; Doherty et al., 2014; Lepoutre et al., 2013). It is a difficult task, for social enterprises are heterogeneous in nature, and the research has recognized a wide array of social enterprises. This variety is likely to be reflected in their growth paths as well. What connects all social enterprises is the co-existence of financial and social missions (Bacq and Janssen, 2011; Defourny and Nyssens, 2017).

The purpose of this chapter is to investigate whether social enterprises can act as a balancing force during economic downturns by generating jobs and tax revenue. The theoretical points of departure are derived from research on small firm growth that contributes to the design of a theoretically sound approach to studying growth trajectories. Social enterprise researchers have been inclined to stress the scaling of social innovations and social impact at the expense of organizational growth. However, understanding the outcomes of growth requires knowledge on the determinants of growth and the qualitative differences in firms' growth trajectories, as they are known to influence the outcomes of growth (Davidsson et al., 2010). To overcome some of the problems in previous studies, here, growth is operationalized with multiple dependent variables, the evolution of which is followed over time. The research gaps are addressed by employing a comparative research design, rigorous quantitative methods and financial data from Finnish small and medium-sized enterprises (SMEs) and social enterprises. Even though Finnish social enterprises are heterogeneous in terms of firm demographic factors, they are highly dependent on market logics and thus form a special type of social enterprise population.

The results indicate that social enterprises are resilient: during the economic recession of 2010–15, they were able to grow more quickly than their commercial counterparts in terms of employment, sales, assets and asset turnover. In economic booms, their growth pace was comparatively slower, and in the long term, the diverging growth trajectories reset each other, resulting in similar growth paces. This study contributes to the social enterprise research by providing new evidence on social enterprises' organizational growth over time. In addition, it demonstrates that borrowing proven theories from firm growth research helps to complement our understanding of social enterprise growth.

SOCIAL ENTERPRISE GROWTH: UNIQUE OR NOT?

Social Enterprise Definition

The concept of social enterprise is fluid and multidimensional. Most often, social enterprises are painted as hybrid organizations combining interests and operational logics from the private sector with those of the public and/or non-profit sectors (Bacq and Janssen, 2011; Doherty et al., 2014). The research field has produced a range of typologies aiming to describe the central dimensions along which different types of social enterprises are situated. Most of the definitions share the requirements of parallel financial and social missions, but the relative weight of the missions varies (Defourny and Nyssens, 2017; Saebi et al., 2019). In addition, the roles, organizational forms and resource bases available to social enterprises vary by region (Bacq and Janssen, 2011; Defourny and Nyssens, 2010).

This study defines social enterprises by following the three dimensions that the European Union (EU) has established. First, social enterprises need to be entrepreneurial organizations and engage in continuous activity of production and/or the exchange of goods and/or services. Second, the social dimension stipulates that social enterprises must have an explicit and primary social aim benefiting society. The priority of the social aim is ensured by limited profit distribution to the owners. Third, the governance dimension is translated as independence from state and private enterprises and participatory governance and/or democratic decision-making processes (European Commission, 2015, pp. 9–11).

The Finnish social enterprise model is assessed as being compatible with the EU criteria. Although there exists heterogeneity vis-à-vis firm demographics and the origins of social enterprises, Finnish social enterprises are some of the most market-oriented in Europe. They are expected to derive the majority of their revenues from markets and cannot rely on voluntary work because they should operate side-by-side with other businesses (Kostilainen and Pättiniemi, 2016; Russell et al., 2014). In this regard, they represent a specific type of social enterprise population.

Social Enterprise Growth

The primary aim of social enterprise growth is to magnify organizations' social impact and contribute to social change rather than to gain a competitive economic advantage (Austin et al., 2006; Dees et al., 2004; Martin and Osberg, 2007). Consequently, in general, the growth of social enterprises is often framed as a unique phenomenon and is distanced from firm growth. This perspective is reflected by the ongoing debate concerning the use of the terms 'scaling' and 'growth'. Some researchers state that social enterprise growth should be conceptualized as the scaling of innovations and impact rather than growth, which bears connotations with organizational growth and financial outcomes that are irrelevant in the social enterprise context (André and Pache, 2014; Dees et al., 2004; Lyon and Fernandez, 2012).

One of the biggest paradoxes within the social enterprise research relates to the outcomes of growth. Although social enterprise growth is predominantly seen as an intermediary process aimed at producing firm-external outcomes, the outcomes of growth are not proven. The drawback applies to both financial and social outcomes. One hindrance is caused by the difficulty of measuring social impact. As for financial indicators of growth, advancements in small firm growth research could prove beneficial if applied to social enterprises. However, the advancements are not utilized, perhaps due to the gap between these two bodies of research, as well as the positive bias within the social enterprise growth literature. Social enterprise growth scholarship is focused on positive social values and success recipes at the expense of investigating, for instance, risks and barriers to growth. Moreover, there are social enterprises whose impact is reliant on the volume of their business (Hynes, 2009; Davies et al., 2018). It appears that especially the social enterprises that are more dependent on markets are in danger of being neglected by researchers.

Uncovering organizational performance and differences among social enterprise populations requires broad datasets and robust statistical analysis. The lack of these hinders efforts to locate determinants, establish cause-and-effect relations and use statistical analysis (Bacq and Janssen, 2011; Lepoutre et al., 2013; Doherty et al., 2014). To the best of the present researchers' knowledge, the studies by Bacq et al. (2013) and Gimmon and Spiro (2013) are the only quantitative studies published in peer-reviewed journals that investigate social enterprise growth using a comparative setting. However, neither of these uses financial data; instead, they rely on informants' assessments of past growth performance or their future expectations. Thus, both the objectivity and the variety of growth measures, as well as controlling for a broader range of independent variables, could be improved.

Furthermore, the studies on small firm growth have established that the operational environment significantly influences firms' growth performance, but researchers do not address this in their work on social enterprises (Davidsson et al., 2010; Wiklund et al., 2009). The closest the field has come concerning social enterprises' performance in economic downturns is a study by Molina et al. (2018). They found that social enterprise creation in Catalonia was fuelled by the economic crisis that began in 2008.

In this study, commercial and social SMEs are compared in order to scrutinize the uniqueness assumption. Based on previous studies, social enterprises have distinctive features that may influence their growth. To begin with, social enterprises' willingness to grow is unclear: as hybrid organizations pursuing multiple and sometimes contradictory goals, they are subjected to a variety of external and internal tensions. Growth may expose social enterprise leaders to situations in which they have to choose whether to promote their firms' financial or social goals (Battilana and Lee, 2014; Smith et al., 2013). Vickers and Lyon (2014) reported that social enterprises can be reluctant to make compromises and form the partnerships necessary to acquire resources for growth. Social enterprises prioritize organizational survival and the sustainability of their social mission over financial growth, rendering them more risk-averse than their commercial counterparts (Bacq et al., 2013; Lumpkin et al., 2013; Weerawardena and Sullivan Mort, 2006).

Besides risk aversion, another feature exerting influence over social enterprise growth is the importance of beneficiaries and multiple stakeholders. Stakeholders broaden the resource base available for social enterprises if they agree on the attractiveness of opportunities that social enterprises recognize. If alignment is not reached, social enterprises may not be able to mobilize the necessary resources (Austin et al., 2006; Lumpkin et al., 2013). Reaching consent is a double-edged sword, for goal alignment with various constituencies is a difficult task and may compromise social enterprises' autonomy and flexibility (Lumpkin et al., 2013; Margiono et al., 2018).

To conclude, in spite of the compelling success stories of social enterprises that managed to scale their social impact (Austin et al., 2006), convincing evidence on the large-scale effects of social enterprise growth is still missing.

To narrow this research gap, this study combines the theoretical insights on SMEs' growth performance with the findings from social enterprise growth research to form hypotheses.

THEORETICAL BACKGROUND AND HYPOTHESES

Determinants of Growth in Small and Medium-Sized Enterprises

The vast body of literature on firm growth is fragmented, and divided into two sometimes intersecting streams (Anyadike-Danes and Hart, 2018; Shepherd and Wiklund, 2009; Cowling et al., 2018). The first, the 'economist' stream, originates from Gibrat's (1931) proposition that a firm's proportional growth rate at any given period is independent from its original size. This stream mainly uses very large longitudinal samples to form empirical generalizations about the effects of directly observable characteristics such as size, age and financial slack, or firm-external factors such as economic cycles.

The other stream, 'managerial', is predominantly based on Penrose's (1959) theory of firm growth or Barney's (1991) resource-based view; it is more focused on firms' internal characteristics as determinants of growth. It seems to be more theory-driven, focusing on resources and capabilities that are harder to operationalize. While the economist stream can shed light on the growth trajectories of SMEs during different macroeconomic cycles, the management stream can help to build theory on the differences in growth patterns between social enterprises and commercial SMEs.

The reviews of small enterprise growth research by Davidsson et al. (2010) and the integrative model for small firm growth by Wiklund et al. (2009) summarize the determinants of growth, the main categories of which are growth attitudes, resources, strategy, structure and environment. These dimensions are now discussed in more detail.

The Penrosean view of growth is built on the function of entrepreneurial and managerial capabilities. Human capital is among the most relevant resources required to enable growth. Macpherson and Holt (2007) systematically reviewed 113 studies and concluded that the research on human capital supports this view. Financial capital, especially the lack of it among small businesses, has been established as a critical factor restricting growth (Wiklund et al., 2009). Nason and Wiklund (2018) conducted an explicit test of the resource-related theories of firm growth. Their meta-analysis of 113 studies found that valuable and versatile resources, such as financial capital, are positively related to growth. Further, they reported that inimitable resources, usually framed as a key component of firms' competitive advantage, were negatively related to growth. It is likely that the importance of resource versatility is highlighted even more in the context of financial crises and small firms.

Several studies have examined the effects of slack resources on firm survival and growth. Slack resources are supposed to have a positive effect, creating a buffer between firms and adverse economic conditions and enabling managers to put resources to more productive use (Penrose, 1959) to facilitate firm growth. The positive effect of slack has gained some empirical support (Bradley et al., 2011; Canarella and Miller, 2018); however, opposite findings have also been reported (Tognazzo et al., 2016).

Recent empirical evidence has emerged that human capital, entrepreneurial experience and access to finance did not significantly influence SME employment growth immediately after the global recession from 2008 to 2009 (Cowling et al., 2018). Only later in the recovery period did external finance have a positive impact on job creation. Growth orientation was a significant determinant of growth in the context of the financial crisis.

Lastly, the strategic growth determinants that were most prominent in the literature were innovation (Audretsch et al., 2014; McKelvie et al., 2017) and entrepreneurial orientation (Lumpkin and Dess, 1996), both of which had a positive impact on growth and were mostly supported by empirical evidence.

In sum, in order to grow, small-firm entrepreneurs must be growth-oriented, have valuable and versatile resources that enable growth, have a strategy that fosters growth, embrace flexible structures and operate in an environment that is conducive to growth. The following section discusses how these characteristics could manifest among social and commercial enterprises over economic cycles, impacting upon their growth patterns.

Hypotheses

The hypotheses for this study are derived from the preceding literature reviews on social enterprise growth and firm growth. The central factors of social enterprise growth are introduced, and the effects of these factors during different economic cycles are theorized. Inspired by Penrose (1959), the factors are classified as either entrepreneurial or managerial capabilities and resources.

Entrepreneurial and managerial capabilities
The importance of social mission
This is thought to cause social enterprises to avoid financial risks and to lessen their competitive aggressiveness, for the survival of the organization and its social mission takes precedence over maximizing financial gains (Lumpkin et al., 2013; Weerawardena and Sullivan Mort, 2006; Vickers and Lyon, 2014). On the one hand, settling for modest financial performance and less growth orientation (Bacq et al., 2013) may backfire in economic booms if social enterprises decline financially lucrative opportunities for fear of compromising their social mission. On the other hand, guaranteeing survival and striving

to serve their social cause may strengthen social enterprises' stamina during economic downturns.

Ownership structure and decision-making
The majority of Finnish social enterprises are collectively owned and operated (Russell et al., 2014; Kostilainen and Pättiniemi, 2016), whereas commercial enterprises tend to have more centralized decision-making that provides them with the flexibility to quickly grasp growth opportunities during economic upturns (Gilbert et al., 2006). Collective management and the importance of stakeholder networks have been interpreted as diminishing social enterprises' autonomy and causing friction in their operations. Reaching goal alignment with a broad range of actors is a demanding task (Lumpkin et al., 2013; Margiono et al., 2018; Tracey and Jarvis, 2007). Again, these dynamics may slow social enterprises down in terms of reacting to growth opportunities.

The nature of opportunities
Social enterprises are typically drawn to opportunities stemming from social needs, the features of which include prevalence, urgency and radicalness, among others. These characteristics can compromise the opportunities' financial potential (Austin et al., 2006; Zahra et al., 2008). Hence, social enterprises operate within Penrose's (1959) 'interstices': less promising niches that are not interesting to commercial enterprises, especially in economic upturns when growing markets offer more easily exploitable opportunities. During crises, however, there are less financially lucrative opportunities, and opportunities based on prevalent and urgent social needs and/or market failures are highlighted (Austin et al., 2006; Zahra et al., 2008).

Resources
Broad stakeholder networks
Even though dependence on stakeholders may slow social enterprises down, it can nonetheless grant them access to a broader resource base (Austin et al., 2006; Lumpkin et al., 2013). Therefore, in recessions, when all types of companies suffer from a scarcity of resources, social enterprises may be able to improve their relative situations against conventional enterprises.

Terms of employment
Austin et al. (2006) maintain that social ventures cannot compete with wage levels on conventional enterprises, but because of their social mission, they are able to appeal to employees motivated by things other than money. Thus, employees' readiness to work for lower wages while maintaining their firm's productivity may give social enterprises the advantage of a flexible cost structure in economic downturns.

As a result of the aforementioned considerations, the following hypotheses were formulated:

H1: In economic cycle upturns, social enterprises grow more slowly than their commercial counterparts.

H2: In economic cycle downturns, social enterprises grow more quickly than their commercial counterparts.

METHOD

Sample and Data Collection

The year range of 2003–15 was selected as the time frame for the study. During this period, Finland experienced one of its history's best and worst economic turns. From 2003 to 2008, the economy boomed, and the annual average gross domestic product (GDP) growth was greater than 3 per cent. In 2009, the global economic crisis severely hit the open economy, and the GDP plummeted by as much as -8.3 per cent in a single year. In the following years, from 2010 to 2015, the economy struggled: the annual GDP growth rate was only 0.5 per cent on average. The following analysis uses the boom period of 2003–2008, the stagnation period of 2010–2015 and the whole time frame of 2003–2015 to analyse social enterprises' different growth paths during these economic cycles.

In order to take a closer look at young SMEs (less than ten years old), an additional dataset was created for the stagnation period of 2010–2015. This study utilizes a combination of three datasets: original survey data, a list of officially registered social enterprises in Finland, and companies' demographic information from Statistics Finland.

This study used an Internet survey conducted from February to March 2015 to differentiate social enterprises from commercial enterprises. The survey was sent out to the chief executive officers of all Finnish companies that employed at least one person and had an e-mail address (33 390 companies in total). Altogether, 6268 companies replied to at least some of the survey questions, resulting in a response rate of 18.8 per cent. The basic demographics of the survey sample were compared to the corresponding total company population in terms of employment and industry composition. The sample represented the overall characteristics of Finnish companies well, and the risk of non-response bias was thus diminished.

Social enterprises were identified from the pool of survey respondents with a commonly used self-recognition method. The screening question, 'Does your company use most of its profits to enhance some social mission?', was used to identify social enterprises. Although not optimal, screening questions based on self-recognition are often used to locate social enterprises for comparative studies utilizing large datasets such as the Global Entrepreneurship Monitor (GEM) (Bacq et al., 2013; Molina et al., 2018) or the Panel Study of Entrepreneurial Dynamics II (PSED II) (Gras and Lumpkin, 2012). Despite being a single question, this screening question captures three of the most distinguishing characteristics of a social enterprise: the existence of a social mission, trading for profit and reinvesting most of the profits.

The social enterprise sample was enlarged and strengthened using a list of third-party-verified social enterprises in Finland (105 social enterprises in total). This comprised enterprises given the Finnish Social Enterprise Mark and/or that contained members of an interest organization for Finnish social enterprises called ARVO. The sample was increased to alleviate potential bias due to self-recognition screening and to include market-oriented non-profits. Exclusion of large companies from the dataset resulted in a final company list of 4151 SMEs, 418 of which were labelled as social enterprises. Finally, the company list was matched with the data on company demographics and financial information on the companies' bottom lines from 2003 to 2015 (retrieved from Statistics Finland's company register).

Measurement of Growth

The measures of growth were selected based on earlier literature on small firm growth. There is plenty of evidence supporting the use of multiple indicators, as the correlations between different dimensions of growth have been found to be rather low (Shepherd and Wiklund, 2009). Furthermore, the determinants of growth might have different effects on different dimensions, as the firm more directly controls the growth dimensions of employment and assets, whereas the dimensions of sales and valuation are generated by the firm but are determined by the external market conditions to a much larger extent (Nason and Wiklund, 2018).

Five different measures of growth were used in the analysis: growth of employment, sales, total assets, sales per total assets and value added per employee. Growth percentages were calculated for the three time periods as follows:

Growth of variable X for company i in period t1 to t2 = $((X_{it2}/X_{it1})-1) * 100$

Each of the growth variables was treated for possible outliers by forcing the top and bottom 2.5 per cent observations into the 2.5th or 97.5th percentiles, respectively.

Matching and Analysis Methods

To control for the effects of the basic characteristics that may affect growth, the comparison of commercial and social SMEs was conducted with the coarsened exact matching (CEM) method created by Iacus et al. (2011, 2012). In the matching process, each social enterprise (treated) was paired with a commercial enterprise (control) that was, apart from the social mission, similar to the social enterprise in terms of the selected matching criteria. The matching criteria included several fundamental characteristics that are known to potentially have an impact on a company's growth. The matching criteria included company size in terms of employment (number of employees) and sales (euros per year), ownership (domestic and private owner 1/0), company age (years) and industry classification (14 industries, 1/0) in the first year of the time period. The cut points of the continuous explanatory variables (number of employees, sales and company age) were defined by the default binning algorithm Sturges' rule.

In the matching procedure, the data were temporarily coarsened; exact matching was conducted with coarsened data. According to Iacus et al. (2011), CEM produces matching solutions that are better balanced, and estimates of the causal quantity of interest that have lower root mean square errors than traditional matching methods, such as those based on propensity scores, Mahalanobis distance, nearest neighbours or optimal matching. CEM for STATA15 was used for matching in the present study.

Two matched datasets were created: (1) companies that had operated throughout the period of 2003–15; and (2) companies that were less than ten years old (that is, 'young' companies) that had existed during 2010–15. The first dataset included 216 matched company pairs for 2003–15; the second dataset included 97 matched young company pairs for 2010–15.

The goodness-of-fit of the matching was tested using Wilcoxon–Mann–Whitney tests for the continuous variables (number of employees, sales and company age). No systematic differences in the matched samples were found. For the group variables (industry classification and ownership), Pearson's chi-squared was used to ensure that the statistically significant differences of the unmatched groups of companies vanished in the matching process. The results suggest that the matched commercial enterprises are similar to the social enterprises in the sample.

RESULTS

First, the level and development of the five growth measures over time were surveyed, and the differences in the average growth percentages between commercial and social enterprises were tested. Then, regression was presented to see whether the initial observations held. Matched pairs of young companies from 2010 to 2015 were investigated. However, the results had small statistical robustness; thus, the findings concerning young enterprises have been omitted to create space to discuss the significant results.

Descriptives

All three volume measures of growth – sales, employment and assets – yielded similar patterns: the commercial firms grew at a faster rate during the economic boom in 2003–08, whereas the social enterprises outperformed them during the recession in 2010–15 following the global financial crisis. Looking at the whole period, the differences evened out. Growth in employment was slower than growth in sales and assets during all the periods of interest.

Table 10.1 depicts the total average growth rates and the compound annual growth rates (CAGRs) for all five measures of growth. When looking at the

Table 10.1   Average growth percentages in the matched samples

Period	Growth dimension	Social enterprises (N = 179–211)		Commercial enterprises (N = 180–214)		T-test
		Total (%)	CAGR (%)	Total (%)	CAGR (%)	p
2003–15	Employment	107.8	5.8	115.4	6.1	0.789
	Sales	158.1	7.6	167.8	7.9	0.833
	Total assets	166.2	7.8	181.1	8.3	0.724
	Assets turnover	12.1	0.9	6.6	0.5	0.544
	Labour productivity	39.8	2.6	18.3	1.3	0.037**
2003–08	Employment	37.9	5.5	77.8	10.1	0.006***
	Sales	85.9	10.9	112.5	13.4	0.321
	Total assets	70.6	9.3	116.7	13.8	0.026**
	Assets turnover	13	2.1	11.8	1.9	0.880
	Labour productivity	37	5.4	28.3	4.2	0.417
2010–15	Employment	24.1	3.7	6.1	1.0	0.027**
	Sales	38.4	5.6	9.3	1.5	0.001***
	Total assets	36.1	5.3	19	2.9	0.044**
	Assets turnover	17.1	2.7	0.5	0.1	0.011**
	Labour productivity	13.9	2.2	13.5	2.1	0.959

Notes: + p < 0.15, * p < 0.1, ** p < 0.05, *** p < 0.01. OLS regression with heteroscedasticity consistent standard errors.

development of employment and sales in social and commercial enterprises, 2009 seemed to be a turning point: while social enterprises kept on growing, the growth of commercial enterprises stagnated (the CAGR of employment was 1 per cent, and of sales it was 1.5 per cent). Social enterprises also seemed to have more resilience in terms of total assets during economic turmoil than their commercial counterparts. Overall, the social enterprises' assets were larger than those of the commercial enterprises during the whole period, but the visualization in Figure 10.1 reveals a drastic dip in 2008. Nonetheless, the social enterprises recovered fast despite bumpy growth in the later period.

Moreover, labour productivity and the sales per assets ratio were used as measures to describe how efficiently the firms deployed their resources in generating revenues. Interestingly, the social enterprises had somewhat higher labour productivity than the commercial firms. The social enterprises were also able to improve their productivity from 2003 to 2015 to a greater extent than the commercial firms, although the increase was minor. The differences were not statistically significant when examining the sub-periods before and after the financial crisis. In contrast to the other measures, the asset turnover of both company groups had hardly grown at all.

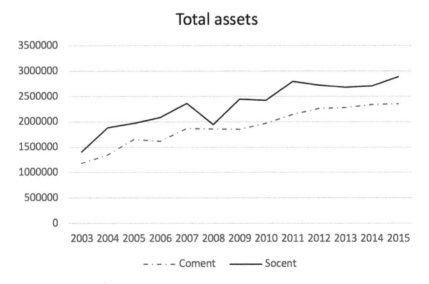

Figure 10.1   Growth of total assets in commercial enterprises (Coment) and social enterprises (Socent)

Regression Analysis

To find out whether the initial findings hold, ordinary least squares (OLS) regression was conducted, where companies' societal motives were separately tested for each growth measure and period. OLS was conducted for the matched company samples, where the basic company demographics (number of employees, sales, ownership, company age and industry classification) were used as the matching criteria. Although testing for the goodness of fit for the matching revealed that there were no statistically significant differences between the two groups in terms of basic company demographics, the companies' first-year employment was included in the analysis as a control variable to improve the robustness of the results. The OLS regressions were run with STATA15 using robust standard errors.

The regression results presented in Table 10.2 confirmed the initial hypothesis: social enterprises' growth was countercyclical, which resulted in com-

Table 10.2   Key results of the OLS regressions

Time frame	Dependent variable	b	P >|t|
2003–15	Employment growth	-5,1	0,857
	Sales growth	-7,5	0,870
	Total assets growth	-12,3	0,769
	Sales per assets growth	5,8	0,525
	Labour productivity growth	21,3	0,039**
2003–08	Employment growth	-38,3	0,007***
	Sales growth	-25,6	0,338
	Total assets growth	-45,0	0,028**
	Sales per assets growth	1,3	0,861
	Labour productivity growth	8,4	0,432
2010–15	Employment growth	18,2	0,025**
	Sales growth	29,5	0,001***
	Total assets growth	17,5	0,038**
	Sales per assets growth	16,8	0,011**
	Labour productivity growth	0,7	0,917
2010–15, young companies	Employment growth	31,4	0,137+
	Sales growth	29,4	0,252
	Total assets growth	12,2	0,593
	Sales per assets growth	22,5	0,146+
	Labour productivity growth	-19,5	0,127+

Notes: + p < 0.15, * p < 0.1, ** p < 0.05, *** p < 0.01. OLS regression with heteroscedasticity consistent standard errors.

paratively faster growth in difficult economic times and, respectively, slower growth during economic prosperity. The differences were statistically significant. Over the economic cycles, these two contrary effects offset one other, and there were very few differences in the growth of the social and commercial enterprises in the long term. Accordingly, there were very few statistically significant differences in the growth of social and commercial companies in the total time frame of 2003–2015. Though not statistically significant, the coefficients for the social enterprises' employment, sales and total asset growth were negative for all three indicators. In terms of labour productivity, the social enterprises managed to improve their competitiveness relative to the commercial enterprises (the difference was statistically significant).

Robustness of the Results

The primary analysis was conducted using one-to-one matching, which resulted in the same number of treated and control companies in each matched strata. As a robustness test, the same analysis was run without forcing a one-to-one matching but enabling many-to-one matching and then utilizing the matching weights in the regression analysis. The main results of the two matching methods were in line with each other.

DISCUSSION

This study indicates that social enterprises can function as buffers in their economy because their growth is countercyclical, unlike the growth of their commercial counterparts. Thus, social ventures create jobs and economic activity during stagnations; but how? In the section where the hypotheses for the study were derived, several dimensions that were central to social enterprises' capabilities and resources were introduced, and the influence those dimensions may have had on social enterprises' growth was theorized (including social mission, ownership structure and decision-making, the nature of opportunities, broad stakeholder networks and terms of employment).

In addition, the findings indicated that social enterprises' larger assets may play a role in the explanation of the results via two mechanisms. First, studies focusing on firm growth during economic downturns or on their recovery from crises reported that slack provided firms with a buffer against recession and had a positive effect on growth (Bradley et al., 2011; Canarella and Miller, 2018). Having large assets means that social enterprise managers have latent resources at hand that can be activated, combined and rearranged as challenges arise. Nonetheless, there are indications that in munificent economic environments, slack hinders growth (Tognazzo et al., 2016). The other potential explanation has to do with valuable and versatile resources that are positively related to firm growth (Nason and Wiklund, 2018). Therefore, if social enterprises' assets can be considered as valuable and versatile resources, their relatively large assets can be flexibly modified and used where needed to survive economic downturns.

To conclude, this study has implications for research on social enterprises by drawing attention to the role of assets and dynamic indicators, such as asset turnover and labour productivity. The dynamic indicators of growth measure the efficiency with which a social enterprise can deploy its resources. Overall, the study completes the perspective on social enterprises' growth by exploring organizational growth. It opens up avenues for accumulating reliable knowledge on the various dimensions of social enterprise growth. Conducting quantitative and comparative studies on different types of social enterprises and on commercial SMEs is a necessary part of this ongoing endeavour. Firm growth research has established that operational environments and firms' demographics are likely to result in qualitatively different growth trajectories, which have different implications for growth outcomes (Davidsson et al., 2010; Wiklund et al., 2009). This chain of cause and effect remains unexplored in the social enterprise context.

This study also contributes to small firm growth research. The application of multiple growth measures implies that volume-based measures, such as employment, sales and assets, have converging growth trajectories. In addition, including asset turnover and labour productivity yields novel insights into growth patterns when employed alongside volume-based measures.

One of the limitations of this study is related to self-recognition, which is not an ideal way to form a social enterprise sample. However, the sample was strengthened with social enterprises that were recognized through third-party verification. The context generates another limitation, as social enterprises are context-dependent; thus, the generalizability of the findings should be verified by replicating the research design elsewhere (Defourny and Nyssens, 2010).

CONCLUSIONS

This chapter demonstrates that social enterprises can live up to the expectations placed on their growth by growing more quickly during downturns in comparison to other types of enterprises. However, this study found that in the boom period, social enterprises grew more slowly, and in the long term, these contrary effects offset one another. In future research, one of the most interesting questions arising from this study is why social enterprises manage to grow faster than commercial enterprises during crises. Researchers should take advantage of this question to determine what could be learned from these experiences. They should also investigate the possible differences among various types of social enterprises.

REFERENCES

André, K. and A.-C. Pache (2014), 'From caring entrepreneur to caring enterprise: addressing the ethical challenges of scaling up social enterprises', *Journal of Business Ethics*, **133** (4), 659–675.

Anyadike-Danes, M. and M. Hart (2018), 'All grown up? The fate after 15 years of a quarter of a million UK firms born in 1998', *Journal of Evolutionary Economics*, **28** (1), 45–76.

Audretsch, D.B., A. Coad and A. Segarra (2014), 'Firm growth and innovation', *Small Business Economics*, **43**, 743–749.

Austin, J., H. Stevenson and J. Wei-Skillern (2006), 'Social and commercial entrepreneurship: same, different, or both?', *Entrepreneurship Theory and Practice*, **30** (1), 1–22.

Bacq, S., C. Hartog and B. Hoogendoorn (2013), 'A quantitative comparison of social and commercial entrepreneurship: toward a more nuanced understanding of social entrepreneurship organizations in context', *Journal of Social Entrepreneurship*, **4** (1), 40–68.

Bacq, S. and F. Janssen (2011), 'The multiple faces of social entrepreneurship: a review of definitional issues based on geographical and thematic criteria', *Entrepreneurship and Regional Development*, **23** (5–6), 373–403.

Barney, J. (1991), 'Firm resources and sustainable competitive advantage', *Journal of Management*, **17**, 99–120.

Battilana, J. and M. Lee (2014), 'Advancing research on hybrid organizing – insights from the study of social enterprise', *Academy of Management Annals*, **8** (1), 397–441.

Bradley, S.W., D.A. Shepherd and J. Wiklund (2011), 'The importance of slack for new organizations facing "tough" environments', *Journal of Management Studies*, **48** (5), 1071–1097.

Canarella, G. and S.M. Miller (2018), 'The determinants of growth in the US information and communication technology (ICT) industry: a firm-level analysis', *Economic Modelling*, **70**, 259–271.

Cowling, M., W. Liu and N. Zhang (2018), 'Did firm age, experience, and access to finance count? SME performance after the global financial crisis', *Journal of Evolutionary Economics*, **28** (1), 77–100.

Davidsson, P., L. Achtenhagen and L. Naldi (2010), 'Small firm growth', *Foundations and Trends in Entrepreneurship*, **6** (2), 69–166.

Davies, I.A., H. Haugh and L. Chambers (2018), 'Barriers to social enterprise growth', *Journal of Small Business Management*. https://doi.org/10.1111/jsbm.12429.

Dees, J.G., B.B. Anderson and J. Wei-Skillern (2004), 'Scaling social impact: strategies for spreading social innovations', *Stanford Social Innovation Review*, **1**, 24–32.

Defourny, J. and M. Nyssens (2010), 'Conceptions of social enterprise and social entrepreneurship in Europe and the United States: convergences and divergences', *Journal of Social Entrepreneurship*, **1** (1), 32–53.

Defourny, J. and M. Nyssens (2017), 'Fundamentals for an international typology of social enterprise models', *Voluntas*, **28** (6), 2469–2497.

Doherty, B., H. Haugh and F. Lyon (2014), 'Social enterprises as hybrid organizations: a review and research agenda', *International Journal of Managements Reviews*, **16**, 417–436.

European Commission (2011), *Social Business Initiative* (COM 2011) 682 final.

European Commission (2015), *A Map of Social Enterprises and their Eco-systems in Europe*, Luxembourg: Publications Office of the European Union.
European Commission and OECD (2016), *Policy Brief on Scaling the Impact of Social Enterprises*, Publications Office of the European Union.
Gibrat, R. (1931), *Les inegalités économiques*, Paris: Sirey.
Gilbert, B.A., P.P. McDougall and D.B. Audretsch (2006), 'New venture growth: a review and extension', *Journal of Management*, **32** (6), 926–950.
Gimmon, E. and S. Spiro (2013), 'Social and commercial ventures: a comparative analysis of sustainability', *Journal of Social Entrepreneurship*, **4** (2), 182–197.
Gras, D. and G.T. Lumpkin (2012), 'Strategic foci in social and commercial entrepreneurship: a comparative analysis', *Journal of Social Entrepreneurship*, **3** (1), 6–23.
Hynes, B. (2009), 'Growing the social enterprise – issues and challenges', *Social Enterprise Journal*, **5** (2), 114–125.
Iacus, S.M., G. King and G. Porro (2011), 'Multivariate matching methods that are monotonic imbalance bounding', *Journal of the American Statistical Association*, **106** (493), 345–361.
Iacus, S.M., G. King and G. Porro (2012), 'Causal inference without balance checking: coarsened exact matching', *Political Analysis*, **20** (1), 1–24.
Kostilainen, H. and P. Pättiniemi (2016), 'Evolution of the social enterprise concept in Finland', in L. Lundgaard Andersen, M. Gawell and R. Spear (eds), *Nordic Contributions to Social Entrepreneurship*, London, UK and New York, USA: Routledge, pp. 59–75.
Lepoutre, J., R. Justo, S. Terjesen and N. Bosma (2013), 'Designing a global standardized methodology for measuring social entrepreneurship activity: the Global Entrepreneurship Monitor social entrepreneurship study', *Small Business Economics*, **40**, 693–714.
Lumpkin, G.T. and G.G. Dess (1996), 'Clarifying the entrepreneurial orientation construct and linking it to performance', *Academy of Management Review*, **21** (1), 135–172.
Lumpkin, G.T., T.W. Moss, D.M. Gras, S. Kato and A.S. Amezcua (2013), 'Entrepreneurial processes in social contexts: how are they different, if at all?', *Small Business Economics*, **40**, 761–783.
Lyon, F. and H. Fernandez (2012), 'Strategies for scaling up social enterprise: lessons from early years providers', *Social Enterprise Journal*, **8** (1), 63–77.
Macpherson, A. and R. Holt (2007), 'Knowledge, learning and small firm growth: a systematic review of the evidence', *Research Policy*, **36**, 172–192.
Margiono, A., R. Zolin and A. Chang (2018), 'A typology of social venture business model configurations', *International Journal of Entrepreneurial Behavior and Research*, **24** (3), 626–650.
Martin, R.L. and S. Osberg (2007), 'Social entrepreneurship: the case for definition', *Stanford Social Innovation Review*, **5** (28), 27–39.
McKelvie, A., A. Brattström and K. Wennberg (2017), 'How young firms achieve growth: reconciling the roles of growth motivation and innovative activities', *Small Business Economics*, **49**, 273–293.
Molina, J.L., H. Valenzuela-García, M.J. Lubbers, P. Escribano and M.M. Lobato (2018), '"The cowl does make the monk": understanding the emergence of social entrepreneurship in times of downturn', *Voluntas*, **24** (4), 725–739.
Nason, R.S. and J. Wiklund (2018), 'An assessment of resource-based theorizing on firm growth and suggestions for the future', *Journal of Management*, **44** (1), 32–60.

Penrose, E.T. (1959), *The Theory of the Growth of the Firm*, Oxford: Oxford University Press.

Russell, S., P. Pättiniemi and L. Koivuneva (2014), 'A map of social enterprises and their eco-systems in Europe. Country Report: Finland', European Commission.

Saebi, T., N.J. Foss and S. Linder (2019), 'Social entrepreneurship research: past achievements and future promises', *Journal of Management*, **45** (1), 70–95.

Shepherd, D. and J. Wiklund (2009), 'Are we comparing apples with apples or apples with oranges? Appropriateness of knowledge accumulation across growth studies', *Entrepreneurship Theory and Practice*, **33** (1), 105–123.

Smith, W.K., M. Gonin and M.L. Besharov (2013), 'Managing social–business tensions', *Business Ethics Quarterly*, **23** (3), 407–422.

Tognazzo, A., P. Gubitta and S.D. Favaron (2016), 'Does slack always affect resilience? A study of quasi-medium-sized Italian firms', *Entrepreneurship and Regional Development*, **28** (9–10), 768–790.

Tracey, P. and O. Jarvis (2007), 'Toward a theory of social venture franchising', *Entrepreneurship Theory and Practice*, **31** (5), 667–85.

Vickers, I. and F. Lyon (2014), 'Beyond green niches? Growth strategies of environmentally-motivated social enterprises', *International Small Business Journal*, **32** (4), 449–470.

Weerawardena, J. and G. Sullivan Mort (2006), 'Investigating social entrepreneurship: a multidimensional model', *Journal of World Business*, **41** (1), 21–35.

Wiklund, J., H. Patzelt and D.A. Shepherd (2009), 'Building an integrative model of small business growth', *Small Business Economics*, **12**, 351–374.

Zahra, S.A., H.N. Rawhouser, N. Bhawe, D.O. Neubaum and J.C. Hayton (2008), 'Globalization of social entrepreneurship opportunities', *Strategic Entrepreneurship Journal*, **2** (2), 117–131.

Index